How Many Words Do You Want?

How Many Words Do You Want?

An Insider's Story
of Print and
Television Journalism

by Leslie Midgley

A Birch Lane Press Book
Published by Carol Publishing Group

20167741
DLC

7-30-90

Copyright © 1989 by Leslie Midgley

A Birch Lane Press Book
Published by Carol Publishing Group

Editorial Offices
600 Madison Avenue
New York, NY 10022

Sales & Distribution Offices
120 Enterprise Avenue
Secaucus, NJ 07094

In Canada: Musson Book Company
A division of General Publishing Co. Limited
Don Mills, Ontario

Manufactured in the United States of America

Library of Congress Cataloging-in-Publication Data

Midgley, Leslie.
    How many words do you want? : an insider's story of print and
television journalism / by Leslie Midgley.
        p.   cm.
    "A Birch Lane Press book."
    ISBN 1-55972-015-8 : $19.95
        1. Midgley, Leslie. 2. Journalists--United States--Biography.
    3. Editors--United States--Biography. 4. Broadcast journalism--
    United States--History--20th century. 5. CBS News. I. Title.
    PN4874.M488A3   1989
    070'.92--dc20
    [B]   89-228085
                                                           CIP

To STEWART RICHARDSON
without whose help
and encouragement
this book never
would have been
finished

Contents

BOOK I

The Word on the Page

Preface

A WEEK AFTER I started as a rewriteman at the *New York World-Telegram* in 1940, Bo McAnney, the city editor, came over to my desk carrying a batch of copy.

"Look this over and see what you can do with it," he said.

It was a long story about hanky panky on the docks of the Port of New York, written by John O'Neill, a veteran Scripps-Howard reporter permanently assigned to the beat. Before the airline and trucking industries took away big chunks of their business, ships and shipping were regular sources of daily news. Often news of violence and corruption.

I read the copy a couple of times, then walked over to Bo's desk.

"Mr. McAnney," I said, "two questions:

"How long do you want this story?

"And what do you want it to say?"

A smile lit up his Irish face. They were the right questions. He gave his answers and the next day the story, as I had written it, appeared with big headlines on the front page. Under O'Neill's byline.

I knew then that a position on one of the great dailies of New York was secure. I was only 25 but I already had been a reporter, rewriteman, composing room makeup man and city editor on daily papers around the country.

Lest there be confusion about the wording of my questions:

First, I wanted to know about how many words or columns the story might run so I could decide what to put in and what to leave out. For space reasons.

When I asked, "What do you want it to say?" I was not seeking any guidance from the boss about how to "slant" the story. I wanted to know what Bo thought were its most important points. The headlines.

Those same questions, unspoken, were my guides through the next 15 years on newspapers and magazines, and another 28 years in television news during what appears now to have been its finest hours.

I began putting down this account of some wonderful years after a fellow worker insisted I should write a book about the difference between print and television journalism. Because, he pointed out, I was one of those who had extensive, inside experience in both.

They *are* different, as any child who has been peering at television since he first opened his eyes, and is now learning to read, knows. But in basic ways all forms of news presentation are alike.

Differences: First class reporting in print requires that information be presented in clear, concise sentences that not only tell the story but illuminate it.

Because the images we recognize as words, received by the eyeballs from a printed page, require the recipient to create, through the exercise of imagination, a mental picture from what has been put on the page.

Good writing, the most essential element in *all* journalism, is a blessing that can stimulate and expand the readers' imagination to make that picture more correct, complete and vivid.

In radio the same process works through the ears.

But television comes complete with its own picture. One that walks and talks. You don't have to visualize in your head a short red dress, a wild ride, a man stopping a tank by standing in front of it. You see them. Like in the movies. (A grand word, movies!)

Here is where television is enormously different from—and more powerful than—the printed word.

Pictures that move possess great power, as the men who pasted together the first crude movies found out. When they made the pictures talk, that power was enormously enhanced. They had then the dramatic tools of the stage to work with, plus the almost limitless power of cameras to go anywhere and look at anything. Literally making come true "All the world's a stage and all the men and women..." etc.

This dramatic power generates, inevitably, EMOTION. Written descriptions of a child dying of hunger in a desert ten thousand miles away can stir emotion, but the sight and sound of it produce a flood of feelings in any viewer.

And today's astonishing technology has made it possible to enhance answers to "What's new?" with the tools of both the stage and the motion picture.

That is the great asset of television.

But printed newspapers and magazines have a great strength of their own. It is the ability to expand coverage of an event to include valuable information about details of just what happened, how it happened, the history of similar events, the natural forces and/or the governments involved, the possibility or certainty of its happening again, and much more.

Bound tightly into today's time restraints, television news must settle for what is all too often just some expanded headlines.

Television news offers pictures that demand attention and with them bring emotion, which is not to be scorned but indeed highly prized.

Printed news offers far more complete information.

Take your pick.

Similarities: The daily newspapers and the daily TV programs select their content from the same enormous pool of available information. Each presents to its readers or viewers what editors select as important and/or interesting.

When really big news breaks—an earthquake, a nuclear power plant leak, a political uproar—the size of printed headlines and the number of columns pre-empted for such a story in newspapers and the amount of time devoted to it on TV reflect the attempt by editors to report, in their own fashion, the seriousness of the event.

The press with big headlines and columns of type, the television news producers with larger chunks of their precious minutes and seconds. The toilers in television really try, often very skillfully, to make their reports as complete as possible. Their technical abilities give them a leg up—making the picture tell a lot of the story—but they are ready and willing to use a lot of time in the interests of accuracy and detail. (I am referring here to serious work, not the foolishness and excesses of programming desperately shoving on the screen any fire or horrendous crime to grab an audience.)

They are doing the same thing. The real difference is that they employ totally disparate mechanical devices to transmit information through the senses into the brain.

The news itself—the fodder—is the same.

My old question "How many words do you want this story?" is still asked constantly every day in newspaper city rooms. And it must also be asked and answered right on the dot in television, bound into a straitjacket of allotted time. For TV, words have become seconds.

(One of the wisest TV practicioners I know says he doesn't believe the question is asked anymore in television news. The "how many words" [seconds] is *told* to him, not *asked* by the writer.)

And my "What do you want it to say?" goes directly to the heart of news reporting by any and all means. It is the first and overwhelming concern of every reporter and editor.

I spent most of my years working as an editor, with occasional forays as a reporter into the world outside. During which I was lucky enough to meet and become friendly with some fascinating characters. Like Frank Costello in New York and Howard Hughes in California and Nevada.

That was fun, but the people who interested me most were not those made into celebrities by newspaper and television publicity, but my fellow toilers in the news business who did the making.

Among them the great news editor John Denson, the finest of city editors, Lessing Engelking, dozens of talented reporters like John O'Reilly, Homer Bigart, Robert J. Donovan, Bob Shaplen, Red Smith, John Crosby, Stephen White, Seymour Freidin and John Lardner. Plus great broadcast journalists like Charles Collingwood, Walter Cronkite, Charles Kuralt. And especially editors—alas mislabeled producers—at CBS News: Don Hewitt, Ernest Leiser, John Sharnik, Philip Scheffler, Bernard Birnbaum.

From them I learned how to work—to play, if the truth be told—in the wonderful world of covering the news.

What, you might well ask, has all this personal stuff to do with the difference between print and television news?

When I faced up to pondering what was really different about television and print, I decided the only way I might make the difference clear was to relate what had happened to *me*. How I had learned to work in both of them.

Bear with me. The answer is here.

Chapter 1

Sneaking into the Circus Tent

DURING THE FALL AND WINTER OF 1934, aged 20, I was lucky enough to spend many nights watching a big city newspaper being put together. The sight of such fun and games being played by grown-ups was entrancing. Like a wonderful movie or a vision. A vision that for me became a reality.

I decided almost from my first look inside the *Washington Post* that if you could actually get paid for doing this there was no reason whatsoever to do anything else. Anything. I never changed that opinion and I wouldn't trade those years for any man's fortune.

I could walk into the city room of the *Post* because I had two friends from Salt Lake City who worked there. Sidney Olson was a reporter, Harold Rhodenbaugh head of the photo department. I worked days as a government typist for $1,440 a year. They worked nights, so I began hanging out there, eating cheap dinners and drinking with them and other *Post* men. I was an unabashed fan, a groupie if you will, and the reporters and sub editors proved quite willing to endure a little adulation.

They talked, of course, about their bosses. The man running the editorial department was Mark Ethridge, who had been hired only a year before by Eugene Meyer. A very rich millionaire, Meyer had bought the failing newspaper, not in a boardroom deal, but during an auction conducted on the front steps of the crumbling stone building facing Pennsylvania Avenue three blocks east of the White House. Meyer wasn't trying to make more money; he wanted to be the proprietor of a high quality newspaper. So Mark, one of the finest editors and publishers of our time, began hiring a new staff.

In the middle of the Great Depression, word got around fast where there were jobs to be had. Peter Kihss came from Brooklyn, my friends from the Far West, others from New England and the South. And 33-year-old John Denson came down the newspaper journeymen's trail.

When I first got a peek inside the city room, Denson was assistant managing editor, the principal news editor. The one who had the last word about what was news and what was not. Which, where and how long stories would appear in the paper. Denson ate and drank with the boys, and it was apparent that the staff viewed his experience and news judgment with something approaching awe.

Listening to them and him I got my first inkling—even a little understanding—of how news editing is done. He had learned it the hard way. In the old newspaper tradition, John had drifted from his native Louisiana to a job as copy boy at the *Washington Herald,* then on to more than a score of papers all across the country. He had done everything, reporter, rewriteman, copy reader, news editor. He always moved on. Even in later years, successful in very important jobs, he would walk away, forever restless.

Times were hard in the Thirties but two businesses that stayed alive were newspapers and movies. Historians say the movies flourished because they were cheap and gave unemployed people something to do—and something to dream about. Newspapers were cheap and provided something to do. I don't know about dreams. Anyway, newspapermen went from city to city seeking work and often finding it.

The *Post* was hiring trained people but not totally inexperienced youngsters. So I went back to Salt Lake, where I had grown up in the middle of a large Mormon family. (With 75 first cousins). I went to public schools, the church high school and finally put in two years at the University of Utah. Beginning in childhood, I read constantly. Magazines and books in my own home and books by the hundred from the public library. And the daily newspaper.

I entered the university too young, at age 16. I got so-so grades but what interested me most was English. In that subject I got A's without effort.

After two years I decided to forgo academe and get out into the world. My parents were distressed but made no real effort to dissuade me. Soon after leaving college, I was lucky enough to be befriended by a reporter on *The Deseret News* named Sidney Olson. Sid was a young intellectual who had been editor of the university humor magazine. He had a good-sized personal library, many of the volumes simply taken without records or permission from the public library. Sid introduced me to writers like George Jean Nathan, H.L. Mencken and James Gibbons Hunecker. This was not the education I would have obtained in college but it served me well enough.

Jobs were very scarce in Utah but many young people had found they could get work in various New Deal offices in Washington. One day, a friend who worked, literally, in the basement of the Capitol while studying law at George Washington University at night, said he was going to drive back after a summer holiday. He offered me a lift in exchange for sharing the driving. In those days, we drove day and night to save tourist camp bills. That was how I came to be in the nation's capital and got a whiff of my future.

The head of my clan was my grandfather, Heber J. Grant, the President of the Mormon church and, as such, a very powerful person indeed. The church owned *The Deseret News,* which as a kid I had delivered to a lot of front porches. I went there and asked for a job as a reporter. I was taken on as a beginner at $5 a week. (Raised to $15 after a few weeks.)

One of the oldest traditions of the newspaper business is that reporters start by covering the police station. And that's just where the city editor sent me.

The dozen other reporters were all older than I and, of course, knew a lot more about the city and county and state governments, what went on in the federal building, how the local stock exchange worked and so on. But I quickly discovered I could "get the stuff and write it," as James Thurber used to describe reporting. Probably because of omnivorous reading, I wrote, from the start, simple declarative sentences and put a story together properly. The old who, what, where, when, why business.

Most young people seeking to become journalists these days have college degrees. Many of them are graduates of schools of journalism. I have nothing against institutions of higher learning and always wished I had a better formal education. But the rock on which all journalism is founded is good writing. You don't need a degree for that. Talent helps.

I covered all kinds of stories after the police beat. Stories from the state capitol, city hall and the federal building, Rotary Club lunches, interviews with visiting politicians and entertainers. When veteran director and actor John Huston died a few years ago, I recalled that I had, as a very green reporter, interviewed his *father,* the great Walter Huston.

Almost everyone on the staff had grown up in Utah, but the "wire editor" on the *News* turned out to be Al Reck, one of the wanderers. His previous job had been city editor of the *Washington Daily News,* a Scripps-Howard afternoon paper. Before that he had worked on various papers in the South. He had been an infantry captain in World War I and retained a certain military swagger. He was tall and sharp-featured, and one of the first things that caught my eye was how women looked at him in the street. They liked what they saw.

Al certainly was untypical of the staff of this church-owned newspaper. How he came to be in Utah and got hired I never found out. He smoked cigarettes, frowned on by church doctrine. Every hour or so, he would walk across an alley behind the composing room and slouch down to light up in a tiny coffee shop which fronted on Main Street. Working on an afternoon newspaper, the staff arrived early and Al was there long before seven every morning. Every afternoon, he repaired to one of various little restaurants and clubs and drank scotch. It seemed to be his only recreation. Although we were products of the Mormon society, Ted Cannon, the city editor, and I sometimes joined him.

On a paper this size, the "wire editor" was the news editor. Reck was no Denson but he knew how to put a newspaper together. I had discovered that watching experts work was how to learn, so I habitually wandered into the composing room in the afternoon to watch him give final approval to columns of metal type locked up on the dollies called "the stone."

After about a year, I told Ted it felt like time to move on. I had tried several times to get a job in San Francisco, which had the finest newspapers in the West. But San Francisco was tightly organized by the unions, and as long as local men were on the street, outsiders were barred. So one day I took the Union Pacific to Denver, spent the night in the Brown Palace Hotel and went around to *The Denver Post.* I told the city editor I had worked in Salt Lake and he said to come in the next day for a tryout.

When I walked into the *Post* city room early the next morning, they put me to work on the usual miscellany: phoning for information to check on wire stories, taking stories from the beat reporters, writing obits.

The *Post* was an afternoon newspaper, the gaudy creation of two colorful characters, Eugene Bonfils and Harry Tammen, who had started informing—and entertaining—Denver citizens around the turn of the century. They were both dead but Bonfils' daughter carried on as publisher and the headlines and front page cartoons were still big and catchy. It was a lively, splashy paper, very popular.

In addition to appearing weekday afternoons, the *Post* put out a Sunday morning edition. Which meant that the staff had to work late on Saturday night but had little to do until the following Monday. But, the city editor told me, there was a standing rule that a *Post* reporter must be on duty at the police station every Sunday. Being the new man, I was it for my first Sunday in town.

I dutifully showed up at the Denver police headquarters Sunday morning and found it even sleazier than the one in Salt Lake.

Figuring correctly there would be little or nothing to do, I brought along a copy of Gene Fowler's book *Timberline,* an hilarious account of the exploits of Bonfils and Tammen. And I discovered right there in Fowler's book why one Les Midgley was sitting in the Denver police station one Sunday in 1936.

In the old days, Fowler wrote, the *Post* newsroom was deserted on Sundays. Except for Bonfils, who couldn't stay away. One Sunday, he was wandering alone around the room when the phone rang. It was a woman who wanted to report she had lost her dog. Bonfils was fond of dogs. The next day he ordered that there must always be a man on duty at the police station on Sunday. So there I was. Checking on lost dogs.

Being around the *Post* was fun, but a few weeks later I got a call from a friend in Salt Lake, John "Soup" Campbell. He was driving to Washington and wanted company. So I thanked the *Post* editors, bade them goodbye and went off to join Soup. They were surprised but I was footloose and 21 years old.

When I got to Washington there were no openings on the *Post*. Sid had moved to New York to write for TIME at the princely sum of $10,000 a year.

A *Post* man told me Rhodenbaugh had gone off to Louisville, Kentucky, as chief of the morgue for the *Courier-Journal* and *Times,* two papers owned by the Binghams. Judge Bingham, the family patriarch, had been sent to London as President Roosevelt's ambassador to the Court of St. James's. The judge had hired Mark Ethridge to be publisher in his absence.

I took the train to Louisville and checked in with Hal, who took me upstairs to meet Mr. Ethridge. He sent me to the managing editor, who gave me a job.

After I got to know some of my new fellow workers, I realized they were all from Kentucky.

"Don't guys come down here from Chicago or Cincinnati?" I asked.

"No," they answered, "How did you get here?"

I realized then that Louisville was a quiet backwater and Ethridge was ready to hire outside talent which might let a few new ideas into the dusty *Courier-Journal* establishment.

I don't know exactly when I got to Louisville, but it was in the spring before the Kentucky Derby because one of my earliest assignments was to do feature stories out at Churchill Downs just before the big race. The smell of big money was as rich as the stable odors.

I picked up a few tips on local customs. One day, I wrote the words "Civil War" in a story. The assistant city editor called me over.

"We call it the War Between the States" he said.

Another day they sent me to talk to a local political bigwig in a suite at the Brown Hotel.

"Would you care for a drink?" he asked, waving toward a sideboard covered with bottles.

When I didn't make any move, he said:

"Son, we have a custom here in Kentucky. A man pours his own drink. If he wants a small drink he takes one. If he wants a big drink he pours it on out."

He had me tagged, correctly, as an outsider.

Who should show up in Louisville one day in October but John and Kitty Denson. John was by then managing editor of a lively tabloid, the *Chicago Times*. The executive editor was Louis Ruppel, a big, tough-talking character who had worked with John on the *Daily News,* Captain Patterson's highly successful New York tabloid. When he got the Chicago job, at the suggestion of President Roosevelt himself, it was bruited around, Ruppel immediately sent for Denson.

John said at dinner that Ethridge had asked him to come to Louisville to talk about joining the Bingham organization. The talks went on for a couple of days, after which we understood John would come to Louisville soon. Several weeks went by and he didn't show up. So one night I got on a sleeper and went to Chicago. John welcomed me cordially, and after the last edition had been locked up, we adjourned to a saloon downstairs on Wacker Drive.

When was he coming to Louisville?

Well, he wasn't. Ruppel had persuaded him to stay in Chicago.

In that case, since I wanted to work for him, was there a job for me in Chicago? One could be found, he said.

So I went back to Louisville and upstairs to see Mr. Ethridge. I told him I was very grateful for the break he had given me but I thought I should move along. Instead of objecting, he offered to get me a job on the *Richmond Times-Dispatch,* where he had been publisher before coming to Louisville. He thought it was a good idea for young men to move around.

I had to level with him. I said I was going to Chicago to work for Denson.

"But he is coming here," Ethridge said with great surprise.

Maybe, I said, adding "I don't think so."

Being a classy guy, Mark said he thought working for Denson was a very good idea and wished me luck. But don't go before Christmas, he added. The *Courier* was going to pay a bonus for the first time in years.

I couldn't resist asking just what Ethridge had had in mind for Denson. He had been slated to be executive editor of both the *Courier-Journal* and the *Post,* Mark replied. I never found out if John gave Ethridge proper notice. I hope so. Probably not.

(Mark himself was an example of newspapermen on the move. A Mississippian, he had worked for various papers and the Associated

Press before taking over the *Post.* He stayed there only two years and another two years in Richmond before going on to Louisville. But he stayed there for many years.)

I got the Christmas bonus, then went home for the holidays. I arrived in Chicago early in January, found a rooming house on Oak Street near the lake and took the Elevated down to the *Times.* John said my job was to be night makeup man, working from 3 A.M. until 10 A.M. mostly in the composing room, making sure that type for the first two editions went into the forms the way they had been laid out by the night editor. Wonderful hours!

The *Post* advertised itself as an afternoon paper but the first edition appeared on the Elevated newsstands in time to be bought by riders on their way *to* work. And the last of eight full editions appeared in the evening, only after final baseball and racing and financial results were in.

And that was not all. If some big story broke between those editions, MAKE OVER PAGE ONE slips would come clattering down the tin chute between the newsroom and the composing room followed by new copy and headlines. And we would, with great gusto, rush hot—literally hot—type into the forms.

Lou Ruppel was brash and loud and he liked his paper to be the same. He and John vied to write splashy banner headlines to fill half of the front page, in New York *Daily News* style. They had some fun doing it.

When Franklin D. Roosevelt ran for re-election the first time in 1936, Colonel Robert McCormick, owner of the *Chicago Tribune,* was bitterly opposed to Roosevelt. He ordered the *Tribune*'s telephone operators to respond to all incoming calls with the words, *"Chicago Tribune.* Only 29 days to save the nation," counting down until election day.

An afternoon newspaper is hard put for real news of an election on the day it is held. So the big headline on the *Times* that day was:

52 DAYS

TIL XMAS

Backed up by a little story on page 3 about the wisdom of doing Christmas shopping early.

After a little grumbling from the boss of the composing room about my lack of experience for this particular job, I began to get along well with the compositors and makeup men in the shop. Here was another job that didn't require genius.

I worked directly for the night editor, Ned Bush, But Denson invariably showed up very early in the morning and would be on hand for the lockup of the first two editions. He trusted Ned but could be extremely critical of news selections and layouts that he didn't think were good enough. After the first edition arrived, he would go over it carefully with Bush and the chief copyreader, dictating changes in layout or headlines. I stood by making notes of changes which would soon be arriving downstairs. So for several hours every morning, I could see how Denson went about editing a newspaper.

He went about it seriously.

He had the background for it. During his journey, John was on the *Herald Tribune* Washington staff and the fabled *New York World*. Legend at the *New York World-Telegram* was that if a man was *fired*, the paper might rehire him. But if he *quit* they would never take him back. Denson quit three times; they hired him back three times.

In later years, he was assistant Washington bureau chief for Time Inc., associate editor of *Fortune*, managing editor of *Kiplinger's*, editor of the *Los Angeles Examiner*, managing editor of *Collier's*, editor of *Newsweek*, which he turned into a genuine competitor of TIME, and finally editor of the *New York Herald Tribune*.

Over the years people have asked me many times, "What *is* the news?" "Who decides what THE NEWS is?" "How?"

There is no really satisfactory answer, although I have read many defintions by learned scholars.

The best answer is a simple one: News is what an editor decides it is.

Exercising judgment and experience, without even thinking much about it because time is short, the best editor selects reports to be printed—or broadcast—which he thinks readers *should* know. Because the information would be of value to them.

As part of the process, he discards items which do not interest *him*. What he thinks is important goes on Page One. What he thinks is not important is buried or thrown away.

At the same time, to make his product livelier and therefore more popular, he also selects items he thinks they would *want* to know. Sometimes merely gossip and rumor.

That is what John Denson did in front of Ned Bush and me early every morning. He selected—by accepting Ned's choices—some of the news and told us to remove some of the stories entirely or change their display. Then he went on through the day as new news showed up, rearranging the paper through six more editions to suit his own taste. Which, believe me, was good.

John was tall and skinny, with a high, wide forehead that made his face look square. He wore thick glasses and was prone to squint through them. His habitual facial expression was one of surprise, even amazement, accompanied by such statements such as "No kidding!" and "You don't mean it!" He had a habit of grinding his false teeth constantly, especially when under pressure. He always wore a conservative dark suit and tie with a white shirt.

He and his wife, Kitty, lived not in an apartment but in the Mayflower Hotel on the Near North Side. They were, I guess, born transients. I never could figure out what Kitty did with her time. They had no children and she seemed to have no interest in anything except John and his work, which was always the sole subject of our conversations over drinks or at dinner. As far as I could see, he had no interest in anything outside the *Times* newsroom except professional football, which he followed meticulously, attending games every Sunday. He apparently had no friends other than newspapermen and no social life outside their world.

Ned and I were principally concerned with getting "boiler plate," regular features such as columns, editorials and so forth, into place and getting the principal news pages laid out. The sports section occupied the back pages. They were the responsibility of the night sports editor whose name was, and is, Irv Kupcinet.

Bush was a competent journeyman and his long experience probably fortified him to put up with our odd schedule. For example, when we finished work at 10 A.M., we usually went downstairs to have a few drinks in a bar. I was free as a bird but Ned had a wife and several children. They must have had a strange family life. One day around noon, Ned said he was going over to a horse betting room on Division Street and asked if I wanted to come along. I had never been in one and was delighted at the prospect. We went in the door of a two-story building and walked up a flight of stairs. A door closed behind us, and for the first and last time in my life, I was frisked for weapons. The frisker was polite but very firm; I guess they had been held up before, even by youngsters. I figured out later that the little room where we were frisked actually was an elevator with doors at the front and rear. If they didn't want you in the place, I assume they just ran the elevator down a flight and ushered you out to the street. Unharmed, I hope.

I never did get used to the weird hours and didn't get much sleep that winter. But Chicago is *a* big town—if not *the* big town—and lots was going on. Being a jazz buff and sometime piano player, before going to work I liked to drop into the Blackhawk Cafe to hear Mildred Bailey sing and her husband, Red Norvo, play the vibraphone. Mildred was one of the great figures of jazz. Billie Holiday and many other women singers copied her style of phrasing. She had a thin voice but knew just how to use it.

I had a lot of time on my hands, and when I heard one day that Hearst's *Examiner* was hiring moonlighting copyreaders, I went over to apply. I had never officially been employed as a copyreader but figured I had been around editorial operations enough to know how to write headlines. And being a rewriteman I certainly knew how to cut copy to size.

The head of the copy desk on the *Examiner* was known around town as a tough curmudgeon, famous both for his high standards of copy editing and for summarily and with relish firing guys whose work he didn't like. I told him I worked at the *Times* beginning at 3 A.M. He told me to come in the next day from 5 P.M. until 1 A.M.

When I walked up to the *Examiner* copy desk for the first time, there sat two copyreaders who worked full time on the *Times*. They said hello.

Although I had only written headlines occasionally at the *Times*—sometimes in an emergency but usually for fun—I knew enough about words to make headlines fit. And didn't get fired. I worked the double *Times*/*Examiner* shift for a couple of weeks, then decided it was just too much effort. The money was nice. The *Times* was paying me $40 a week. The *Examiner*, which was maneuvering to keep the new American Newspaper Guild from organizing its staff, had upped copyreaders to $65 a week. So for a while, I was getting the unheard-of sum of $105 a week. But working all the time, I couldn't spend it.

Denson had been at the *Times* for only a couple of years but I could detect he was getting restless. When the Newspaper Guild organizers came around to the *Times,* John, for one of his unfathomable reasons, joined. He was clearly part of management and Ruppel and the owners protested. John just quit and went back to New York.

I had learned a lot in Chicago and had fun, but without Denson there wasn't any particular reason for me to stay there. I heard that Ted Cannon had gone to the *Salt Lake Tribune* and the city editor's job on *The Deseret News* was open. I went back and asked the managing editor, Mark Petersen, for the job. He didn't like either me or the idea but he gave it to me anyway.

I spent the next three years running a staff of a dozen reporters. I knew how to do the work and I knew the town from top to bottom and lots of its people, of high and low estate.

But the wide world called. One day in 1940, I went down to the Greyhound Bus depot and took off for New York. Cold, without any letters or introductions. When the vehicle got to Chicago, I had had enough of buses, spent the night in the Blackstone Hotel, and took the 20th Century Limited to New York the next morning.

I couldn't help recalling during that bus/train trip something Duke Ellington said six or seven years before, when two friends and I were lucky enough to sit up all night drinking gin and ginger ale and listening to him play the piano.

Duke asked where we went to do and see things not to be found in Salt Lake. The answer was that we called San Francisco "The City." In our eyes it was the big town.

"Forget it," he said. "Go to New York. San Francisco and Chicago and London and Paris are okay. But New York is the BIG town. To make it you have to make it there. Nothing else really counts."

Well, that's where I was going.

Every newspaperman in the country probably wished then he could work at the *New York Herald Tribune*. Its high standards of writing and editing, its famous staff of reporters, its classy appearance, all made the paper Number One for professionals.

The *Daily News* was livelier and funnier and had a much bigger circulation. *The New York Times,* was fatter and richer, but poorly written and dull.

It seems almost unbelievable now but when I arrived, nine newspapers carrying world, national and local news were published in the city. The *Herald Tribune, Times, Daily News* and *Mirror* appeared in the morning and the *Journal-American, World-Telegram, Post, Sun* and *Brooklyn Eagle* in the afternoon. Plus others like financial and sports papers, the *Staten Island Advance, Bronx Home News,* etc.

It being the best, I walked into the front door of the *Herald Tribune* on West 41st Street and asked to see the city editor, Lessing Engelking. He turned out to be a big, shambling Texan who courteously explained that he had only four rewritemen on duty every night and none of them showed any inclination to leave. But he encouraged me to keep in touch.

So I went to see John Denson.

In the CBS building at 485 Madison Avenue, where he and Ruppel were running, not the news division but, of all things, the publicity department. John didn't seem surprised to see me for the first time in years. He said one of his writers had a lunch date the next day with Bo McAnney, the city editor of the *World-Telegram* and I could go along to meet McAnney.

We ate at a saloon in Barclay Street, where the *Telegram* was located in a dingy building near the Hudson River. McAnney said he could give me a tryout if I wanted to come in the following Monday. I did.

An afternoon newspaper with tight deadlines, the *Telegram* had a staff of eight rewritemen to handle news stories phoned in by reporters. Morning papers had time for most reporters to write their own stories. The *Telegram* rewrite bank was a classy crew. H. Allen Smith had just finished his first book and was nervous about whether it would sell. It did. Asa Bordages sat behind me and Floyd Taylor and Elliot Arnold across the way. All were published authors. Mel Heimer joined the staff soon after I did.

Rewrite was easy, and I got along fine for three days until a particularly officious assistant city editor told me to take the next day off. I tried to explain that I was on trial for a week but he just walked off. When I came back after the skipped day, Bo said there had been a misunderstanding.

"You told me you were a copyreader", he said. "I can use one next week but are you sure you want to do it?

"Absolutely," I replied.

I showed up on Monday morning to find Tom Dafron sitting in the copy desk slot. Tom had been one of Denson's assistants at the *Chicago Times*. So I had no trouble working on the rim for a week. Tom probably gave me a break but I wrote my share of headlines.

On Friday, I went back to Bo and said I would like to work at the *Telegram* but I wanted to be a rewriteman. He told me to wait and walked over to Lee Wood, the executive editor. Then he came by the copy desk. "You're on," he said. "Come in Monday."

So I had a job in New York. On one of its most famous papers, the flagship of the Scripps-Howard chain.

And, as it turned out, that was the last time I ever asked anyone to hire me. During the next 42 years, I worked for two more newspapers, two big national magazines and CBS and NBC News. All of them sought me out.

I like that.

Chapter 2

Herald Tribune Nights

ONE AFTERNOON about six months later, I got a call at the *Telegram* from Mr. Engelking, city editor of the *Herald Tribune*. He suggested I come uptown to see him. I went.

After greeting me at his desk, he walked over to a long rack of files that held recent issues of various newspapers and asked me to point out stories I had done for the *Telegram*.

Then we adjourned downstairs to the bar of the Artist & Writers Restaurant, a combination saloon, club and second home for the *Herald Tribune* staff. After we got our drinks, Engelking said one of his rewritemen, Eddie Lanham, had asked for a leave to write a book. I could have the job if I wanted it. Wow!

I was making the Newspaper Guild minimum of $65 a week. Mr. Engelking said he could pay me $70.

"How about $75?"

He just smiled. I accepted.

The newsroom of the city's finest paper was on the fifth floor of a dirty brick building that ran through the block between 41st and 40th Streets just west of Seventh Avenue. It was at the northern end of the garment center, and the building had all the physical charm of a sweat shop dress factory. But the neighborhood was wonderful. Times

31

Square was a gaudy parade day and night, and safe then, even in the middle of the night. Which is when we wandered through it. The National Theater was next door and the Metropolitan Opera in the next block. Most important, Bleecks was right downstairs, with the town's most expert bartenders standing by to refresh body and spirit.

The *Telegram* city room was filled with the kind of drab green steel furniture that you associate with government offices. The *Tribune* was not that fancy. The desks were ancient wooden relics scarred with cigarette burns. The walls were a dirty beige. The windows apparently never had been washed.

The big L-shaped room housed the city staff, the sports and society departments, plus working space for the various news editors and copyreaders. Probably a hundred people in all. Managing Editor George Cornish had his own room in a corner, the only private office on the floor. Off to one side was the morgue, the indispensable library of clippings. The financial department was on an upper floor as were the sanctums of the editorial writers, the advertising department and the office of the publisher, Ogden Reid. In the usual fashion, the composing room was on the fourth floor, directly beneath us, and the stereotype and press rooms beneath the compositors. The work flowed down like water.

Engelking sat hunched over a desk too small for his big frame, facing one of his assistant city editors. At his right during the afternoon was Dick West, day city editor, who was replaced at 5 P.M. by Joe Herzberg, night city editor. Next to Joe was a row of four desks, the rewrite bank.

At the first desk sat Bob Peck, the dean of New York rewritemen, known for his skill at writing fast with great class. The others were John Watson, a dark, brooding Irishman with genuine literary gifts, and John Durston, a consummate professional. Some company! We worked together most pleasantly until Watson was overcome by drink and a romance with young Marguerite Higgins and went off to join the *Daily News*.

Along with acceptable publicity handouts and wire copy, a surprising amount of what the reporters turned in wound up in a battered wire basket into which Herzberg tossed copy to be rewritten. We picked up copy from it in turn. By redoing the stuff, we found out very fast which reporters wrote well and which did not.

There were 100 lines of type in a column of the *Herald Tribune*. Copy for the rewrite desk was marked by the desk man with a number,

"25", "50" or "75." This told the rewriteman how long a story should be. "50" was half of a column. About 500 words.

Speaking of lines, some time later I heard that the *Daily News* had spots open for moonlighting rewritemen and I went over to try my hand on a day off. The *News* city desk had the same kind of basket for copy to be rewritten. As they finished one story, the writers picked up whatever was on top of the pile.

One of the first sheets I picked up was marked "25." It was a piece of wire copy about a small fire in Queens.

"You sure you want 25 lines on this story?" I asked the desk man. He looked at me like I was crazy.

"That's 25 words, not lines," he said.

About enough space to say it was a fire and give the address. That was the *Daily News*.

The *Tribune*'s staff of reporters was the best in the city. Many of them went on to become famous for their work on newspapers, magazines and/or writing books.

Homer Bigart was a stocky, hustling general assignment reporter who stuttered constantly and couldn't see a thing without his spectacles. He gave a touch of style to any story, even a few paragraphs about a fire or a robbery.

Robert J. Donovan was a talented young man who would go on to become the *Tribune*'s Washington bureau chief and biographer of Presidents like Truman and generals like Eisenhower.

Robert Shaplen was for many years the finest American correspondent covering Asia. He left the paper to become a staff member of *The New Yorker* and wrote many serious books about the Far East.

John O'Reilly, "Tex," was a nature buff and humorist. Later a great war correspondent.

There were dozens more.

The city desk routine went like this.

West came in at 9 A.M., looked over news prospects for the day and started to fill a big sheet of lined paper with assignments. Unless they had been given overnight tasks, all the reporters showed up at 1 P.M. and Dick told them what to do. Many promptly adjourned to Bleecks for lunch.

When the reporters drifted back from wherever, they described their stories to Herzberg. Joe suggested how long they should write a piece and began going over copy as it was finished and brought to him by bustling copy boys. Engelking talked to reporters whose stories particularly interested him.

At 6 P.M., the most important meeting of the day convened in Managing Editor George Cornish's office. Around a long conference table sat one of George's assistants, Al Davies, Henley Hill or Everett Kallgren, the news editor, the foreign editor, the national editor and our city editor. Plus a photo editor who displayed offerings from *Tribune* photographers or the wire services.

They met to make up the front page. The big game.

The foreign editor described, briefly, what major stories he had in hand or in prospect. In 1940, his first offering was almost always from the war zones in Europe, Asia and Africa. The national editor followed, proposing this or that story from Washington or elsewhere. Engel had Herzberg present the local news, but sat in to make his own comments. All were, of course, parochial advocates for their assigned areas.

If a story important enough to make the front page surfaced in the financial or sports or other areas, editors from those departments were called in to brief the meeting. They loved to make Page One.

After discussion among the group produced concensus on what was big news and what was not, Kallgren sketched a layout of Page One on a big sheet of paper and Cornish gave his final approval.

What they decided was news *was* the news, at least for readers of the *New York Herald Tribune*.

A lot of our work on the rewrite desk was routine. Taking information from district men over the phone, rewriting handouts or city news service material or whatever. Also writing obituaries, which I always enjoyed, especially those of celebrities or people of accomplisment. Not necessarily statesmen or tycoons; often writers, artists, musicians and entertainers had far more interesting lives.

One slow night, I got out the file of clippings about a still-living man named Heber J. Grant and wrote an obituary about him which filled a whole column. It was duly placed in an envelope marked with his name, to await his death. It was standard practice to have such material ready for prominent persons, especially those of advanced age.

President Heber J. Grant died in 1945 when I was in Europe and the *Tribune* published the obituary as I had written it. Some officials of his church protested that the article was not serious enough, that it should not have described him as a "speculator" or pointed out that his sermons were most often descriptions of his own financial and other temporal triumphs. Or that he had been married to three women at the same time. After marrying one one day and another the next day. The *Tribune*s answer to his Morman champions was that it had been written by one of his fifty grandchildren.

Over the years, I formulated a theory which crystalized in New York. The theory was that a man sitting at a desk in 40th Street in Manhattan could describe how it felt to be standing in a doorway in the rain in Brooklyn better than the wet man in the doorway could describe it.

Stephen White, who joined the *Tribune* the next year and became my best friend, says he saw Bob Peck write a story for the first edition about a fire at the Palisades Amusement Park across the Hudson River in New Jersey. When Margaret Parton, a new reporter, later a famous foreign correspondent, came back from covering the story in person, she was astonished to read the early story.

"Where did you get this stuff?" she asked. "It's just what happened over there."

Bob had, over the years, written several stories about fires at Palisades Park. He had taken a brief item from the city news service wire and fleshed it out.

Steve White was a genuine intellectual, a product of the Boston Latin School and Harvard, plus a stint at the fabled *Boston Transcript.* I met his wife under unusual circumstances only a few weeks after he joined the paper.

When the night's work was done at 1 A.M., I habitually adjourned to Bleecks to sit in a contest, already in progress, known as the "match game." Over the years the game had grown into serious business and often hundreds of dollars changed hands. One night, I had been very lucky, stayed up until mid-morning and slept only a few hours.

About an hour after I started work the next afternoon, a small, dark woman came up behind me.

"I'm Miriam White, Steve's wife", she said. "He's sick and I had to take him to a hospital. They want money and Steve said to come to you."

Telling the story in later years, Miriam said I reached in my jacket pocket, took out what she described as "a big wad of bills," handed it to her without a word and resumed typing.

It probably happened that way. It was a busy night and that's what I usually did with winnings, stuffed them in my jacket pocket.

Steve and I began to eat and drink together. He was and is a superb writer and I suspect he consciously set about to improve my sadly neglected education.

One night, Herzberg asked me to sit in as assistant night city editor. All went well and my work there became more and more frequent.

Then when Joe went away for a week, Engel told me to take over as night city editor. I knew the ropes well enough—until the national editor came out of the news conference and told me it was my turn. I had never sat in on the meeting and didn't know just what went on.

I sat down at the end of the long conference table, looked around and asked.

"What can I do for you?" There was a long pause.

"You're supposed to tell us what stories you have for Page One," someone replied.

"It's a slow night, I don't have anything worth Page One," I answered.

They looked very surprised. But no one said anything so I picked up my papers and walked out of the room.

Engelking came out later and said he was sorry, he should have explained that I was supposed to go in and pitch some stories for good play, no matter what I thought of them. The game, for the city editors, was to get big display for local news, he explained. After that, I knew how to work the news conference.

But one night a couple of years later, things went wrong in there and revealed some flaws in the great *Tribune* news operation.

It was a Sunday and I was night city editor. Our district men at police headquarters and uptown Manhattan had warned the desk during the day that things were getting dangerous in Harlem. It was a blistering hot day and there were demonstrations and rumbling about rioting. The cops, who ran Harlem in those days, were getting nervous and getting ready.

As night fell, black men, women and children began smashing windows and looting shops along 125th Street, almost all of them owned by whites.

I told our street reporters in Queens and the Bronx to get to Harlem fast to help the Manhattan man. They all reported back that the rioting was out of control, too big for the police to handle.

When I went into the news conference, I said it was a very big story, worthy of big banner headlines. Cornish was not there and the meeting was chaired by one of his assistants, Henley Hill. Everett Kallgren, the news editor—called "The Count" by one and all because of his pretentious manner—was skeptical.

"Every time anything happens in Harlem it is called a riot," he said. "Let's not go overboard on this."

All I could do was relay the information from our reporters, whom I trusted.

With obvious reluctance, Kallgren and his night assistant, Al Davies, laid out big banner headlines.

The district reporters and the rewrite men did their usual fine job, and the first edition, which came up from the presses at 9:30, had a full and satisfactory account of the riot, which was still going on.

But then the first edition of the *Times* arrived. Its story had smaller estimates of the damage and the numbers of people involved, under much smaller headlines.

"That's just what I was afraid of," crowed Kallgren. "Let's get this cut back."

I protested that we must believe our own men, but Henley Hill went along with the Count, why I don't know. I suspect he was unsure of his own judgment.

I did everything I could to convince them of the validity of our story. I pleaded, I begged them to trust the *Tribune* staff. To no avail.

And, to my sorrow, when the final editions of both papers were in hand, after 1 A.M., the *Times* story had been expanded many-fold. The play of the two papers had simply been reversed in size, impact and, I am sorry to say, degree of truth.

When I came in the next day, Engel asked what happened. When I told him, he said he had already guessed the circumstances. He was deeply troubled that his staff had not been believed.

I was acting night city editor again that night, and when I walked into Cornish's office, there sat Kallgren and Davies looking, I must say, somewhat sheepish.

I have never forgiven myself for not saying, loudly, "I don't see any reason to be reporting to these incompetents." *Esprit de l'escalier,* yes, but they were incompetents and had no business being responsible for the news judgments on such a fine newspaper. The *Tribune*'s "second day" story was, of course, correct and complete, filling several pages.

My schedule finally shook down to being day city editor on Saturday and Sunday and night assistant on my other shifts. Sunday was always a slow news day, and my routine was to make out the assignment sheet and then go over to some place on Broadway for lunch, Bleecks being closed on Sunday.

I was about to go off on December 7, 1941, when bells on all the wire service teletype machines began to ring steadily, a signal that something big was going on. The AP, UP and INS bells clanged without stopping for several minutes then simultaneously printed out:

> BULLETIN BULLETIN BULLETIN
>
> JAPANESE PLANES BOMBED THE PEARL HARBOR NAVAL BASE EARLY THIS MORNING.
>
> HEAVY CASUALTIES HAVE BEEN SUFFERED.
>
> STAND BY.

We stood by. For 10, maybe 15, minutes while nothing else came over the now-silent tickers. We began wondering why no details were arriving. Was it possibly a hoax?

We found out later that the bulletin had been phoned to the wire services by Steve Early, the President's press secretary, from his home. The blank interval came while he was being driven to the White House.

I didn't have to call anyone to come to work. Shaplen and Peck, both of whom lived nearby, showed up in minutes. Engelking lived in Forest Hills and it took him a while to get to the office. Dick Tobin, the weekend night city editor, arrived in an hour or so and was shuffling impatiently behind my chair, dying to get into action.

I turned over the local command post to Dick and was thinking of leaving when Engel called me over. Get together a background piece about Campbell and Short, the Army and Navy commanders at Pearl Harbor, he said.

I got out the clips and wrote a story about how we were in good hands, etc. etc. Sort of a euology for two guys who were later court-martialed. But a full story, 75 lines of type, three-quarters of a column.

Pearl Harbor meant that America was in the war all the way and started a rush by almost everyone on the staff for assignment as war correspondents, the most glamorous job in journalism. I asked Joe Barnes, the foreign editor, about my chances for a spot but he indicated I was pretty far down his list. After all, he had all those great reporters panting to go.

There was a poker game twice a week in the sports department bullpen. One night after work, I sat in a game with some sports writers, two guys who worked in the mailroom, and a young city reporter named Seymour Freidin. After one pot had been won with an excellent bluff, one of the mailroom types said, "That's a real Jew trick."

Freidin looked at him coldly and said, "That's how people get their noses broken."

The guy looked very flustered and bowed out of the game in a few minutes.

"That's how to handle that," I thought. "Mr. Freidin, you're my kind of guy." We became good friends and spent a lot of time together in New York and later in Paris after the war.

Chapter 3

Mr. Bleeck's Mission

ONE OF THE MOST AGREEABLE THINGS about the *Herald Tribune* was that almost everyone who worked there, the city staff, sports writers, society and fashion reporters, theater, music and film critics, editorial writers, columnists, copyreaders, advertising salesmen, financial editors, even the publisher, gathered happily day and night in their club, Jack Bleeck's (pronounced Blake's) saloon.

Some denizens called it "The Mission," because it provided a refreshment not only for the body but also for the soul. A group which met every Saturday for lunch at one of the long tables called itself "The formerly Club," after the sign which swung above the door on 40th Street:

ARTIST & WRITERS RESTAURANT (formerly Club)

Note there was only one artist. "The formerly Club" referred to its origin as a speakeasy. Jack Bleeck always was nostalgic for the days of prohibition. Because it was against the law, he happily served us booze in coffee cups on election day.

The *Tribune* people really owned Bleecks, got the best tables and were served promptly. H.L. Mencken once wrote that a good restaurant always had arms on the chairs and sold fine cigars. Bleecks did.

Mencken also wrote that you never really knew a place until you called the waiters by name. We did.

In proper saloon tradition, the bartenders, Henry, Harold and Leo, were our best friends in the place. Although we tipped the waiters, modestly, we didn't tip the bartenders and they didn't buy us drinks. It was an accepted standoff.

There were lots of other regulars: the Lardner brothers, John and David, from *Newsweek;* musicians and technicians from the Metropolitan Opera; Dick Maney, Broadway's ace press agent. Novelist John O'Hara, a *Tribune* alumnus, always came by when he was in the city from Hollywood. Obstreperous when drunk. And the place was mobbed at lunch time by men and often very attractive young ladies from the garment center down Seventh Avenue.

The shabby old joint had a long bar just inside the door on 40th Street with a single row of small tables along the wall facing the bar. Past the bar were two dining rooms separated by a partition in front of which stood a full size suit of armor, a prop from some long-forgotten play. The tables and chairs were battered dark oak and the walls a particularly ugly shade of brown, darkened by years of exposure to billowing cigar smoke. It was grand.

Jack was German and so were his chef and food. Heavy stuff like red cabbage and potato pancakes. Prices were right. Four-ounce Manhattan and Martini cocktails were 25 cents each. A man could—and I saw a lot of them do it—get reasonably drunk for a dollar. A steak sandwich, actually a very good steak on toast, was 85 cents. A minute steak was $1.35.

I was formally introduced to the place by the day city editor, Dick West, who suggested, within an hour after I arrived, that we adjourn to the bar. There he informed me that anyone on the staff automatically ran a tab for all his drinks and meals and settled up on payday. So, he pointed out, I could buy him a drink. Sure enough, as soon as Dick told Henry Shiffgen, the head bartender, that I was now working upstairs, Henry wrote down what I owed and tossed the chit in a cigar box.

The place really was a physical part of the newspaper. Very few guys from the *Times* came around, although it was only a few blocks away. Russell Porter, one of the *Times'* best reporters, was a regular and

Turner Catledge, later executive editor of the *Times*, came in occasionally.

The New Yorker offices were farther away, on 43rd Street between Fifth and Sixth, but a lot of its staff members managed the trek to 40th Street. I met and drank with Joe Liebling, Jim Thurber, St. Clair McKelway and Wolcott Gibbs.

About the match game.

It is a variant of the old children's game "rock breaks scissors, paper covers rock, scissors cut paper." It can be played by any number—we often had seven or eight—but it works just as well with two. Each player is equipped with three wooden matches. He puts both hands behind his back, then puts one clenched fist on the table. Inside the fist can be anything from three to no matches. The players guess, in clockwise order, the total number of matches in all the hands. If a player guesses the total correctly, he drops out and collects any side bets he may have made. The game continues until all have dropped out except two, who then play two-out-of-three. The loser pays off all of the others, usually a drink and one dollar. But there can be many side bets between players contesting which one of them will get out first.

As previously noted, the game got a little out of hand over the years and the side bets got into the $10 and $20 range.

For some reason, this simple game was a big part of life at Bleecks. It is illegal to permit gambling in a bar but Jack never said a word, although it could have cost him his liquor license.

The game encouraged excessive drinking, and many a night it went on until the legal closing hour of 4 A.M. When Henry would finally manage, despite loud protests, to oust us into 40th Street, Lardner, Maney, Gibbs, Porter, Stanley Walker and others, I among them, would often proceed by cab to an after-hours place run by Jimmy Carr in a beautiful old mansion on Fifth Avenue. Jimmy wasn't doing very well and he always welcomed us for more drinks and often breakfast.

"We'll be staggering around the streets at 10," Maney crowed one night when we arrived. We were.

Sometime in the Thirties, Thurber drew a panel of cartoons illustrating the match game, ranging from "horse and horse," which showed two players locked into final combat for the privilege of paying everyone off, to "possible 27" which showed nine guys sitting around a table with their hands behind them. (Twenty-seven was the maximum number if every one of them held three.) One of the nine faces is unmistakeably that of Jim Thurber.

In 1953, Jack Bleeck decided to retire and sold the place to two chaps named Hitz and Fitzsimmons. Jack wrote into the contract that all the dubious art in the place (including a painting by Clare Briggs, the *Tribune* cartoonist, of a golfer raising high his glass on the "19th hole," which I eventually acquired) went with it except the Thurber match game panels. Those Jack took off to his home in Manhasset, L.I.

But he had underestimated some of his old customers and their attachment to the saloon and their favorite game. These were members of the aforementioned "formerly Club." Among "formerly" regulars were John Crosby, Lardner, cartoonist Walt Kelly (who created "Pogo"), an investment banker named Fred Allen (we called him "the real Fred Allen"), and a television sports producer named Hugh Beach, known to his friends as Meathead.

One afternoon, Maney hired a limousine and he and Beach drove out to Manhasset, confronted Bleeck on his doorstep, and demanded possession of the drawings so they could be returned to their rightful place on 40th Street. The pair had been sharing a bottle of scotch on the way, and Jack handed over the drawings.

John and Beach had insisted to Bleeck that the drawings were not his at all, but in truth the property of "The formerly club," which was duty bound to carry out Thurber's wish that they remain forever in the saloon. But instead of placing the drawings back above the armored knight, Maney took them to his office and hung them on his own wall.

When this was reported to the club by Meathead, a great row ensued and dark threats were uttered about legal action, including the claim that Maney had falsely represented himself as a member of the club. After a few days, Maney capitulated and the drawings went home.

If the truth be told, the real reason most of these fellows showed up for lunch on Saturday was that they had no other place to go and several had no desire whatsoever to stay home with their wives. I joined them from time to time when I was around that early on Saturday.

Despite his lapse in the matter of the Thurber panel, Maney was one of the most popular and constant members of the Bleecks gang. A big man with a shock of white hair, a red face and a booming, gravelly voice, he was a marvelous raconteur and an ornament of his perhaps dubious profession. He had a house and a wife in Westport, Connecticut, but slept every week night in the Hotel Astor, right on Times Square. He knew everybody in the Broadway theater and was loved by one and all.

Probably because *Herald Tribune* critics Dick Watts and Howard Barnes were regulars at Bleecks—and perhaps because Maney was always to be found there—a lot of actors used to show up in the place. Tallulah Bankhead, one of Dick's many clients, was there often, every night when she was starring in *The Skin of Our Teeth,* around the corner at the National.

A marvelous dame with a voice and a laugh that could go through a wall, she joined in the match game and went drink for drink, or better, with the players. One night, I was awed by a Bankhead after-hours performance.

When Henry finally managed to get us out of the door sometime after 4 A.M., she announced loudly, "We're all going over to the Elysee." She lived then in the small Elysee Hotel in 54th Street between Madison and Park.

Among the gamesters that night—or morning—were Stanley Walker, Gibbs, Porter and Lardner. When we all trooped into the lobby long after closing time, Tallulah stalked up to the desk clerk and waved toward the closed door of the Monkey Bar.

"Open the bar," she thundered. And I do mean thundered.

The clerk didn't say one word. He reached for a key, unlocked the door and turned on the lights. We helped ourselves from bottles behind the bar and got back to the game.

It was an exhibition of raw power. The hotel could have lost its liquor license by serving booze at that hour, but the clerk knew he didn't have a chance.

One night, Humphrey Bogart came in with his then wife, Mayo Methot. They were both wearing rumpled army fatigues and we found out later that they had just been bounced out of the Mediterranean theater of war, where they had gone to entertain the troops. It turned out they did more drinking than entertaining and the USO command got tired of them.

When he realized that Howard Barnes wasn't around that night, Bogart wanted to leave but they ended up sitting against the wall in the front room with Mrs. B. beating up on him. Literally. With her fists.

The *Tribune* sports editor was Stanley Woodward, a huge bear of a man who had been a fullback in college. He was a fine writer and the kind of editor beloved by his staff. Mrs. Helen Reid became the company powerhouse after her husband, Ogden, died. One day, she told Woodward he would have to reduce his staff by two men. Stanley's reply was: "The two will be Red Smith and me."

Red—Walter Wellsley Smith to his mother—was one of the finest prose writers of his time. His stuff was so classy even non sports fans like me read it faithfully. He hung out at the bar and drank his share. A slight man, unfailingly good-humored, courteous and gentle of speech and manner.

Red's columns were so well written that most readers probably thought turning them out was easy for him. (The sure sign of any professional is to make it look easy.)

But many times I heard Red say that, for him, writing was "only like opening up a vein and letting the blood flow." After covering a sporting event, he would sit down and literally sweat until he had it right.

No one left the sports staff then, despite Mrs. Reid.

One of the regulars at the bar was John Crosby, the talented radio—later television—critic for the *Tribune*. John and I became friends and were together a lot in later years.

Among *The New Yorker* contingent gracing Jack Bleeck's "store," as he called it, were Joseph Mitchell and A. J. Liebling. Liebling was a fine writer and critic but his passion was eating. Some of his classiest prose was devoted to descriptions of meals he had eaten all over the world.

It is literally true that Joe ate himself to death. Tim Costello told me Joe would come into his "store" on Third Avenue and ask for the special of the day, say boiled beef. After finishing that, he would then say he might just try the steak. When the steak was gone, he would announce that the boiled beef was better and have another portion. Finally his legs became so swollen it was hard for him to get around and his heart just gave up.

I never worked for him, but in the early Forties, I spent a lot of time, almost all of it in Bleecks, with Stanley Walker. He was a legendary character in New York journalism, most famous as the city editor of the

Herald Tribune. He had left the paper to work for Hearst's *Daily Mirror.* By the time I got to town, he was writing editorials for the *Tribune* on a free-lance basis.

Stanley was in the saloon almost every night, playing matches. He had written several books, the most famous being *City Editor* and *Mrs. Astor's Horse.* He was a Texan from Lampasas, a stop on the old cattle trail to Kansas City.

Around 1942, Governor Thomas E. Dewey was set to run against Roosevelt in 1944, and the Dewey forces hired Walker to write an official biography of their candidate. His fee was rumored to have been $10,000, and I saw him lose huge chunks of it over the tables at Bleecks. He carried a lot of cash, and as the evening wore on, some of the less savory types in the game began to bait him to wager more and more on side bets. Hundred dollar bills appeared out of his pockets, something few newspapermen had ever seen.

Walker had a problem. It was that he was older than most of the players and alcohol affected him faster. A lesson we all learn eventually.

Although sometimes sarcastic and sardonic, he was fine company, a man with a head full of knowledge about the big city and lots of other things. One night, he gave me a cigar and I punched a hole in the end with my knife.

"What kind of a thing is that to be doing to a good cigar?" he growled. "The way to open a cigar is to pinch it until the leaves open up. Pinch it gently, like a tit."

A couple of days later, the *Tribune* ran an editorial deploring increasing ignorance among the young about how to smoke cigars. I was glad my own ignorance got him $50.

Walker finally went back to a small ranch near Lampasas, which he had never sold, stopped drinking and became a serious breeder of black-faced sheep. The move probably saved his life.

One night, an encounter in the saloon started a new chapter in my personal life. Among the regulars was the garden editor, Jack Johnston, married to a savvy dame named Jean who had been fashion editor of the *Tribune* before Kay Vincent moved in. Around the spring of 1943, she began to meet her two stunning daughters for dinner. Jean, the older, was a classic Irish redhead so lovely she could have been a model. Katherine, two years younger, was black-haired and also a beauty. The patrons loved the sight of them.

One night, Jean introduced me to the girls. She said the family was going to the race track the next day and why didn't I come along? It must have been Tuesday because I went, although I knew nothing about racing or horses.

In the *Herald Tribune* tradition, I not only knew Jean's mother but her grandfather, Rand Anderson. He was the boss of the mailroom and often played in our games at the bar. A crusty Scotsman.

The young Jean and I got married that fall and moved to a drafty apartment on Riverside Drive, just down the block from Riverside Church. It was freezing in winter, famous as the coldest and windiest spot in Manhattan.

Jean was lovely and perfectly at home with our lifestyle; she had grown up in it. She wasn't one bit surprised to find her own grandfather in a group that showed up around 4 A.M. to continue the game.

"Bring on the drinks and something to eat," her grandfather would order. And she did, quite content. I have seen some pretty frosty wives in exactly the same circumstances.

Of all the shining lights gracing The Mission, I judged the brightest to be John Lardner and Walt Kelly. John was one of the very best writers and reporters of his time and Walt was a comic genius. They were fine companions and conversationalists about all kinds of things and great fellows all around. Their friendship was one of the best things that ever happened to me.

Walt was the first comic strip cartoonist to take on the likes of Joe McCarthy and get involved in political commentary. But most of his stuff stuck to the funny antics of the denizens of his beloved Okefenokee swamp.

He used his friends as models for many of the characters. John O'Reilly was the terrible-tempered bear. I was depicted as a tall bird, "Mr. Miggle," a storekeeper who always wore a broad-brimmed hat and smoked a long, thin cigar.

I liked the name—and cherished the connection with Walt—so much I put it on the transom of my boat and now use it as the license plate on my car.

I wish he could see it.

Eddie Lanham told me one night he was often amused to see me and John drinking together at the bar.

"You guys look like an unanimated cartoon," he said. "You stand there saying nothing for a long time, then chat a bit, then stop talking and just lean on the bar. And seem to like it. Crazy."

I had never thought about it but Eddie was right. I am by nature somewhat shy and reserved and so was John. We simply were comfortable in each other's company and had no reason to be chattering away.

John Lardner wrote beautiful stuff, whether about sports or war or whatever. So good it looked easy. He didn't talk a lot but he had a wonderful quiet humor. He was tall and sturdy, black-haired, very attractive. He spent his nights in Bleecks, and his wife, Hazel, spent most of hers in a bar in the Village named Chumleys. Apparently by mutual agreement. But I never saw John with another woman.

A great deal of guff has been written about the uses and abuses of alcohol. For myself, I hold with Winston Churchill that alcohol did more for me than I did for it. I started to drink early and, being shy, found it made social situations easier. Sometimes it got me into trouble but it was, and is, my drug of choice.

What highly vocal seers of alcohol abuse don't seem to understand is that many of the most creative people, such as John's father, Ring Lardner, had a real need for this drug and probably couldn't have done their work without it. Walt and John were bright stars and both were dependent on the crutch of whiskey. In my opinion, it was good for them; I can't conceive of their lives without it.

John and Walt were the closest of friends. When Lardner died in 1960, he was laid out in an open coffin at Campbells on Madison Avenue. I was looking into the coffin when Walt came up behind me.

"I put three matches in his hand," he said.

When Walt died in October 1973, and was laid out for a wake, guess who put three matches in *his* hand?

Chapter 4

Mr. Bugeja's Newspaper
Paris Nights

VINCENT BUGEJA was a native of the island of Malta who grew up in England. He was a fine scholar who aspired to the Roman Catholic priesthood. He entered a Jesuit seminary and had almost completed the rigorous seven year period of training when his superiors circulated a letter notifying all seminarians they must sign a statement that the theory of evolution was false. Bugeja protested.

"To swear to this runs against everything you have been teaching me all these years," he told his Jesuit masters. "You have been telling me to study hard to understand the world and the heavens. I just can't swear that this is false out of hand."

"Sign son," he was told. "Within your lifetime it will be recognized that the theory is probably true, not false. It will make no difference to you."

But young Vincent was adamant, and within a few days, he was released from his vows and left the seminary.

Having nothing in particular to do, he went to Paris. One day, he walked in the door of the European edition of the *New York Herald*

Tribune and asked Eric Hawkins, the managing editor, for a job. Hawkins asked if he had any newspaper experience.

"No," he replied, "but I have been reading your paper for a few days and don't see anything particularly difficult about it."

He was hired, of course, and was still on the staff when I walked through that same door dozens of years later. Buge was chairman of the Socialist party of Malta in absentia, an intellectual, a nudist. A grand man.

After Pearl Harbor, the war dominated the news and the best *Herald Tribune* people were going overseas to report it. O'Reilly was covering battles in Africa; Bigart and Russell Hill and Joe Driscoll had gone to London and then on to Europe after the D-Day invasion of Normandy.

Some were drafted. Bob Donovan went into the infantry along with Bob Crandall, a fine news editor. I received a notice to report to the induction center in the old Grand Central Palace where I stripped for the medical examiners and assured the psychiatrist that I did indeed like women.

I didn't hear anything for a while, then got a notice that I had been given a limited deferment, revocable at any time by the Selective Service. Only then did I discover that the paper had asked for the deferment because I was considered a "necessary employee." I hadn't asked for any such thing but I didn't rush off to enlist. I probably should have but, like many others, I was hoping for an assignment to cover the war.

My prospects of going overseas looked very slim. But in November of 1944, George Cornish called me in and waved toward a new horizon. He told me the European Edition of the *Herald Tribune* was going to resume publication in Paris the following month. Everett Walker, an assistant managing editor, had gone to Paris to help get the paper going and one copyreader, Frank Webb, the very best man on the rim, was already there. They needed help and wanted me to join them. Would I like to go?

Well, yes.

I knew very little about the Paris paper then, indeed I had never seen a copy. I knew it had suspended publication when the Germans occupied Paris and was therefore legally entitled to resume publication. The *Stars & Stripes,* the Army newspaper, already was being printed on the *Herald Tribune* presses at 21 Rue de Berri.

Cornish told me the War Department did not want to give the paper any more war correspondent credentials. But, he said, the State Department would issue me a civilian passport which would be stamped to permit travel into the war zone. I would have to live on the civilian economy, since the military would have no responsibility for me. I didn't know the difference then; I sure found out what it was later.

I got a passport and waited. Finally, after Christmas, I got a call to go out to Floyd Bennett Field and catch such and such a flight of the Military Air Transport Command.

I took a cab out there one night carrying a canvas flight bag bulging with clothes and wearing a long, heavily-lined trench coat, both purchased, of course, at the late, lamented Abercrombie & Fitch. Plus a duffel bag filled with books, bottles and cigars. The plane turned out to be a DC-4 hospital transport, fitted out with hammocks that could be hung up or dropped down to form beds for wounded men being ferried back from Europe.

There were about 20 men on the plane. I was the only civilian. It took the propellor-driven DC-4 eight hours to get to Bermuda. We stayed in officers barracks for 48 hours, then flew another 12 hours to the Azores. It was overnight there and then on into Paris the next day. I got a lift on a truck into the city and found Geoffrey Parsons, Jr., and Eric Hawkins were waiting for me at the ATC depot. Parsons was editor of the paper and Hawkins the managing editor. Both wore correspondent's uniforms, which meant they were "assimilated" captains in the Army.

Accredited correspondents for newspapers, wire services, magazines and radio services lived in the Hotel Scribe, hard by the Paris Opera. Daily briefings were conducted in the hotel ballroom, sometimes including an appearance by the Supreme Commander, Dwight D. Eisenhower.

Why the press in the Scribe? Because that is where the German press had been during the years of occupation. The American Army which entered Paris on the heels of the fleeing Germans simply moved into the same places that had been used by their enemy counterparts.

Where, some general asked, had the German press been billeted? The Scribe? Then American correspondents were sent to the Scribe. General officers of high rank, including Eisenhower, were assigned to the luxurious George V, where German generals had lived. Naval officers were sent to the same luxury hotel the Germans had used to house their Navy officers.

It was probably practical, but hardly good manners. Practical because at the Scribe the clerks and maids and waiters had become accustomed to serving journalists during the last four years. The only difference was that this bunch spoke English.

Being a civilian, I could not stay at the Scribe; I had been booked by the French Ministry of Information into a small hotel named the Lincoln, in a lovely neighborhood just off the Avenue Montaigne. I also got a ration card and French press accreditation. The card authorized me to purchase very small amounts of bread, butter, etc. each week. I don't remember ever using it.

The hotel was perfectly comfortable but with one big drawback: It had not been heated at all for the past four years and this was the middle of winter. It was very cold.

One day in the lobby, an English woman introduced herself as Mrs. P.G. Wodehouse. She and her husband lived in the hotel and they were having a hard time. Then I recalled that Wodehouse had been accused by the British of making propaganda broadcasts for the Germans during the occupation.

When British liaison officers arrived with the French and Americans, they didn't know what to do with the humorist, who had spent the war years in France. He had indeed made some broadcasts but always insisted they had been innocuous and that he had meant no harm. Apparently he was not considered guilty enough to be given any kind of trial or punishment.

But at the same time, for home front morale reasons, the British authorities didn't want him back while the war was still on. So they asked the French to stash the couple somewhere. Like in the Hotel Lincoln. Mrs. Wodehouse was very distressed that they had been there for six months since the liberation and had no idea when they might be permitted to leave. I met them both in the lobby a few days later. They said they knew a few black market restaurants in the *quartier* and gave me the names of some. They finally were permitted to go home and Wodehouse continued to write his enormously successful comic novels.

After getting settled in the hotel, I walked up the Champs-Elysées to the corner of the Rue de Berri and down to number 21, where I would work for almost four years. The building was Twenties modern, with large glass windows. Above the first floor, the structure was U-shaped, with open space in the middle. The left wing of the U on the second floor was Parsons' office and in the right wing were offices of correspondents of the New York paper. The newsroom was at the back of the building on the second floor. It had been divided by a partition. The larger room was the editorial office of the *Stars & Stripes,* the smaller housed the tiny *Herald* staff.

The composing room was at the rear of the first floor and the stereotype and press rooms were on below-ground levels. The printers had all worked there before the war. They didn't speak English and I have no idea how much of it they could read, but they were fine craftsmen, a pleasure to work with.

Some of the upper floors were occupied by the business offices of the *Herald,* one was rented to the Associated Press and others to correspondents of foreign papers.

The *Herald* had resumed publication a few weeks earlier. It consisted of a single page of newsprint and it looked—and read—like a tiny version of the *New York Herald Tribune.* (After a few months, when the war news got hotter, we began printing a FOUR-PAGE paper.)

I was put to work as Hawkins' assistant, with the title of night editor. Frank Webb was the whole copy desk. Also on hand was the aforementioned Vincent Bugeja, and an Englishman named Lewis Glynn, who had been financial editor of the pre-war paper. Both had remained in France throughout the occupation.

We were a small band of very lucky people.

Lucky because nothing could be more wonderful than having your own newspaper to put out every night. One that printed the work of the *Herald Tribune* reporters and had all the resources of the Associated Press, the United Press, Reuters and Agence-France Presse. We had been given a glorious toy, a newspaper of our own.

In New York, for example, decisions about major news of the day and how it should be displayed were made in that big solemn conference in the managing editor's office.

That function was performed every night by just Eric and me. And I dare say a comparison of the New York and Paris papers during 1945— one of the greatest news years in this century—would make us look good.

Eric and I were almost always in complete agreement about the play of the news, although I had habits of news judgment ingrained in 40th Street style while Eric, having always worked for the *Herald* in Paris, was not quite sure we were doing it right.

Because, I now discovered, the pre-war paper had been an entirely different animal.

The little newspaper had an exotic history. It was founded in 1887 by James Gordon Bennett, Jr., famous playboy son of the publisher of the *New York Herald*. He had fled to France to escape social opprobrium after some scandalous prank and started an English-language edition of the *New York Herald* in Paris, because he liked to have a newspaper to play with. After Bennett's death, the paper was bought in 1920 by Frank Munsey, the publisher of the *New York Sun*. A reporter for the *Sun*, Lawrence Hills, was in Paris covering the peace conference and Munsey told him to take over as editor of his new paper. Four years later, Ogden Mills Reid bought it from the Munsey organization.

The pre-war *Paris Herald*—as everyone called it—was then a small, undistinguished newspaper whose principal function seemed to be publishing the New York stock market prices so Americans in Paris could keep up with their money, and interviewing social, literary and theatrical figures when they showed up on holiday from the USA.

It was a glamorous place for young Americans to work between the world wars and many, like Eric Sevareid and William L. Shirer, put in stints in the Rue de Berri, then went on to become journalistic and literary giants. Although it was owned by the Reids, the *Herald* was a French corporation. Because youngsters came clamoring to work on it, wages were very low. But Paris was a great place to live, the girls were agreeable, prices were low and the food was heavenly. They loved it.

The problem with the *Herald* was that, oddly enough, it had been edited and published in almost total isolation from the parent in New York. Hills had gone his own way. For example, as war neared in the late Thirties, the New York paper was strongly on the side of England and France, obviously allied against Germany and Italy. But the Paris paper often contained large advertisements for tourist resorts in the Axis countries. Some of its readers in Paris thought that the paper kowtowed to its advertisers.

Hawkins wrote years later that Hills was very surprised to be told in 1939 that editorials in the *Paris Herald* thereafter would be required to conform with the policy of the New York paper. Both Hills and Bugeja, who wrote many editorials, apparently believed that the Nazis were not bent on war. As Hawkins put it, they thought the Nazis "were engaged in promoting a new and improved form of socialism."

In any event, Hills then gave orders that only editorials written in New York would be printed if they concerned political matters.

Many European newspapers of the period were corrupt in small or large ways; most of them had no tradition of integrity such as guided the best London and New York newspapers.

The paper closed down when the Germans marched into Paris and no decisions had to be made about it until after the French—and Americans—re-took the capital. Then serious consideration was given to abandoning it. A building had been erected for the paper in 1930 in one of the most fashionable sections of the city and the real estate was very valuable. Some Reid financial advisors wanted to take the money and run. But the paper's advertising manager, William E. Robinson, demurred. A hearty, red-faced salesman of the old school, Bill Robinson put down drink for drink with us in Bleecks and was a tough competitor in the match game.

After the liberation, Bill got himself into uniform as a war correspondent and flew to Paris to look the situation over. He went back to New York and proposed that publication be resumed as soon as possible but with one big difference: The paper would henceforth adhere strictly to New York standards in every respect, including news coverage, commentary and advertising policy. It would publish editorials cabled from New York. Its opinions would mirror those of the parent paper. News judgments would be made by people familiar with the New York operation; that was why Frank Webb and I were there.

Robinson also made a decision which had enormous influence on the paper's future. The pre-war sales price had been one franc. Bill decided the post-war price would be three francs, against stiff opposition from the business manager, a Frenchwoman named Renée Brasier, who had been a great and good friend of the late editor Larry Hills. Production prices, wages, newsprint, etc. were frozen at pre-war levels and Mme. Brasier pointed out that the paper could operate profitably with a one franc price. And she thought *she* should be running the paper.

But Bill calculated, correctly, that the market for this English language paper was not going to be Frenchmen at kiosks but the diplomatic community, staffs at military headquarters and Army, Navy and Air Force men in hotels all over the city. Plus GI's in barracks. They couldn't care less about the price, he figured. One franc or three was the same to them.

Apparently Mme. Brasier got one small concession from Robinson. When publication was resumed a box at the top of the front page read, "TEMPORARY Price 3 Francs." By July, it read simply, "Price 5 Francs." The paper was making an excellent profit.

(Incidentally, Bill Robinson knew how to get along with the right people. During this trip, he sought out Dwight D. Eisenhower and they became close friends. After the war, they were constant golfing companions at Augusta and elsewhere.)

Before I arrived, I knew that old friends were already installed in the Rue de Berri. O'Reilly was bureau chief for New York and Joe Newman, Carl Levin and Russell Hill were based there. Sy Friedin was in and out.

But a surprise was to find *Herald Tribune* men on the other side of the partition, in the *Stars & Strips* office. Both Bob Donovan and Bob Crandall had managed to get themselves transferred from the infantry to the *Stripes*. And there were other experienced and capable journalists on that staff.

During the early months of 1945, Webb had the toughest job on the paper because he was our only copyreader. When we went to four pages every day, his work load was too much and Eric hired moonlighting *Stripes* men to help him. Soon we had better copyreaders than were working in New York. Crandall sat alongside Frank and was joined by Lewis Jordan, a *New York Times* editor. They were delighted to pick up some spending francs for a little night work.

The copyreading worked out so well I got some rewrite help. Donovan came in, asking that whatever he earned be held in New York to be paid after the war. Ernest Leiser, from Chicago, gave us a hand. I was later to work for and with Ernie for years at CBS.

That winter was a rough one for Parisians, most of whom did not have enough food or drink or heat. Although we were civilians sleeping in freezing hotel rooms, Frank and I had one invaluable prerequisite: We could eat at the enlisted men's mess set up for the *Stars & Stripes* staff. Lunch at the mess was breakfast for us but the greatest blessing was that it served a hot meal late at night. That *was* a perk!

As spring brought warmer days, it became apparent that, despite the bitter winter battles in Germany, the war was finally drawing to a close. But less than a month before it ended, we had a story under a double banner headline.

ROOSEVELT DIES OF STROKE IN GEORGIA
TRUMAN SWORN IN AS NEW PRESIDENT

I wrote the story, "Special to the European Edition," incorporating wire service and *Herald Tribune* material.

"WASHINGTON, April 12—Franklin Delano Roosevelt, President of the United States and Commander-in-Chief of its Armies and Navies sweeping to victory around the world, died today in a bedroom of his cottage at Warm Springs, Ga." And so on for more than a column.

The off-lead story was about the "final Allied drive" with Generals Omar Bradley, William Simpson and George Patton advancing on a broad front toward Berlin. It seemed unfair that President Roosevelt had not lived to see the victory in Europe.

The *Stars & Stripes* had a tradition that its editors were not officers but enlisted men. The tradition went back to its founding during World War I by the first editor, Harold Ross. The same Ross who founded *The New Yorker.*

We were ourselves "assimilated enlisted men" and Frank and I always had excellent relations with the *Stripes* editors and staff. Some of them, like Leiser and Andy Rooney, became and still are close friends. But during the final weeks of the war, the treatment of the big story was markedly different in our paper and theirs. The *Stripes* kept running very big tabloid-type headlines indicating that the war was over, or at least almost over. We were far more cautious.

One day, one of the few officers connected with the *Stripes* asked me to have dinner with him. He wanted to talk about the difference in news treatment in the two papers. I explained that in my opinion the last thing a soldier wanted to hear was that the war was over unless it really *was* over. Therefore the *Herald* was playing it conservatively.

I guess officers did have some influence, because the *Stars & Stripes* changed managing editors two days later.

We did not, of course, underplay the story when the facts were evident. Five days before the official end of the war, the *Herald* had triple eight-column headlines:

GERMANY'S WAR MACHINE COLLAPSES

ALL IN ITALY SURRENDER, REDOUBT GONE

HITLER BELIEVED DEAD AS BERLIN FALLS

Imagine having to squeeze the words "as Berlin falls" in at the very end of a headline!

But the whole enormous war enterprise was rushing to a conclusion, no matter who wrote what about it. On May 8, 1945, the *Paris Herald* had a single banner headline four inches high:

VICTORY

(and under a ten-point boldface byline)

By Leslie Midgley

"The German Army announced yesterday that it had surrendered unconditionally, laying down its arms in defeat after five years and eight months of bitter warfare raging over Europe..." And so on and so forth.

A few paragraphs down in the story was the account of how the news had reached the United States, in a dispatch by Edward Kennedy, chief of the Associated Press bureau in Paris, continuing, "As a result, all transmission facilities of the AP in Europe were suspended yesterday afternoon by the Army Public Relations Division, which claimed that the news should have been held for official release..."

It was a classic snafu, trying to put a time and date on a "release" which would announce the end of a great war when everyone knew the surrender had been signed.

Ed Kennedy was a hero to the press corps for his feat of getting the story past censorship and into the London office of the AP. There was a lot of speculation about how he had done it. We soon found out that he had used *Herald Tribune* equipment.

What happened was that Mort Gudbrod, Ed's assistant, knew we had a telephone line which could reach London directly. We used the line both to send stories on to New York and to receive voice transmission of stories from London for the Paris paper. The transmissions were recorded on discs—crude by today's standards—and transcribed by a typist.

Ed got his story of the surrender at Rheims to Mort, who used our line to call not the *Herald Tribune* London bureau but the AP office. The censors in London assumed the story had been cleared in Paris and let it go through to New York.

Anyway, the suspension of facilities for the AP lasted only a day or two. The agency issued strong statements of support for Kennedy, but not long afterward a place was found for him as editor of a newspaper in Santa Barbara, California.

My rewrite story led the paper with type set three columns wide. The off-lead on the left side was under a headline: "EYEWITNESS TELLS OF BERLIN RUINS/ Nothing Left, Says Correspondent, Except Mountains of Debris and a Few Shell-Riddled Walls." The story was signed by Sy Friedin, who had managed to get into Berlin with the very first Americans. But his dispatch started out "BERLIN, Thursday, May 3, (Delayed)" The censors had held it up for four days. The same thing happened to Ernie Leiser, who was on the scene for the *Stars & Stripes*.

So the war was over in Europe and our friends in the office next door looked forward to going home. It would be months before they would be dispersed either back to the USA or up to Wiesbaden, Germany, where the *Stars & Stripes* set up its new European headquarters.

Food and fuel were still strictly rationed for Parisians but it was summer now and life was a lot more pleasant for everyone. The race tracks were open in the Bois de Bologne and the city looked drab but lovely.

The war was still going on in the Pacific, although dispatches from Homer Bigart, Mac Johnson and other *Herald Tribune* correspondents reported that the Japanese were taking a terrible beating.

Then on August 7, a story came over the wires that changed everything. Frank Webb wrote over it a truly classic headline:

ATOMIC BOMB REVOLUTIONIZES WAR
HITS JAPAN LIKE 20,000 TONS OF TNT
Secret of Nature Solved
To Rain Ruin on Enemy

I rewrote everything we could get from our own Washington bureau and the wires. The story was adequate but nothing could match those headlines. The *Tribune* in New York and almost every other American paper headlined the "20 thousand tons of TNT" because that had been in the official release but their insights didn't go to "revolutionizes war." That's genius.

Because physics was one of his hobbies, Bugeja was of great help in assembling the story but even he was baffled. After the paper was locked up that night, I asked our French "cycliste," Paul, to get us a bottle of brandy and told Bugeja to explain what this was all about.

"I just don't know," he said. "We were always taught that if you started an atomic chain reaction there would be no way to control it. It might just end up by destroying every thing on earth, maybe the planet itself.

"I can only conclude that the Americans have found some way of terminating the chain reaction after they have obtained a certain amount of energy from it. It's an enormous event."

I am very proud of the work we did in Paris that year but I don't think we ever topped the handling of that great, and mystifying, story.

It was, of course, the beginning of the end. On August 8, our headline was, "RUSSIA WARS ON JAPAN." On August 10, it was "JAPAN OFFERS SURRENDER," and on August 15, "TOKIO SURRENDERS UNCONDITIONALLY." The war was over.

There was a lot of celebrating in Paris that night because now all the troops knew for sure they would not be going to the Pacific war zone.

After work we again ordered up a bottle of cognac and sat around the office talking about the final edition.

"Frank," I said, "you and I will never see another year for news like this one. Roosevelt died, the war in Europe was won, the first atomic bomb was exploded with God knows what consequences, and now the Japanese have surrendered after overrunning the Pacific. Some year."

And we never did see another like it. We had a ball, and when I write that, I am well aware that our big news was of terrible death and destruction.

We were, indeed, a small band of lucky men. Because we had a newspaper of our own. And enormous events to report in it. Who could ask for anything more?

Chapter 5

War Is Hell
But Not for Some Characters

IN ADDITION TO the always eye-catching parade of Parisiennes on the avenues and past the sidewalk cafes that summer, there were characters worth watching in the swollen press corps. Many of them had a ball, the best time of their lives. Their war was not exactly hell.

Jack Belden was one of the finest TIME-LIFE correspondents but what he did best was play poker. One night after work, I asked Boris, the night driver, to take me to the Hotel Scribe. In O'Reilly's room, number 400, I found the dregs of what had obviously been a big game, now down to O'Reilly, Belden and Colonel Kenneth Downs, a dapper former INS correspondent. He was the only American officer I ever saw who actually carried a swagger stick under his arm.

When I sat down at the table, John suggested I watch a hand first. The last bet on that hand was more money than I had in my wallet. I had a drink instead of getting in the game.

They were playing stud and the next hand ended with Belden versus Downs. The colonel made a very large bet and Jack began an oration.

"Goddamit, you got me," he wailed, standing up and walking around the room, pounding his fists on the walls. Ken sat quietly and watched the performance. Then Jack abruptly sat down and raised. Downs called, but guess who had the right hole card?

After the war ended, this game began to get bigger and bigger with what were, to me anyway, enormous stakes. One of the reasons was that the Army finance office on the Champs-Elysées transmitted money orders back to the States for officers, which included accredited correspondents. Some sharp type had figured out this was a way to stash cash at home.

Correspondents, and some of their friends in the military, began to drift back from Germany with odd kinds of money, including currencies which had been printed by the occupation authorities, spearhead money orders and other esoterica. One night, I couldn't help noticing that one of the Army types was more interested in getting his hands on dollar-convertible money instruments than he was in winning the game. He was laundering money. I found out the next day that he had been in Wall Street as a civilian and was shipping tax-free money home.

One day, Belden had a lot of winnings. He went to the finance office and filled out a fistful of applications for money orders. Told he could buy only one at a time with, I believe, a $200 top, Jack asked how many times he could come back.

"I don't look at who is in the line," was the answer.

He spent most of the afternoon going from the window to the end of the line handing in forms one at a time.

More and more correspondents in uniform kept arriving in Paris enroute to take a look at the ruins in Germany. Among them was the mentor of my youth, Sidney Olson, now a principal writer for LIFE. The TIME-LIFE contingent lived high on the hog, not in the Scribe with the ordinary working press. The Ritz was more to their taste. Even fancier than the Ritz was the Lancaster, a small hotel in the Rue de Berri just down the block from the *Herald*. Charlie Wertenbaker was the senior TIME man and he lived in this elegant little hostelry, reputed to have been *the* place British duchesses went to have a fling in Paris. Charlie had a suite, complete with grand piano, which had formerly been occupied by Marlene Dietrich.

Wertenbaker was away when Sid arrived so he moved into the suite. One day, he announced he was giving a cocktail party. For me. We invited the *Herald* and *Stripes* gang and other friends and a fine time was had by all. Nice thing to do for an assimilated corporal.

Among the TIME-LIFE group I met a genuine war correspondent hero, the photographer Robert Capa. He liked to stay up all night and took to dropping around the paper about the time we were wrapping up. I think he knew every bistro and club in the city and was hailed with glad cries everywhere we went.

Short and stocky, with eyes as black as those of Pablo Picasso, Capa enjoyed the pleasures of life as much as anyone I ever met. He did indeed have a girl in every port and, I suspect, wanted a "friend" from every country. One day, he showed up in the Ritz bar with a truly lovely Israeli. New country, new friend.

We left the bar, on the Rue Cambon side of the hotel, to walk through to the Place Vendome. The corridor was—and still is, I guess—lined with showcases glittering with pieces from the most expensive jewelers in Paris.

As the lady began to slow down in front of the cases, Bob kept calling out, "Eyes straight ahead, Pita. Eyes straight ahead."

During the summer, Geoffrey Parsons and Drue Leighton, the lovely lady he had been living with, got married one afternoon and had a grand reception in their beautiful flat on the Ile St. Louis just behind Notre Dame.

Frank Webb and I were holding drinks and chatting when in walked a tall, handsome man with wavy hair wearing what was called an Eisenhower jacket, a short style favored by the Supreme Commander. The jacket was usually made of olive drab wool, worn with trousers called pinks, a lightly tinted tan. But this beautifully tailored outfit was all made of pinks, complete with *brown suede shoes*. Shoulder patches identified the wearer as a war correspondent.

"Frank," I said, "what on earth is that?"

"I have no idea," he answered.

A few nights later, Bob Capa stopped by long after midnight, seeking company. After I finished up, we got in his jeep and he started to drive toward the Seine and Montmarte. I made some comment about the vision Frank and I had seen at the wedding reception. Capa fixed me with those black eyes.

"Les," he said, "Charlie Collingwood is one of the finest and bravest correspondents covering this war." I had been properly chastised. By one qualified to judge. Years later, Collingwood and I worked together on scores of shows for CBS News and became close friends. He was indeed a remarkable man.

As noted, the *Stars & Stripes* had some very solid citizens on its staff, like Bob Donovan, Bob Crandall, Ernie Leiser, Lew Jordan, Ben Price, Andy Rooney and many others. Along with some offbeat types. Like Junior Gordon. Junior had been a sports writer on the Hearst paper in Boston before he found himself fighting with the infantry across Normandy. He got transferred to the *Stripes* in Paris and from then on life was a ball. (His name was David Gordon. He was called Junior because there was another David Gordon on the staff. Who was, of course, Senior Gordon.)

When I got to Paris, Junior was living, not in the barracks assigned to the *Stripes* staff, but in a seedy French hotel at the end of the Rue de Berri, rooming with another character named Fred Fererra. They paid for the room and some meals and lashings of cognac with cigarettes and other Post Exchange items such as soap, Kleenex and tinned food.

Junior was a short, dark wiseguy, and Freddy was a tall, dark wiseguy who had been a bartender in New York before the war and went back to being a bartender after it. He eventually became head of a bartenders union local and, in the great tradition, went to jail for misusing union funds. Junior and Freddy had a lot of fun in 1945. They had jeeps to get around, not to cover stories but to go to the racetracks. The PX was a reliable source of stuff which could be converted into francs. Living was easy. They were not all that eager to be shipped back to the USA. Amusing and dependable companions, day or night.

Also residing in the hotel was a blonde named Gay Orlova, who was reputed to have been one of Lucky Luciano's girls in New York. She had somehow been stranded in Paris during the occupation. She was very, very friendly with a series of *Stripes* staffers.

Junior and Freddy were only little operators on the fringe of the huge black market that flourished after the war, especially in Germany, where cigarettes became the true currency of the country. But they fancied themselves big operators. One day, they showed up with a barracks bag stuffed with currency. The notes were French francs printed in occupied Germany. But not by the French; these francs had been run off by the Russians. Freddy had obtained them for a pittance and brought the bag back to Paris in an Army vehicle. They expected to make a killing but were nervous about holding the stuff in the barracks or in their room. I agreed to stash it for them. They finally did sell the money for about what they had paid. Not the glittering haul they expected.

One of our good friends was a Czech who drew political cartoons for French newspapers. He had an unpronouncable name but signed his work "Woop" and that is what everybody called him. He was a huge man, 6'4", with a big black drooping moustache grown, I was told, to hide some of the enormous damage inflicted on him by gestapo torturers. Almost everyone in France claimed, after the war was over, to have been in the Resistance, but there was no doubt about Woop. He was a genuine hero. He was marvelous company and loved to bring his accordion to parties to squeeze out corny Parisian dance tunes.

Woop lived in Paris with his English wife for a year or so, then bought an old mill in the countryside outside the city which he began remodeling into a pleasant house. One day, he asked me if I had a gun. I told him yes, O'Reilly had given me one. It was a small Italian Berreta pistol wrapped in oilcloth, along with a supply of ammunition. I told Woop he was welcome to it; I had no use for firearms around the house. But he did. If someone came looking for him again, he wanted to be ready.

Chapter 6

After the War Is Over

IN THE SUMMER OF 1945, a new general manager for the European Edition had arrived in Paris. He was Kenneth Collins, a high-powered advertising man who had been a vice president of Macy's in New York and was a long-time friend of Bill Robinson.

Jean and I had been writing about the possibility of her coming to Paris, and I was looking for an apartment. Geoffrey Parsons said one was available in his building, at 18 Quai d'Orleans. The building, a Paris landmark, was owned by Tudor Wilkinson, an American expatriate, who lived in a beautiful duplex above the Parsons. His wife, still lovely, had been the original Dolores of the Ziegfeld Follies.

Wilkinson was quite willing to rent me the place, which had a two-story living room on the ground floor complete with huge cathedral windows facing the sidewalk along the Quai. Staircases led to bedrooms on either side of the second floor. The furniture was huge and old; a refectory table must have been 12 feet long. A showcase, as they say.

The catch was the Wilkinson wanted to be paid in dollars, deposited in New York. Since I worked for a French corporation and was paid in francs, I didn't see how that would work. And the price, $2,000 a year, seemed astronomical. I told Ken Collins I just couldn't afford it. He said to take it; he would arrange for the payment in New York. So I moved out of the Hotel Lincoln, to which I had become quite accustomed, and into this grand place on the Ile St. Louis.

With the war ended and the American armies streaming home across Europe and the Atlantic, more and more Americans were showing up in Paris. One day, Edgar Mowrer, a famous foreign correspondent for the *Chicago Daily News,* arrived and announced he was there to publish a Paris edition of the *New York Post.* The *Post* was a second-rate afternoon tabloid which wasn't doing very well at home.

Mowrer asked me to have a drink with him and suggested that I become managing editor of the new paper. It so happened that Mowrer's appearance coincided with a visit by Mr. and Mrs. Ogden Reid, their first since the war ended. Mr. Reid visited the newsroom one night and I overheard him asking Eric which one of these people was Midgley. He then came over and chatted cordially. The next day, Parsons told me they would raise my salary and I said I would stay at the *Herald.* The *Paris Post* did indeed appear but it wasn't much of a newspaper and only lasted a year or so. (The *Herald Tribune* really had a lock on the town; several years later *The New York Times,* no less, tried to publish there and failed ignominiously.)

Ogden was visibly fading by then and often got into arguments in public with his wife, usually about her refusal to let him have a bottle of brandy.

Jean finally wrote that she had obtained a passport and could get passage to France on a cargo ship. She did, and to meet her, I traveled all night with a courier who drove down to Le Havre with bundles of our paper to be put on channel steamers enroute to London. That night, we were together in Paris in the rococo flat that was to be our home for the next four years. Where two girls with dual French and American citizenship would start their lives.

One day, the Army announced that Americans living in Paris could buy jeeps from the huge surplus stocks parked just outside the city. So I bought a jeep. Then I could work for a few hours in the afternoon, go home for dinner and back to the Rue de Berri until the wee hours. And we could get around the city and nearby countryside on weekends.

Jean and her sister had spent most of their teenage years on a farm on the Eastern Shore of Maryland. They had several dogs on that place and she was anxious to have one now. Since we were in France, it must be a caniche, a French poodle. We found a breeder and she picked out a tiny brown ball of fluff that turned out to be the finest dog I ever knew. He had a grand pedigree but we named him Mike. He was the family's constant companion for the next 14 years.

One day, I felt terrible and Jean said I looked sallow. We got the *Herald* driver to take me out to an American Army hospital in the suburbs. They took one look and put me to bed. I was literally unconscious for two days, and when I came to, found that my skin and eyeballs were a rich shade of yellow. Jaundice, probably from contaminated food or water, the doctors said. I was in a ward with 20 or so GIs, all of them various shades of yellow. The doctors said the only treatment was a diet of hard-boiled eggs and white bread. The fact is they had no idea what caused the hepatitis or how to treat it.

The guys in the ward were good company; all they wanted was to get out and go home. The patients—including me—especially appreciated the sight of Jean on her frequent visits. She was pregnant, but the GIs hadn't seen anything like her for a long time.

After a couple of weeks, my color was something resembling normal and I asked the doctor in charge of the ward if I could go home. He said he couldn't let the soldiers go because they had to eat in a mess and couldn't stay on a proper diet, but since I had an apartment it would be okay. No drinking, he warned.

A few weeks later, I wandered into the Ritz Bar around lunch time and asked for a dry martini.

"I thought I told you not to drink," came a voice from down the bar. It was the doctor.

"But I feel okay now" was the only answer I could think of.

"Oh well, let me buy you one," he said. "I'm going home tomorrow."

Drue Parsons, Geoffrey's wife, knew a gynecologist who was reputed to be the finest such specialist in the city. He was a charming Frenchman named Jacques Varangot, who was delighted to take on the case of Mrs. Midgley. He practiced at the American Hospital, but recommended instead a specialized clinic at Bologne-Billancourt run by a very stern Catholic sister. Leslie Rand Midgley was born there in June, 1946. Rand for her maternal great-grandfather, Rand Anderson, the old boss of the mailroom in New York.

In the fall, we decided to make a trip home for a change of scene and to show the baby to her grandparents. Planes were now available for civilian transatlantic travel but I wanted to go by ship. Eric had friends at the United States Lines, and one day they said we could have a tiny cabin on a ship registered in Scandinavia that was in the Havre-New York run. It had been converted to a troop ship during the war and there were only a few cabins.

Once again, Collins arranged dollar payments for our passage and also for the price of a used car I wanted to pick up in New York to drive out to Utah. When Ken heard we had been booked on the ship, he decided to make the trip himself.

Other passengers on the ship, we discovered, would be Nicky Raymond, the teenaged son of Allen Raymond, a *Tribune* correspondent who lived on our island, and Virgil Thomson, the gifted composer and music critic of the *Herald Tribune*. Virgil had lived in Paris for years before the war and maintained a flat there.

So one day, we boarded the boat train for LeHavre with an infant in a laundry basket, assorted luggage and a smartly-coiffed brown poodle. Other passengers in our compartment seemed surprised to see the dog and one provided an inkling of what was to come by asking if we had a rabies certificate. We didn't.

When the US Lines ticket agent came through the train, he glared at Mike and warned that we couldn't board the ship with a dog and not to try it.

The conductors only asked whether the dog was French, smiled when told he was from Gascony, and politely asked for 120 francs for his train ticket.

When we found the ship, Virgil and Nicky were waiting in line to board. Nicky and I found some sailors playing catch nearby and noticed that a small dog was with them. They said he lived in the crew's quarters. One of the sailors said he would take Mike aboard, feed him and deliver him on the pier in New York for $20. I had misgivings about getting him back on the other side but slipped off his fancy collar and leash and turned him over to the sailor.

We got settled in a tiny cabin which contained two bunks, two chairs and a chest which could hold the baby's basket.

After the ship pulled out of the harbor and headed across the English channel for Southampton, a shaken Mr. Collins showed up at our door. He had found himself in a cabin with 50 bunks. Not his idea of how general managers should travel. We gave him a few drinks and he went off unhappily to his troopship accommodations. The next morning, he left the ship and went to London enroute to New York via Pan American Airways. First Class, I imagine.

Virgil Thomson, on the other hand, was *delighted* to be in a cabin with 49 other men. We saw a lot of him during the voyage. It was my first Atlantic crossing by ship but old stuff to Virgil.

Nicky checked on the pooch during the voyage and said he was okay but not getting any exercise. The day before we were to land, word came from the crew that the first mate had found Mike, knew immediately he did not belong to a crewman and ordered him impounded.

When I sought out the mate, he explained they could not land without entering all livestock on the ship's manifest for quarantine purposes. Also, I'd have to buy a ticket for the dog's passage from the purser.

The purser was sympathetic but happy to take $35 from me. He said the quarantine officers would require a rabies certificate, and that if we didn't have one, we would have to get a veterinary to come aboard and administer an injection before Mike could go ashore.

We got our luggage and the baby through customs and into a room at the Waldorf-Astoria. I found a vet listed in the yellow pages near the pier on 46th Street. He gave the dog an injection ($15), the quarantine officers filled out their forms and I walked Mike down the gangplank.

He was a mess. Apparently thinking his whiskers were too long, some sailor had trimmed them, making his snout pointed instead of properly square. He was a tub of fat and what was left of the whiskers were clogged with chewing gum. The first port of call next morning was a dog beauty parlor near the hotel.

Jean showed off baby and dog to her mother and sister and I visited the *Tribune* city room and Bleecks.

I picked up a Chrysler sedan with about 50,000 miles on it and we started the drive west. Although he had eaten in the best restaurants in Paris and spent a few nights at the Waldorf-Astoria, Mike was banned by hotels and motels in Middle America and spent his nights in the car. On we went, through Ohio, Illinois, Iowa, Nebraska and Wyoming. In Cheyenne, I stopped, as was my invariable custom, to have a drink at the bar of the Plains Hotel. (I always have maintained that the West begins at Cheyenne.) We crossed the Continental Divide after a four-inch snowfall with no chains on the tires and came down to the Salt Lake valley.

We left the dog with a friend and the baby with her grandparents and went on to San Francisco with my brother, Grant, and his wife, Marsha. Returning in a few days, we picked up both and crossed the country again, this time by a southern route. In Washington, we had a pleasant evening with John and Kitty Denson. He was now the assistant chief of the TIME-LIFE bureau in Washington.

We had a couple of days in New York, then boarded the Queen Mary—the great old Queen Mary Number One—for the voyage back to Europe. First class. It was very grand. The huge liner had been a troop ship during the war and the British had rushed to refit her for civilians because they badly needed the foreign currency she earned.

No trouble about dogs on this ship. It had a bank of kennels on the top deck, along with an exercise area and stewards to take care of them.

We stayed at the Dorchester in London for a few days, then took the boat train for Paris. When the conductor came through, he told me our dog was fine and in the baggage car. He had been quarantined in British customs. After the train pulled up on the dock alongside the channel steamer, I walked up to the front of the train and there he was, leaping and barking with joy at seeing me again.

Late that afternoon, we were back home on the Quai d'Orleans and delighted to be there. John Crosby wrote a column about Mike's trip to America and his return to Paris. (Columnists, I had discovered, often are desperate for material.)

Both British and American newspapers had complained about restrictions on the amount of newsprint they could use during the war but they had been rationed into prosperity willy-nilly. Their incompetent business managers could not understand that smaller papers with the same advertising rates and the same newsstand price would be very profitable.

So the *Herald Tribune* had prospered, and during the late Forties, it maintained large and excellent news bureaus throughout Europe. There were four or five correspondents in each of the bureaus in London, Rome and Paris. Marguerite Higgins and Russell Hill were in Berlin, Higgins busily making a killing in the black market by selling cigarettes imported duty-free and in case lots through the military postal system. Cigarettes had replaced marks as the currency of Germany, and visitors to her villa in Berlin reported in was packed with furniture, china, jewelry, etc., all acquired from desperate Germans in exchange for cigarettes.

Our little transcription room, used to record and pass on to New York over voice circuits the work of these correspondents, was now operated by a former WAC named Stiva Berger, a charming and efficient young lady. On holiday in Paris from his beat in the Balkans, Sy Friedin asked me one night, "Where is that girl I have been talking to on the phone?"

I took him next door and introduced him to Stiva. So a few months later, they were married. And still are.

Among *Herald Tribune* correspondents arriving in Paris was Bill Attwood, who had been a Marine in the Pacific theater during the war. Bill spoke excellent French, having spent childhood years in Paris. He began living with a beautiful young lady named Simone, whom he had known as a child. They were married and had a good life until he died in April 1989.

In the summer of 1947, John and Gladys O'Reilly decided to return to New York and we put together a great gag edition of the Paris paper to bid him farewell.

John's successor as bureau chief was Walter Kerr, who had been a correspondent in Russia and the Balkans as well as several European countries. He and his wife Vivian had leased a very fancy apartment on the Ile St. Louis owned by Helena Rubinstein.

One night at dinner, we got into a heated discussion about postwar politics. Walter insisted that Tito was going to knuckle down to the Russians. No way it could be otherwise, he insisted. He had been a correspondent in Russia and was a friend of the then Secretary of State Edward R. Stettinius.

I didn't fancy myself as an expert in Balkan affairs but I insisted that Josip Broz, having won his own war and with a tough army totally committed to him, had no reason to take orders from someone else. We bet a dinner at the best restaurant in Paris on the issue. I won but I don't remember collecting.

Incidentally, there was another Walter Kerr—same spelling—on the *Herald Tribune*. He was the drama critic in New York, and a fine one.

Our man was thus called "the foreign Walter Kerr." He later became the foreign editor in New York and then editor of the ill-fated Paris edition of *The New York Times*.

Among other events of 1947, Jean discovered she was pregnant again and it was back to Dr. Varangot. When the time came in November for her to return to the clinic at Boulogne-Billancourt, the directress was sharply disapproving. "It's too soon," she sniffed at me.

When the hour came for delivery, she ushered me into the room and I first saw Andrea Susan with the umbilical cord attached.

Jean had been driven to the hospital in a fine car at the disposal of the TIME-LIFE bureau chief. He was Andre LaGuerre, who had left the French information ministry for *Time* and, as "Eddie Snow," was an occasional racing columnist for the *Herald*. Andre always insisted she was named for him. I don't remember where the Andrea came from. The Susan we selected because our landlords, the childless Wilkinsons, were crazy about the name.

So we had two citizens of France in the house and an increase in an odd feature of French life, the family allowance. After Leslie was born, a man in uniform began to show up at our door in the courtyard of 18 Quai d'Orleans with a leather satchel over his shoulder. From it, he would extract a wad of banknotes and hand them to Jean. Only to the mother. Never to the father or a maid. The payments came because I was working for a French company and the children were French nationals.

Also in 1947, my close friend Stephen White and his wife Miriam showed up in Paris. When the atomic bomb was dropped in 1945, Steve was the only member of Enkelking's staff who carried a slide rule. Engle persuaded him to become the *Tribune*'s science reporter. As such he started out in the manner of good reporters everywhere to learn the subject and know the people involved. Along the way, he became friends with such luminaries as J. Robert Oppenheimer, I.I. Rabi and many other great physicists of the time.

After the furor about the atomic bomb died down, Steve wrote editorials until Ogden Reid died in 1947. At which time Ogden's widow installed her oldest son, Whitelaw, as publisher. "Whitey" brought some of his pals from Yale into the operation and wanted one of them to write editorials. When Steve was told he would no longer be working for the editorial page, he resigned. Mrs. Reid thereupon called him in and asked what he wanted to do. When he said he would like to be a foreign correspondent, she said okay and he was off to France.

Great things were happening during those postwar years, of course. Such as the organization and operation of the Marshall Plan and the economic revival of western Europe.

We dutifully reported such big matters in the style befitting a serious major newspaper. That was our basic assignment. But we could find space for only limited accounts of the news of Paris itself.

One afternoon, I got an intriguing view of what the *Paris Herald* had been before my time.

Eric was off on a trip to New York and I was filling in for him when a very handsome man, accompanied by a lovely lady, came to visit the *Herald* office in the rue de Berri. He was, he explained, George Balanchine, the dancer and choreographer.

"I came over because the *Herald* always interviews me when I come to Paris. No one has called on me at the Ritz," he said.

I got the point and had one of the newsroom staff sit down to ask him what he was working on in Paris and how he had found postwar Europe.

I trust he was pleased at the story in the next morning's edition.

Some of the Americans who visited Paris had backgrounds slightly different than that of the ballet master Balanchine.

One day, a story came over the wires that Benjamin Siegel had been shot to death through a picture window in his home in Las Vegas, Nevada. Siegel, popularly known as "Bugsy," had built the Flamingo Hotel in Las Vegas, the first big gambling casino operation along what was called "The Strip." It was assumed by all the cognoscenti that his backers in the criminal syndicates, had been displeased by the way he was running the place. The wires also reported that his constant companion, a striking lady named Virginia Hill, was not in Nevada at the time, but in Paris.

Well! That was a *Paris* story.

Bob Yoakum, a young reporter, found her registered at the Ritz and she consented to be interviewed. She tearfully lamented the passing of "dear Ben," said she had no idea why anyone would want to do such a thing, and explained she just happened to be in Paris on a pleasure trip. Yoakum, who subsequently wrote columns for the *Herald* and in the years since has written many humorous pieces for American papers, turned in a very funny story about the lady's reaction to "Bugsy's" demise.

That night after work, I wandered around the corner to a small night club/bar frequented by our staff and visiting Americans. I was sitting at the bar when the door opened and in walked a short, stocky young man with a square face and very bright eyes. He made a point of staring at the patrons, one by one. He seemed to be trying to play the part of the young gunman in *The Maltese Falcon*.

One of Virginia's vacation staff, I thought.

Chapter 7

Transit
Back to New York

THE PARIS YEARS were fun and very satisfying, but in October of 1948, I decided to visit the New York office to see if I could get some idea of my future at the *Herald Tribune*. Neither Geoffrey nor Eric would be leaving Paris so there seemed little prospect of advancement there.

I flew back to New York at the beginning of November and went to stay with the Olsons, who had bought a beautiful old house in suburban Larchmont.

Time Inc. had decided to sponsor election night on NBC over the new thing called television. Part of the deal was that Sid would appear on camera with Ben Grauer, an NBC announcer.

The contest was between Governor Thomas E. Dewey of New York, who was expected to win by a landslide, and Harry S Truman, the incumbent President.

NBC had given the Olsons a television set, a big brown box with a tiny screen in the middle. So Mrs. Olson asked some neighbors to come by on election night to watch. What we saw was a fuzzy little picture of Sid and Ben talking about the returns, which were printed on blackboards. Yes, BLACKBOARDS, just like those in grade school. On which numbers were chalked and erased, chalked and erased.

As the night wore on, the totals for Truman ran ahead of those for Dewey. Ben kept saying "Wait until the big states come in and we'll see Dewey win." Sid kept saying it didn't look that way.

Finally, the neighbors went home and went to bed. I got up the next morning, made a cup of tea and wandered into the living room. For some reason I turned on the TV set and SID AND BEN WERE STILL THERE.

Obviously exhausted and unshaven and still talking about a Truman lead.

I walked down to the station, took a train for New York and walked over the the *Tribune*. The city room was a shambles, deserted except for three or four people answering telephones.

I sat down at my old typewriter on the rewrite bank to write a letter. A few moments later, I looked up to see a woman coming down the corridor leading to the big room. She walked across it and looked toward the managing editor's office. It was empty. She turned and went away.

The woman was Helen Rogers Reid, the paper's boss since her husband died a year earlier. It was a scene straight out of *Citizen Kane*. The Reids had been absolutely sure that this time—after 16 long years of Roosevelt and Truman—they would win. And the *Herald Tribune* would then be not only the voice of the Republican party but the voice of an Administration. They lost. Mrs. Reid didn't look exactly like Orson Welles but it was a dramatic scene he would have loved.

A couple of days later, Whitey Reid asked me to have lunch with him at Bleecks, apparently at his mother's suggestion. His opening remark made some instant decisions for me.

"What do you do in Paris?" he asked.

Well, I thought, it's perfectly clear how well your work is known in New York. It is time to get out of there.

We talked about the papers and I had the temerity to suggest that the success of the Paris edition might be duplicated if a format of smaller size was adopted to cut costs in New York. This publisher had no interest whatever in such a zany idea.

Jean liked living in Paris but she was perfectly content to return to her native New York. Our lease on the apartment expired the following

March and we booked passage for her and the children on the Queen Mary for that month. Eric had longstanding plans for an extended visit to New York at that time so I would have to remain behind for a month or so.

So one morning, we said fond farewell to the Quai d'Orleans and were driven down to Cherbourg to put the family on the ship. The next day, news came that the Queen had run aground trying to get into the harbor at Southampton. With a hole stove in her bottom, the liner lay in Southampton harbor for a week while they poured cement into the breach. Jean said later it was no hardship living in luxury at the expense of Cunard Lines.

I went back to the Hotel Lincoln to see if they could put me up. The woman manager said *certainment* and escorted me upstairs to Room 21.

"This is my old room," I exclaimed.

"But of course," she said. "Where else should you stay?"

About the time my tour in Paris was ending, a short, owlish-looking guy showed up in Paris and Eric started letting him write articles reviewing food and service in restaurants. On the cuff, in the old *Paris Herald* tradition. He was Art Buchwald, and unlike the rest of us postwar *Paris Herald* alumni, he is now rich and famous. Deservedly.

Homer Bigart was doing an interim stint in the Paris bureau, and one Sunday, he and I and the Whites drove down to look at Chartres cathedral, which I had never seen. A few days later, Homer and I boarded the Queen Elizabeth for the voyage home. It was just as grand and luxurious as the Queen Mary.

Bob Jones, my boyhood friend from Utah, now art director of Columbia Records, and his wife Kay had found a furnished house for us in Southport, Connecticut, not far from where they lived in Fairfield. It was a nice place but a long commute, more than an hour on the New Haven railroad.

On my first Monday morning as a commuter, the train stopped two stations south at Westport, where none other than Dick Maney came aboard. He spoke to me but walked right past where I was sitting in an almost empty car and took another seat up front. When I got off the train at Grand Central Station, he was waiting for me on the platform. What you did on the train, I gathered, was read newspapers, not talk.

Apparently they didn't quite know what to do with me on the paper in 1949. I imagine Cornish and Herzberg, who had succeeded Engelking as city editor, thought I would expect some kind of editor's job. Joe brought the matter up somewhat hesistantly. I suggested that he just make me a general assignment reporter. He was obviously relieved and that was what I did for the next year. One of the pleasantest and most satisfactory periods of my life. I got to cover some big stories, got my share of page one bylines and had a wonderful time.

The long commute wasn't practical and I soon found a two-bedroom railroad flat in 82nd Street only a half block from the East River. It was on the second floor of what can only be described as a tenement. We painted the place and bought enough furniture to sleep on and eat off of and found the neighborhood very congenial. The rent was $57.50 a month.

One of the joys of being a general assignment reporter is that something new comes along each day. I covered stories about the weather, various kinds of strikes, theater ticket scalping scandals, the installation of the first broadcasting antennae atop the Empire State Building, and so on.

Occasionally, I did pieces for the Sunday entertainment section. The one that entertained me the most was an interview with my old match game opponent Tallulah Bankhead, done in her dressing room in a theater in Brooklyn, of all places. She was playing the "subway circuit" there.

The biggest breaking story I covered was in September, when a concert by Paul Robeson in a meadow near Peekskill, N.Y., attended by 15,000 people, mostly black, was followed by a huge riot.

It was a dreadful affair. Driving back to the city with Nat Fein, a *Tribune* photographer, we passed dozens of children standing on their front lawns throwing rocks at buses filled with people leaving the concert site. Their parents sat in lawn chairs and cheered while rocks smashed through the windows of the buses as glass shattered.

Robeson, a great singer and actor, had returned a few months earlier from Europe. During interviews on his arrival, he had been quoted by reporters, including me, praising Russia and the Communist regimes in Eastern Europe. After which he had been widely denounced as betraying his native land.

I wrote several follow-up stories about the Robeson riot, covering investigations which went nowhere. One of the stories involved a black writer I had never heard of before. He was W.E.B. Dubois, the leading black philosopher of his time. One of the dividends of the trade is that you get a continuing free education.

I had one reportorial experience which was not so satisfactory. *The New Yorker*, which I had read avidly since childhood, was celebrating its 50th anniversary and I suggested that we interview the editor, Harold Ross.

"Go right ahead if you can," the day city editor said "but Ross doesn't give interviews."

I called *The New Yorker*, asked for Ross and was put through to him. When I told him I wanted an interview, he said to come to his apartment on Park Avenue the following afternoon. I did and after a few minutes he suggested we adjourn to the bar of a hotel on Madison Avenue.

I was fascinated to meet this man, in my opinion the greatest living editor and a personal hero since boyhood. I knew many of his talented staff of writers but not their boss. It turned out that he had been willing to talk to me because he had grown up just one block away from my grandfather's home in Salt Lake City and had known my father and my uncles when they were boys.

Ross said, with a straight face, that his own father had moved the family from Colorado to Utah because his principal pleasure was arguing religion and he took special delight in baiting Mormon bishops.

I went back to the office and wrote a long piece, more than a column. Only to find it cut way down and printed with no byline. It was not, as a matter of fact, very well done and the editorial decision was right. I don't know why I fell down on this one. Bob Crandall, by now the Sunday editor, came by to chide me for not offering him the piece. He said he would have had me rewrite it and see that it got proper display. What a thing to do to a hero of one's youth!

Leslie Midgley at his desk in the city room of the *New York Herald Tribune* in the early Forties.

Midgley at work as night editor of the *New York Herald Tribune* European Edition in Paris in 1945, when World War II ended.

Frank Webb, the one-man copy desk, and Midgley checking a page proof in the *Paris Herald* (as everyone called it) office at 21 Rue de Berri.

William Attwood, Seymour Freidin, Leslie Midgley and John Denson, friends and *Herald Tribune* colleagues over many years, at a quai on the Ile de la Cite in Paris, 1948.

LARDNER'S WEEK

The Missing Masterpiece

by John Lardner

A CRITIC once described "The Match Game," by James Thurber, as one of the conspicuous art treasures of our time. "It is conspicuous," he said thoughtfully, "by its absence," and, sure enough, it had been missing since 1953. One day last week, the artists and writers who eat and drink, respectively, at New York's Artist and Writers Restaurant on West 40th Street were startled to see "The Match Game" hanging once more in its traditional place, on a wall above the suit of armor that Ziegfeld wore at Gettysburg. They didn't know, most of them, the how or why of its reappearance, but they sensed that a dark chapter had been brought to a happy close.

And a fitting close. The A&W Restaurant ("formerly Club") is the mother temple of match-game play today. If match-game art belongs anywhere, it belongs there.

The picture consists of two rows of panels of match-game action. At first glance, these might be taken for sections of frieze-work excavated in Crete or Samos. A second look shows them to be the work of one of the Ohio primitives—almost certainly Thurber, since his name is signed to them, as it seldom is to anyone else's work. They illustrate certain aspects of a sport that is said to have come from China to 40th Street, which is eastbound.

There have been a few small cults of the game in other places—in Hollywood, for instance, and Saratoga Springs. But mainly, since 1929, the game has found its focus in two 40th Street cockpits. After one of these, the Type & Print Club, was closed by the sheriff in 1933, the A&W carried the torch more or less alone. In its oldest form, the game is played for drinks. But on 40th Street, especially in the 1930s, side bets have been common, and there have been historic special matches of ten or 50 rounds played for purses of up to $100, under the auspices of the old Match Game Commission.

The only player ever formally recognized as champion was a newspaperman named Bruce Pinter, whose fame is noted in a fragment of a ballad ("The Dutchman's Stag Saloon") of the time:

The matches clicked at the middle wheel
As the players picked their spots,
And out went Bruce, the champion,
And out went Richard Watts,
With a guess of three, and a grin of glee,
When the other guy said four;
Though he had to leave a match in his sleeve
To hit that ugly score.

There are said to be similarities between the match game and the Italian finger game of Mora—and also the child's marble game mentioned in Poe's "The Purloined Letter." No other game of the species, it is agreed, compares in psychological richness with matches. In its traditional form, it can be played by any number of players, each equipped with three matches, preferably wooden. Each player may hold any number of matches in any round, from zero (also known as "bupkis" or "nada") to three. The players guess in turn at the total number of matches in all hands, which, in a nine-handed game, for instance, may be as high as 27—hence the caption in the Thurber sketch of "Possible 27." (see sketch).

THE total must be guessed exactly. Each winning guess eliminates the player who made it. The last player left picks up the check for the drinks and loses all his side bets, while the winners give exultant shouts, like the war cry of the great picaresque player of the 1930s, M. Jay Racusin: "C'est la vie! Pay la me!"

As noted, the racy, if rococo, sketches of Thurber show certain highlights of the game. As the only known example of match-game art, they had a sentimental and cultural value for players at the old A&W, who pined and sickened noticeably when the pictures disappeared in '53. The break in the case came some weeks ago, when "The Match Game" turned up in the private collection of the noted sportsman and philanthropist, John Bleeck, founder and former landlord of the A&W. Breaking up his collection, preparatory to a pilgrimage to Tibet, Mr. Bleeck offered one of his friends a choice of two *objets d'art:* The Thurber panels, and an autographed photo of Mickey Rooney. The friend, a writer of autobiographies named Richard Maney, though a lifelong admirer of Rooney's work, chose the Thurber as a matter of sacred duty—for he knew it belonged to the people.

And not just to any people. Mr. Maney, consulting with the artist himself, found that it belongs specifically to the formerly Club, the separate, autonomous, match-playing entity of the A&W Restaurant. Last week, restitution was made. Today, "The Match Game" hangs in its old place, and the players are happy again, as they study its vast, harmonious scope and wonder what they can get for it in cash in the open market.

February 10, 1958 ▫ 71

Home Is the Match-Game Art

How Bleeck's Regained The Thurber Sketches

By Richard C. Wald

There was this set of drawings by James Thurber hanging in the back of a local saloon where he was a patron in days gone by and it gave delight to the players of the match game, because that is what it was about. But the saloon changed hands and the drawings disappeared, and thereby hangs a tale unfolded last week when they popped up once more amid charge and counter-charge of dirty cricket.

The saloon is Jack Bleeck's old place on W. 40th St., known by the sign outside as "Artist and Writers (formerly Club) Restaurant," and by those inside as "the drugstore," "the mission," and a place to while away a pleasant lifetime.

For Elite and Oddballs

The match game is an intensely psychological pastime, difficult to describe but like opium for some people. Mr. Thurber put pen to typewriter-paper one early morning in the late '30s and captured the main ploys of the game in ten separate panels.

Jack Bleeck, by his own account, grabbed them off the table and had them framed and hung over the suit of armor that is a permanent guest in the establishment along with some of New York's best known writers, editors, actors, actresses, bankers and oddballs. It's the place where Tallulah Bankhead stood on her hands and sang "God Bless America."

Anyway, the drawings went with the decor of stuffed fish, fading photos and a framed letter from a member of the Swedish royal family. When he sold the place in 1953, though, Mr. Bleeck wrote into the contract that the buyers, Ernest Hitz and Tom F. Fitzpatrick, got everything — fish, photos and armor—except the drawings. Those he took home to Manhasset, L. I.

There they rested until November, when Mr. Bleeck (pronounced Blake) got a hankering for "Fanfare," an autobiography by Richard Maney (pronounced money), a publicist currently beating the drum for "My Fair Lady." He asked a friend and former customer, Hugh Beach, a sports broadcaster known to his best friends as "Meathead," to mediate the swap—pictures for words.

Bleeck Surrenders

Mr. Beach and Mr. Maney met at noon, Nov. 12, in a saloon, Mr. Maney paying for the drinks and a chauffered Cadillac. By the time they reached Manhasset they were oiled and Mr. Bleeck was horrified. He tried to turn them away with an autographed picture of Mickey Rooney.

They would settle for nothing less than Thurber, though, and returned, after a dry visit, to Mr. Maney's Manhattan aerie at 137 W. 48th St., where the drawings were nailed to the wall. Two days later, a gathering of the underworld was held at Apalachin, N. Y.

Although no direct connection with this event has been proved, Mr. Beach was seen to be a double agent. He is a member of the formerly Club, which takes its name and capitals from the sign outside the saloon and is an organization of match-game players who meet every Saturday in Bleeck's and imbibe vitamin-fortified waters.

The Game

The match game is as follows: any number of players, each provided with three matches, put a clenched fist up in plain sight and then attempt to guess how many are in all the fists present. Winner is the player who guesses right. Procedural nomenclature is as obscure as the game's origin. Some of its players are centuries old.

The formerlys, numbering among them John Lardner, of "Newsweek" (the president); John Crosby, radio and television critic of the New York Herald Tribune; George Wells, Walt Kelly and numerous other lights were aghast at Mr. Beach's tale.

"Anonymous Swine"

Mr. Lardner, more aghast than most, promptly called Mr. Maney and accused him of receiving stolen property and misrepresenting himself as a member of the club. According to Mr. Maney:

"Various members called me up and menaced me. A campaign of terror was instituted. They wouldn't have the panels if it wasn't for me. Of all the members, I am the only one mentioned in the panels. The rest of them are anonymous swine."

However, he called Mr. Beach and said, "Take them away. I am now in the mood." Mr. Beach whisked them off to Bleeck's where the formerlys also have a pink and black plaster pig as real property.

Question of Payment

Now Mr. Maney expects to be paid. "I put out fifty-three clams, I figure, for the Cadillac and the liquor and the book, and all I get in return is a hangover and abuse. There have been jocular offers that they would pay off 50 cents a week. Hah!"

Mr. Lardner is opposed to payment. "Maney is a receiver of stolen property and Beach was his fence," is Mr. Lardner's attitude. Walt Kelly, creator of "Pogo," doesn't even want the panels back. One cartoonist is too many for any saloon, he feels. The first day they were back he hung a sign on them saying, "This is a fake Thurber. A Friend."

Thurber's Stand

Mr. Thurber has remained outside it all, a calm elder statesman. He doesn't think the formerly Club has any claim on the drawings though.

"My idea, although nothing specific was stated, was that I was giving them to the place as Bleeck's, not to any one person. They belong back on the wall there. . . . They are very special ultra-murals. I never put them in a book or anything because it is too difficult to explain what they're about. If Maney had kept them it would have been o. k. with me. I love him. He is a brilliant ferocious player. He would say: 'I shall slay you!' and then he'd lose."

Maney's Last Word

Asked whether the pictures had any objective monetary value, Mr. Thurber said: "Somebody once did offer me $300 for them one night. But there had been a lot of drinking that night and I thing he was referring to drinking money."

Mr. Maney tossed in the last word:

"If I was sent to the clink for this, I will not go alone. I will blow the whistle."

"Match Game" Redivivus

"The Match Game" is a sport almost entirely indigenous to a restaurant called Blake's, although it is spelled Bleeck's, and its official name is "The Artist and Writers (formerly Club) Restaurant." Its habitues and sons of habitues, over the years, have included virtually all ink-stained wretches of the press and particularly the Herald Tribune, which is next door.

After Repeal, the inveterate players of the Match Game constituted themselves a kind of inner Sanhedrin of Bleeck's, and styled themselves, in a nostalgic nod to speakeasy days, members of "The Formerly Club." Their crest was a panel of 10 cartoon studies of the Match Game by a chronic loser and daw-plucker named Thurber, who described them as "intra-mural murals." Most of them featured a ferret-nosed character supposed to be Richard Maney, famed Broadway press agent (far right in all cartoons below), while the Man with the Hair is Thurber himself. When Jack Bleeck sold his restaurant in 1953, he took the Match Game murals with him. The other day a rescue party restored them to their proper place, above the suit of armor into which visitors of the Formerly Club sometimes toss pennies. Why? Why do people play the Match Game? Well, the answer to that is, for drinks mostly, though heavy side-bets have been made ("fifty fish"). Don't ask us what the pictures mean. As Thurber says, about these drawings: "I never put them in a book or anything because they're too difficult to explain what they're about."

James Thurber did a panel of ten drawings depicting players of the Match Game in action at Jack Bleeck's saloon beneath the *Herald Tribune.* He put himself in this one. He is the one with the hair.

POGO

By Walt Kelly

Walt Kelly's depiction of Midgley as "Mr. Miggle" in the comic strip Pogo. Kelly named denizens of the Okefenokee Swamp after his friends and put their names on boats in affectionate recognition.

NEW YORK Herald Tribune EUROPEAN EDITION

Price 5 Francs

PARIS, TUESDAY, AUG. 7, 1945

Atomic Bomb Revolutionizes War;
Hits Japan Like 20,000 Tons of TNT

?-Way Plot By Petain Is Detailed

750 B29s Raid 5 Warned Cities Of Japan at Cost of One Plane

Lone Enemy Fighter Watches Tokio Attack and Flees; Photographs Show Toyama, 5d Largest City on Honshu, Is Totally Destroyed

Capitol Hill Now Cold to Peace Draft

Backers of Compulsory Training After the War Concede Plan Is Dead

Blame Is Placed Squarely on Army

Congressmen Declared Alienated by Pentagon

Hiram Johnson Dies; Senate Isolation Chief

California Veteran, 78, Fought to Keep American Out of European Affairs

Secret of Nature Solved To Rain Ruin on Enemy

Reich Science Gave Birth to Atomic Bomb

Jewish Woman, Banished Later by Hitler, Was First To Hit on Correct Theory

Truman Reveals Harnessing of Basic Power of Universe; Blast Is 2,000 Times That of Any Other Bomb

WASHINGTON, Aug. 6.—President Truman announced today that the Army Air Forces have released on the Japanese an atomic bomb containing more power than 20,000 tons of TNT.

Atomic Test

The great headline written by Frank Webb under deadline on the composing room stone the day the atomic bomb was dropped.

Other headlines--and bylines--from the *Paris Herald* ...

NEW YORK Herald Tribune EUROPEAN EDITION

TEMPORARY PRICE 3 Francs

PARIS, TUESDAY, MAY 8, 1945

VICTORY

Eyewitness Tells Of Berlin Ruins

Nothing Left, Says Correspondent, Except Mountains of Debris And a Few Shell-Riddled Walls

Victory Crowd Cheers in Flag-Draped Times Square

Nazi Surrender Unconditional

By Leslie Midgley

The German Army announced yesterday that it had rendered unconditionally, laying down its arms in defeat after five years and eight months of bitter warfare raging over Europe.

While no official announcement of the surrender came from Supreme Headquarters, Allied Expeditionary Force, the British Ministry of Information announced that today will be celebrated as Victory in Europe Day and that Prime Minister Churchill will make a broadcast statement at 3 p.m. Agence France-Presse announced officially last night that General de Gaulle, President Truman and Premier Stalin will make statements at the same hour and it is believed that the De Gaulle message "will be the official announcement of the victory." The White House confirmed

SHAEF Silence Fails to Halt

New York's Emotional Binge Leaves Hangover for Today

Price: 5 Francs

Subscription Rates
Listed on Page Two

NEW YORK
Herald Tribune
EUROPEAN EDITION

58th Year—No. 19,442   PARIS, THURSDAY, AUG. 9, 1945

Russia Wars on Japan

200,000 Believed Killed By Single Atomic Bomb

Photos Show Hiroshima Wreckage and Confirm New Era in Warfare

60 % of Hiroshima in Ruins From New Weapon's Blow

Enemy Surrender Now Is Expected

Raids Can Ruin Whole Cities, Armies, Fleets

By Homer Bigart

General Spaatz Says Additional Damage Is Shown Outside the Completely Destroyed Area; Five Major Industrial Targets Razed

By Mac R. Johnson

Molotov Tells Japanese Envoy Russia Fulfills Duty to Allies

Says Moscow Enters War With Conviction It Is The Only Way to Speed Peace; Tokio's Earlier Request for Mediation Is Revealed

By Joll Dareton

Hitler Ordered Top Priority to

Red Move Seen Shortening War

By Leslie Midgley

Russia declared war on Japan yesterday, throwing her vast military might against a nation stunned only a few hours earlier by the impact of the terrible new atomic bomb.

In Moscow, the Japanese Ambassador was summoned to the Kremlin and told that since his nation had refused to capitulate to the British, Chinese and American ultimatum of July 26, the Soviet Union had joined her Allies in the Pacific war.

In Washington, President Truman called reporters to the White House at 3 p.m. "I have only a simple announcement to make," he said. "Russia has declared war on Japan. That is all."

Truman Asked Stalin to Act in

The ultimatum referred to by Foreign minister Vyacheslav M. Molotov in his note to the Japanese was delivered during the tripartite

---

... as the war ended in both Europe and Asia.

Price: 5 Francs

Subscription Rates
Listed on Page Two

NEW YORK
Herald Tribune
EUROPEAN EDITION

80th Year—No. 19,444   PARIS, SATURDAY, AUG. 11, 1945

Japan Offers Surrender

Reds Drive 130 Mi. Into Manchuria

Junction Town Is Seized As Climax of 130-Mile Push on 3d Day of War

Korea, Sakhalin Invaded, Foe Says

Million Men Locked In Possibly Last Battle

G.I.s Need No Dictionary to Translate 'Le Japon Capitule'

Gleeful Soldiers Greet News With When Do We Go Home?'

Japanese Move Touches Off Paris Celebrations, But Big Demonstrations Wait; Redeployment To Continue Pending Word to Contrary

By John O'Reilly

Smoke Pall Enshrouds Nagasaki

City Hit by Atomic Bomb Is Obscured by Vapor Rising 20,000 Feet High

Scattered Fires Seen Outside Area

Damage Believed Equal To That of Hiroshima

By Mac R. Johnson

U.S. Halts Raids Against Japan By Super-Forts

Announcement in Guam Tells of Termination Of Missions by Bombers

By Homer Bigart

Tokio Wants Ruler Retained

By Leslie Midgley

Japan offered yesterday to surrender under the terms of the "cease or be destroyed" ultimatum given her on July 26, during the Potsdam Conference.

Silently, through diplomacy's protecting powers and publicly, through her own Domei radio broadcasts, the Pacific aggressor offered to capitulate if her ruler-god, Hirohito, lost none of his sovereign prerogatives. The ultimatum doomed militarists but did not mention him.

The 'Son of Heaven' Bows Low

The offer was sent to Britain and Russia via Sweden and to America and China via Switzerland. The State Department confirmed last night that the proposal had been delivered in Bern to the United States Minister, Leland Harrison. He transmitted it to Washington

Frank Costello, thought by cognoscenti to have been the Boss of Bosses of the mob, testifying before a Senate Crime investigative committee in 1951. He admitted he had "burned his fingers" arranging a state supreme court nomination. (UPI/Bettman Newsphotos)

Howard Robard Hughes, Jr., an enigmatic genius, as he appeared in 1955.

Chapter 8

The Boss of Bosses

Frank Costello

THE MOST FASCINATING STORY I covered that year involved a man I had written about back in 1943.

One night on rewrite, I had taken a story over the phone from the district attorney's office about Frank Costello, notorious as one of the city's top mob bosses. Many believed he was THE big boss, the capo de capo. (I got to know him well years later and I shared that belief.)

The 1943 story was that Thomas Aurelio, a Democratic candidate for state supreme court justice, had telephoned Costello at home and thanked him profusely for help in obtaining the nomination.

"Franceso I will never forget what you did for me," Aurelio said.

"I told you everything would be all right and it is," Costello replied.

The call, which had been recorded on a wiretap, obviously would be a bombshell in the coming election.

I wrote the story and Herzberg told me to call Stanley Brown, the *Herald Tribune*'s lawyer, and read it to him.

(Let me interpose. I have been reading for years claims by many people who write about television that TV news is strictly supervised and indeed probably controlled by the desires of advertisers. Nothing could be further from the truth.

(During the more than four years I spent as executive producer of the CBS Evening News, no procedure existed to refer news stories to lawyers. I decided whether the visual material was free of error and libel, and Walter Cronkite either wrote or closely edited everything he reported on air.

(There were lots of lawyers around CBS and plenty of expensive "outside counsel" on retainer from the greatest Wall Street law firms, but I cannot remember ever calling on them in connection with a breaking news story. They did sometimes screen documentaries if the producer suspected some legal question might be involved. But not news stories.

(On the other hand, the finest newspapers in their heyday—which for the *Herald Tribune* was the Thirties and Forties—were very careful to refer news stories to their lawyers and to abide by their decisions. Too many critics of television news have the story exactly backwards.)

I called Brown at home and said I had a story to read to him.

"Wait a minute, let me get a chair," he said.

I read the story, which ran more than a column.

"Read me the first two paragraphs again," he said. I did.

"It's absolutely libelous," he said, "and you have to print it."

"Mr. Brown," I told him, "you are my kind of lawyer."

There is a postscript.

Because it was too late for Aurelio's name to be removed from the ballot, he continued to be the Democratic candidate.

There were enormous fulminations, of course, by the bar association and other pillars of the community who urged the electorate to reject this hand-picked candidate of an infamous mobster.

But, on election day, the voters chose Aurelio over whoever was running as a Republican and he was duly sworn in for a 10 year term as supreme court justice. And during that time he made an excellent record and came to be regarded as one of the most valuable and hard working members of the New York bench.

Maybe they should have let Frank appoint all the judges. He probably did pick quite a few.

Back in New York six years later, I kept hearing about this Costello, now routinely described as the most powerful gangster in the city, maybe even the "prime minister of the underworld." According to people who should know, Costello and his partner, Frank Erickson, made enormous amounts of money "laying off" big bets for the city's bookmakers. A layoff is what a bookmaker does when too many of his clients have bet on the same horse or the same team in a baseball game and he faces disastrous payoffs if the bettors turn out to be right. It works just like the insurance business. Costello and Erickson took on the big risk. For, of course, a commission.

Costello also was reputed to be a power in the larger structure of organized crime, not only in the city but all over the nation. One day, I suggested to Joe Herzberg that we interview him.

"Forget it," Joe said, "We've tried many times. He won't talk to anybody."

I still thought it was a good idea but he was the boss.

Imagine my surprise when a week later Joe called me over to the desk and said,

"Get to work full time on that Costello story. We want to go all out on it."

I was mystified but he WAS the city editor and I didn't mind following up my own suggestion.

So I started doing what is now known as investigative journalism. We just called it reporting.

My first call was at the Manhattan district attorney's office where the assistant D.A.'s in charge of racketeering said they did indeed believe Costello was a great power in the underworld but they had no information on which to bring any charges against him.

There had been some allegations Costello was connected to the drug traffic, so my next call was on Colonel Garland Williams, the head of the Narcotics Control Division of the Treasury Department.

The colonel greeted me by saying, "I know why you are here."

"Tell me," I cried.

"I was talking to Brownie Reid a while ago," he said, "and I told him about Frank Costello, the most powerful racket boss in New York and the *capo de capo*, the boss of bosses. Brownie was very interested."

Now it was all clear. Brownie, the publisher's younger brother, was involved in the *Herald Tribune* management, at that time in some undefined manner. He obviously had gone to the city editor to advise that Costello would make a good story.

And Joe was, quite legitimately, able to answer something like, "I think you are right. As a matter of fact we already have Les Midgley trying to get an interview with him." Sure.

First, I read every word about Costello in the files of the *Herald Tribune*. The stories went back for years, connecting him to various charges of bookmaking, racketeering and influencing elections through Tammany bosses. He apparently had been close to a former Tammany mayor, Bill O'Dwyer. He had only been convicted once, when he was very young, on a charge of carrying a pistol.

The *Tribune* files, and others in the New York Public Library, revealed he had been a very successful rum runner during prohibition—he never made any secret of that—and was doing very well now in the gambling business.

Various law enforcement figures have said over the years that illegal gambling runs into the billions, maybe as high as 15 big ones. Bookies say the total gross is "known to God alone." But there were some figures on record.

Despite the fact that bookmaking was illegal, in 1945, New York City attempted to collect from bookies the local gross business tax ($1/20$ of one percent on receipts exceeding $10,000). The idea of collecting a business tax to cut in on proceeds from criminal activity is somewhat startling, but I guess the city's finance people simple thought that if they could get the money, why not. And the bookies were in a bind. The federal government had passed a law that gamblers must purchase licenses and the law applied to bookmakers. A lot of them did buy licenses; they preferred a little trouble with the city to big trouble with the feds.

Investigators determined that Frank Erickson and his associates banked $27,613,014.64 from January 1, 1943 through March 31, 1945. That was only in banks, in New York, and did not reveal anything deposited in New Jersey or tin box hoarding, of which there must have been a huge amount.

A few years later, Erickson, while stoutly maintaining the city could not collect a tax on his illegal business of bookmaking, paid $36,317.42 in gross business taxes on admitted receipts of $30,208,143.23. He said he was tired of squabbling.

The basics about Frank Costello were:

Born in southern Italy in 1891 with the name Sevarria, Severio, Castellano or Stello (take your choice). Brought to New York as an infant and naturalized in 1921. Grew up in East Harlem, then mostly Spanish/Italian. Had an early reputation as a hoodlum in Greenwich

Village and East Harlem, where he was arrested in 1915 on the gun charge. Was sentenced—as Frank Severio—to a year in prison. (He always resented the description "ex-convict," explaining that it was a youthful peccadillo.)

Costello then got into the rum running business with a brother and they became rich bringing high-powered speedboats loaded with booze from ships at sea into protected landings around New York. A dangerous business but very profitable.

He lived in the Majestic, a large luxury building at 72nd Street and Central Park West with his wife, the former Loretta Geigerman. He had married her when she was a 17-year-old showgirl. They had no children. Two of her brothers, Harold and Dudley, operated slot machines in Louisiana with Dandy Phil Kastel. Costello had an interest in their business, which was legal.

Costello had been dubbed "prime minister of the underworld" by Herbert Asbury, a *Herald Tribune* alumnus, in a series of articles in *Collier's*. Asbury claimed Costello's power stretched across the country, that he had presided at a grand convention of gang leaders at Atlantic City in 1929 where "zoning" was established and territorial rights defined for crime empires. He persuaded the big hoods there was plenty of money for all and that it was safer to cooperate than to go gunning for each other.

Costello admitted under oath in 1943 in supreme court, during hearings on the Aurelio matter, that he knew Joe Adonis, Lucky Luciano, Al Capone, Lepke Buchalter, Owney Madden, Ben Siegel, Dutch Schultz and every other mob type mentioned by District Attorney Frank Hogan. Just friends, he said.

He claimed then his business was operating slot machines where legal, investing in real estate—he owned a large office building at 79 Wall Street—gambling for himself and as a commissioner for others, and part ownership of the Piping Rock Club in Saratoga Springs with Joe Adonis.

Erickson, brought to America by Norwegian parents, was a bookmaker and apparently nothing else. While working as a busboy at a restaurant in Coney Island, he ran bets for customers to a bookmaker in the neighborhood. One day, he got stuck in the restaurant and couldn't get to the bookie. When he got clear, the races were over. He looked at the slips and found that almost all the bettors had lost. He paid off the winners, kept the losers' money and from then on was a bookie instead of a busboy. He apparently was something of a mathematical wizard, able to do complicated sums in his head. Which came in handy before the days of computers.

The clips revealed that Costello's lawyer was named George Wolf. I called Wolf to ask if he could arrange for me to interview his client. Forget it, Wolf replied. Mr. Costello would not talk to me, and neither would he, George Wolf.

Several years previously, Costello had been represented in a tax case before the Internal Revenue Service by another lawyer, Morris Ernst, a prominent member of the New York bar who often appeared in civil rights cases. Costello had retained Ernst to negotiate a deal with the IRS under which he would pay a certain percentage of claims for income tax arrears and in exchange be given a clean slate. It was a common method of settling claims.

I was a bit surprised that Morris Ernst would represent such a notorious man. I rang Ernst's office and arranged a meeting; lawyers often in the public eye like to talk to reporters. But Ernst wasn't happy when he found I wanted to talk about Frank Costello. He said I should go to George Wolf. When I explained that Wolf wouldn't see me, Ernst picked up the phone. Wolf, it seemed, *would* see me.

I went to Wolf's office on Madison Avenue and we had a long talk. He explained that Mr. Costello was a business man who owned real estate and other property, that he led a quiet life and had no desire to see his name in newspapers. I persisted, pointing out that very few New Yorkers thought of Frank Costello as a businessman. Finally he said that if I would give him a written list of questions I wanted to ask Costello, he would see what could be done. I drew up a list of questions that night and dropped it off at his office.

A few days later, I called Wolf and he told me to come to his office on a certain afternoon. When I arrived, he introduced me to a short, dark, husky Italian man with a big nose, dressed in an expensive suit, white shirt and dark tie. He smoked English Ovals constantly and his voice was a hoarse croak with an Italian/New York accent.

The boss of bosses.

Wolf said Mr. Costello had decided to respond to my questions and handed over the answers, all typed up.

The 29 questions were pretty simplistic but the best I could come with. Like:

Q. "What comment do you have on reports that you are chairman of a board which directs organized gambling nationally?"

A. "Those reports are untrue and without any foundation. I do not know of the existence of any organization which controls or engages in national gambling and, therefore, know of no individual or individuals who are chairmen or members of a 'board' which directs organized gambling nationally."

Q. "How would you describe your principal business activities?"

A. "I do not care to describe my business activities other than to state that all the income from my activities is reported on my income tax returns."

Answers obviously written by a lawyer.

He did state, in response to one of the questions, that he had had an interest in slot machines in New York City from 1929 to 1933 and in New Orleans from 1935 to 1937 and from 1943 to 1946.

Another answer stated he had never met Mickey Cohen or Pete Licavoli. He had met Paul Ricca on several occasions but had no business dealings with him.

Q. "Any relations with Vito Genovese, Mike Coppola, Joey Rao or Joe Adonis? If so, how would you describe them?"

A. "I never had any business relations, directly or indirectly, with these four men, excepting that some years ago, Mr. Adonis and I each had a small interest in a gambling operation in Saratoga."

All the rest of the answers were similar, simple denials of any involvement in criminal operations. I was not surprised; Costello had nothing to gain by revealing anything derogatory.

"Well," I said after reading the answers. "I don't think the paper is going to print this. But I'll tell you one thing. If they print it, they'll print it all." I don't know why I said that. I didn't have any authority to do so.

Costello and I left Wolf's office together and when we were going down in the elevator he said, "I'd like to send you a case of Kings Ransom scotch. It's the very best."

No thanks, Mr. Costello" I answered. "That's not how we do things."

One of the answers in my pocket flatly denied that he had any interest in the Whiteley Distillery, makers of Kings Ransom. I discovered later that he had indeed owned a large interest in Whiteley, along with Joseph P. Kennedy.

I went back to the paper, told Joe Herzberg what had happened and turned over all the questions and answers. I said frankly that I didn't see this as much of a story.

I stayed in the city room for a while and then went down to Bleecks. I was standing at the bar when Joe came in after the first edition had been put to bed in the city room but was not yet rolling off the presses.

"You better go up and look at the bulletin board," he said.

So I did and found a notice tacked to it which announced I had been awarded a bonus of $20 for getting the Costello "interview." Some interview! I was astonished; I don't remember any other such cash bonus being awarded during my years on the paper. I was, of course, pleased but still thought the story was not much, certainly not worth the big Page One play it had been given.

I couldn't help wondering if Brownie Reid's interest in the matter had any influence on the news judgment about it.

There were some sequels.

I was off for the next two days and on returning, I found in my old battered metal mail box three separate messages that Mr. Costello had called.

I asked the not-too-bright day city editor, Dick West, what kind of an operation would let such messages go unanswered. He blamed it on dumb copy boys.

By now, I knew how to reach Mr. Costello. He spent every morning until lunch time at the Waldorf-Astoria barber shop, getting shaved and talking quietly with various men who came by to see him. It was his office.

I called the barber shop the next morning and got him on the phone. He was very cordial and proposed that we have lunch. I said I always ate at Bleecks and suggested he join me there. He said okay, he had known Jack in Saratoga. (I proposed Bleecks because I was curious to see if he really would show up there.)

The bar was always three deep at lunch, crowded with *Herald Tribune* people and types from the garment center nearby. At 1 P.M., the door swung open and there stood Mr. Costello in the flesh. The place was too crowded for any conversation and he suggested we go up Broadway to Dinty Moores, a great old theatrical restaurant on 53rd Street. So we walked together up through Times Square. He seemed to be alone and I wondered at the absence of any bodyguards.

At Moores, we were ushered to one of the big corner tables in the rear, facing the dining room and the door. Just like in stories about mob guys who always sat with their backs to a wall.

We had a most agreeable conversation during which he said it was a pleasure, at last, to meet a reporter who was as good as his word. He was referring to my statement that the paper would print all or nothing.

He liked to talk about politics, the city administration and life in general. It was long after 3 P.M. when we stood up to leave. He said he was going over to the Sherry-Netherland Hotel to see his good friend George Raft and asked if I would like to come along. I would.

When we got into a cab, another man got in behind us and I realized then that he had been sitting at the opposite corner table while we were having lunch. Maybe, I thought, he had followed us up Broadway. He was introduced as Joe Baker. I found out later from a police inspector who was a regular at Bleecks that, as Joseph Benedetto, he had a long "yellow sheet," record of arrests.

At the hotel, we found Raft sitting around in a bathrobe drinking and talking to four or five men. He was in town for some movie promotion.

I was fascinated to see Raft and Costello together. It was fact and fiction face to face. Raft, whose specialty was playing tough guys in the movies, no doubt thought of himself as a genuine hard man. And Frank very likely saw himself as the glamorous character Raft depicted on the screen.

Raft was very cordial and told me that if I ever wanted anything to get in touch with him. "Any friend of Frank's, etc. etc."

When we left, Costello and I agreed to get together again and he said I could reach him almost any morning at the barber shop.

The whole matter of Frank Costello was, for the *Herald Tribune,* restricted to that one "interview." I left the paper not long afterward. If I had remained, a real investigation of Costello and Erickson might have been conducted. Might have.

Brownie told me a week or so later he was very pleased with the story and I asked him if he would like to have lunch with Costello, whom I now called Frank. (He called me Midge.)

Brownie said he would love to so I had the temerity to ask the managing editor if he would like to join us. Mr. Cornish replied very frostily that he certainly would not.

We met at the Oak Room of the Plaza, and both Frank and Brownie seemed to have a good time. I guess young Mr. Reid saw this as a glamorous adventure and Frank always liked to be seen with as he put it "the right people in the right places." The service was very, very good.

We left Brownie outside the hotel and Frank and I began walking south on Fifth Avenue, past Van Cleef & Arpels, the fancy jewelry store.

"We ought to buy you something," he said, looking in the show window.

"I wouldn't know what to do with it," I answered.

"Mrs. Midgley would," he said.

We didn't buy anything.

Hanging out with Frank was intriguing and we began to have lunch several times a month. I'm not all that great company socially but I was obviously more interesting to him than the "dese and dose" guys he met in the barbershop. Sometimes we had dinner together, usually at Toots Shors. One night, I was walking east along 52nd Street and ran into him walking west.

"Come with me," he commanded, steering me into Shors.

There we joined Mrs. Costello, "Bobbie," at a corner table. I got the impression he was happy to have someone else there. After I had several lunches and dinners in the place with Frank, Toots was always very happy to cash my checks or get me a table or whatever. I think Frank had an interest in Shors or at least had helped Toots expand it. Which was a great mistake, Costello always insisted.

I told Frank we should go out on the town some night. We did, ending up with our wives in the Blue Angel, where Pearl Bailey was appearing. I had known Curt Weinburg, the press agent for the joint, when he was on the *Stars & Stripes* in Paris. Curt was used to having me in the club but was quite surprised to see who I had brought along this time.

Curt alerted Pearl because in the middle of one number, she walked off the little bandstand and wandered down through the audience, still singing. She wound up standing behind Frank, running one hand over his shoulders. He was furious. I don't think Italian tough guys liked to have black women caressing them in front of their wives.

At the Waldorf barber shop and often at lunch, his constant companions were the aforementioned Joe Baker and a tall, ruddy-faced man named Big Jim McConnell. Who, it turned out, had been a captain on boats plying Long Island Sound. Boats whose cargo was scotch whiskey. The pair went wherever Frank went. Not bodyguards exactly, but...

One morning a few years later, a bulletin came over the wires at CBS News that Albert Anastasia, the mastermind of Brooklyn's Murder Inc., had been shot dead in the barber shop of the Park Central Hotel. While his face was covered with a hot towel. The shop was jammed but no one was able to give the police any description whatsoever of the two men who sent "Albert the Barber" to his final reward.

I saw the bulletin around noon and then wandered up to the Waldorf to the Bull & Bear bar. Frank was not there, which was unusual. But Big Jim was, with a wide smile on his face.

"Did you hear what happened?" he asked. I said I had.

Frank was a complex character. He obviously had great natural talent for organization and was very shrewd about getting people to do what he wanted done. He had very little formal education; I got the impression his wife read the *Daily News* to him at breakfast.

He liked to frequent places like the Waldorf-Astoria and Madison hotels because that is where "the best people" went. He told me once that he was very annoyed when some young boy asked for his autograph. He said his answer was:

"You shouldn't be asking for autographs from people like me."

He enjoyed telling tales about the days of prohibition. He said one winter he and his men bribed a butler who had been left in charge of one of the great mansions on the north shore of Long Island. They used the private docks and boathouses to bring in loads of booze from ships lying outside the 12-mile limit. Their fast speedboats could outrun the Coast Guard, Frank claimed.

"You know," he said, "that was a tough business. What you did was pull alongside a big ship anchored and bouncing up and down in the ocean. They would drop a net down and you put your order in it, so many cases of scotch or whatever along with the cash to pay for it. They hauled up the net and dropped the booze down in it.

"One day, two guys I knew pulled alongside a French ship. It was really cold and one of them talked the crew into letting him come aboard for some coffee. When he got on deck, he pulled out a gun and held up the ship.

"That really takes a lot of guts. But it worked and they got away with all the scotch they could carry. They got it ashore safely...and then lost the whole wad in a crap game in Brooklyn."

I had two unspoken reactions to that story. 1.) Did they lose the money in a game operated by Frank? and 2.) Wouldn't the story make a wonderful scene in a musical?

One day at lunch, the subject of slot machines came up. Frank recalled that when he was operating a casino at Saratoga, the big month was August, when the lovely old racetrack was operating.

One of his best customers, Frank said, was Joan Payson, a very rich lady, sister of John Hay Whitney. She later bought the Mets baseball team. Mrs. Payson used to lose a lot of money at the roulette tables, and one night, Frank decided to cheer her up a little. The corridor leading from the club entrance to the casino was lined with slot machines, and when Mrs. Payson arrived, she habitually played the one-armed bandits on her way to bigger action.

Frank gave me a solemn look. "You can adjust those things you know," he said.

"Yes, I heard you can," was my answer.

"Well," he went on, "I had my nephew fix the machines, and that night when the lady walked in, she won several jackpots. She was delighted. Then she went into the casino and dropped a big bundle."

It just sounded like good business practice to me.

I certainly never was on intimate terms with Mr. Costello; I don't think anyone not an Italian could have been. But I did see him over a period of years and got a pretty good idea of how he ticked.

For what it is worth, I think he was—for a time at least—indeed the boss of bosses. He may have been deposed by Vito Genovese, for whom he gave a great party at the Copacabana nightclub on January 24, 1949, to celebrate Geneovese's release from prison.

I think he was the most powerful boss because he was smarter than Luciano or Adonis or Longie Zwillman or Meyer Lansky, but just as tough.

He always insisted he had nothing to do with drugs or prostitution and advised his associates to leave them alone. Because, he said, there was plenty of money, first in booze and then in gambling, which were "clean" operations, merely providing things most Americans wanted despite laws against them.

It was obvious that he had great influence in his world, and I finally decided that it probably worked this way:

If someone wanted to operate numbers or dice or whatever in a certain area such as Greenwich Village or Harlem, he went to see Frank and told him what he had in mind. Costello would look the situation over, and if there seemed no big reason why the handbook or whatever should not operate, he would give the petitioner the nod.

But I think he added:

"Okay, go ahead. I don't need any of your money but since you ask my advice, do as I say in the future." He was the boss.

One evening, when he walked into the lobby of the Majestic, a man came through the door behind him. "This is for you, Frank," he said, shooting him in the head. The bullet only grazed his head and the wound was not serious. The police determined that the shooter was one Vincent "Chin" Gigante, who was regarded as a minor, overweight hood. Frank said he could not identify who had fired. Gigante went free and, surprisingly, rose in the ranks to be a very big boss now.

About the Copacabana. A few years later, Sy and Stiva Freidin came home from Europe for a vacation. I ran into Frank one day and told him I would like to take them to the Copa, then at its heyday as most popular night spot in town. All he asked was when did we want to go.

When we arrived for the late show, the place was packed but in the center front row of the balcony, overlooking the dance floor, was one empty table. When I gave my name to the maître d', Jack Entratter, he waved toward the table and said to one of his assistants, "A friend of the boss." Frank owned the place.

There was some evidence he also had holdings in Las Vegas. Entratter left the Copa to run the big show room at the Sands in Vegas and was a celebrity in Nevada for years. A surrogate perhaps?

One day, Frank left a thick wad of banknotes—he always carried one and paid for everything in cash on the spot—in a taxicab. The cabby took it to the police, who found folded in it a list of numbers which corresponded exactly to the total take at the Tropicana casino in Las Vegas the previous week. Why did he have it and where did he get it? He didn't say.

In December 1950, I mentioned to Frank that I was going to make a swing through the South and West and would be visiting New Orleans for the first time. He told me to call Dudley Geigerman, Bobbie's brother, who would fix me up. He did. When I added I would be coming back through Las Vegas he said, "I wish I could go with you. They have wheels I can beat." He was telling me he had a piece of the action.

He was then in litigation on what the government claimed were income tax violations and had been ordered by a judge not to leave the Southern District of New York.

That tax case gave what I thought was a revealing look at his character. It made no sense for a man of Frank Costello's savvy to get in serious trouble over income taxes again. Morris Ernst had managed to get him a clean slate. All he had to do from then on was be careful to pay his taxes in full.

But people like Frank simply can't bring themselves to play it straight. They HAVE to cheat, or at least try to. That's the way they are made.

And this case took him back to prison in 1952. He came out all right and was a familiar figure around town until he died in bed at the age of 82.

In February, 1950, Mrs. Reid was interviewed by the trade magazine *Editor & Publisher* about plans for a new "early bird" edition which would cost some $5 million. During the interview, she denied the *Herald Tribune* was for sale and said it would concentrate on giving major local stories big play. My Costello "interview," she recalled, "made Page One easily."

"Mr. Midgley worked more than a year to get it," she added. Asked how, she said, "Well, he made friends."

I suspect Brownie was more impressed than I was by that original story; at the time I hadn't even been back from Paris a year.

But I did make friends.

A POSTSCRIPT.

I never could pick up a check when lunching or dining with Frank.

But I did do him one small favor. We were having lunch one day several years after I had joined CBS News.

"You know a lot about newspapers," he said. "Some of my friends from out of town say they have seen a very nice story about me in Walter Winchell's column. But it never has appeared in the *Daily Mirror*. How about that?"

I told him I'd ask around.

I went back to the office and sought out a guy who had recently come to work on the CBS News assignment desk from the *Daily Mirror*. I asked him how I could check on the story.

A couple of days later, he came by to tell me the story was set in type, ready to be printed, but was lying on the makeup stone at the *Mirror*. Space had not been found for it.

"How can I get it into the paper?" I asked. He said he would find out. He came back the next day.

"Two hundred dollars," he said.

I gave him 200 in cash and he said the item would be in the paper within the next two days.

I knew Frank could be found at the Waldorf barber shop any morning before lunch but I did not know where he might be in the afternoon. I went over to the Waldorf and sought out a diminutive, hard-working Italian gent who shined shoes and ran the checkroom at the barber shop.

"Do you know where I can find Mr. Costello?" I asked.

"Sure," he said. "He's at the Regency Hotel bar."

I realized that this man was Frank's secretary. If he knew you, he would take messages or send you along to see him. If he didn't, forget it. He had known me for years.

I went to the hotel and found Frank having a drink with Big Jim McConnell, Joe Baker and a couple of other guys. When I told him to check the *Mirror* for a couple of days, he said thanks, but looked skeptical.

The item appeared in Walter Winchell's column the next morning. Only $200!

Those were the days!

Chapter 9

Collier's
Mr. Denson Again

BEING A GENERAL ASSIGNMENT REPORTER was just plain fun. But it
didn't pay enough money for a family with a third child on the way. We
needed a house in the suburbs; the girls were approaching school age.
Joe Herzberg said a raise might be arranged but it could only by in the
$10 range.

So I went to see John Denson.

Who else?

After that stint at CBS publicity and a shot at ABC News, Louis
Ruppel and Denson were now editor and managing editor, respectively,
of *Collier's,* a big weekly "general interest" magazine. It published
both fact articles and fiction stories but needed more and more fact
pieces because the news magazines and the picture magazines LIFE and
LOOK were clobbering it.

John had asked me some time before if I wanted to move to the
magazine. When I came in to say yes, he made me an "associate
editor" at a big raise over my *Herald Tribune* salary. So, back to
rewrite.

Crowell-Collier was in a tony neighborhood, on Fifth Avenue at 51st
Street, with St. Patrick's Cathedral right across the street and Toots
Shors and the 21 Club down the block. I had to share a small office with

Bill Emerson, a young writer and editor from Atlanta, but it was luxurious by *Tribune* standards.

When I joined *Collier's,* it was publishing a series of articles signed by Lowell Thomas, the lecturer and radio broadcaster, describing his adventures in Tibet. Newsstand sales were very good during the series and Ruppel wanted more pieces from Thomas.

Lowell Thomas was a very smart operator. Although he was on CBS radio every night reading a news broadcast, he had his own setup. Not at CBS but in Rockefeller Center. His staff consisted of a lawyer, some secretaries and one very facile writer named Prosper Buranelli, who turned out the radio script every day plus various articles published under Thomas' name.

Louis sent me over to see Prosper, who promptly produced from his desk the unpublished manuscript of a book about the exploits of Air Commandos on the Chinese-Burma border during the late war.

It was a good story. Gliders of the 1st Air Commandos, led by Colonel Philip Cochran (Milton Caniff's "Flip Corkin" in the comic strips), had transported British, Burmese and Ghurka troops under the command of General Orde Wingate, a legendary genius of unorthodox warfare, into jungle clearings behind Japanese lines in 1943. It was one of the few victories for the Allies in the Pacific theater at that time.

Prosper didn't exactly say so, but I gathered that whoever had published the Thomas book about Tibet had turned this one down.

I had a series of lunches with Prosper at the Red Devil, an Italian restaurant he frequented. He was a short, chubby type with a luxurious mustache. The scoop was that he loved to eat and drink and was not all that careful about providing for his wife and *nine* children. Mrs. Thomas had made it her business over the years to see that they were taken care of. But he was fast and clever with words and I admire professionals.

I rewrote three articles out of the manuscript. The first was headlined "They Called It JUNGLE BROADWAY. By Lowell Thomas, Part I." I don't know how it did on the newsstands.

Among the associate editors listed on the *Collier's* masthead was Gordon Manning, a bustling, funny Boston Irishman who had been a United Press sportswriter. I was on straight salary but some writers, including Gordon, were on retainers which guaranteed them a certain amount, say $25,000, a year. In return for the guarantee, they contracted to produce a certain number of articles. Some of them, Gordon, among them, were so industrious that their quotas were filled in six months and they went on to earn a lot more in the second six months.

A weekly magazine chewed up a lot of material. The September issue that carried "my" Thomas piece also had seven other articles, five fiction pieces and four features. The magazine simply had to have a sizable "bank" of material.

Louis, who ranted and roared around the office like he was back in the city room in Chicago, decided to go for big name writers, hoping they would boost circulation. He began to pay very large sums for material; free-lance writers said he was the most generous editor in the business.

Among the *Collier's* contributors were three old friends, Sy Freidin, Bill Attwood and Dave Perlman. They had left the *Herald Tribune* and formed a group venture in free-lance foreign reporting. Louis liked their work and gave them enough assignments to permit travel around the world and residence in places like Paris and London. They provided *Collier's* a quality foreign service.

I did various rewrite jobs and spent quite a bit of time in Toots Shors with writers like Gordon and Collie Small and Bill Davidson. Fine fellows all. Denson was on and off the wagon. It became increasingly difficult for him to work properly while drinking and sometimes he didn't show up at the office for days at a time.

Louis finally told Manning to sit in the managing editor's office, and after a few weeks made his appointment official. He gave John a writer's contract and sent him off to the war in Korea. John did good work there but his heart was in editing. He came home and was made *real estate editor* of the *Miami Herald*. It was reputed to be the best real estate section in all of journalism. I don't doubt it, but what a waste!

Later, he became editor of *Newsweek* and did an impressive job of making it into a serious competitor of TIME. Much of the attraction of *Newsweek* came from its excellent graphics displays.

After the Reid family turned the *Herald Tribune* over to their rich friend Jock Whitney, John became its editor. In search of increased circulation, he changed the whole tone and appearance of the paper with various tricky forms of makeup. I didn't like it but what I didn't like most was that he didn't call me to come back.

He finally got into a row with Whitney's business manager, Walter Thayer, because Thayer and his staff kept insisting on earlier and earlier deadlines to save money. When it got to the point where John thought the deadlines were damaging the newspaper, he resigned. Yet again.

Ruppel called me in one day and said he had made a reservation at the Oak Room of the Plaza for me to have lunch with a Boston newspaper columnist named George Frazier. Louis said Frazier had been given a lot of money to do a series about Time Inc. He had delivered a manuscript which wasn't worth publishing and the company was holding up a final payment of $10,000. Louis wanted me to get the material from Frazier and see what might be done with it.

I met George at the Plaza as per instructions and found him visibly nervous. He said he didn't know what had gone wrong. He had been told the *Collier's* brass didn't like his work.

I was very surprised to learn from Frazier that what he had been doing was rewriting a series by none other than my friend A.J. Liebling. Imagine having George Frazier rewrite Joe Liebling!

What happened was that as part of his campaign to enlist "name" writers, Louis thought Joe would enhance one of his pet projects, a profile of Time Inc., and Henry Luce. Why Ruppel thought a profile of another magazine would interest his readers I don't know.

After lunch, we walked over to Frazier's apartment and he showed me the manuscript. It became perfectly obvious that he didn't care what happened to the story. What he wanted was the ten grand as soon as possible. He needed money.

I took the material back to the office and confirmed Frazier's story. Then I called Liebling and we met at Bleecks. It turned out Joe really didn't give a fig about what had happened at *Collier's*. He thought *The New Yorker* was the only magazine worth writing for. He had taken Ruppel's cash because he wanted to get a quick divorce. He got a big advance, went to Pyramid Lake, Nevada, for six weeks and then wrote a series about Time Inc. As far as he was concerned that was that.

I lunched with Frazier on a Wednesday. When I told Ruppel the material might make a good three-parter, he asked if I could have it done by the following Monday.

Typical Ruppel. This series had probably been in the works for a year and now he wanted it in four days. I said if he would spring for a hotel room in town and have a secretary come in to type it up on Sunday, I would give it my best shot. He happily agreed.

I already had in my head some personal impressions about TIME going back to when I used to hang out there on the closing night, Monday, while Sid Olson waited for page proofs to come back from the printers in Chicago. I got to know other TIME writers then and, to tell the truth, remembered big hunks of Wolcott Gibbs' fine *New Yorker* profile about Luce.

The most famous line was Wolcott's description of early TIME prose: "Backward ran sentences 'til reeled the mind."

But my own favorite was: "They think they've got the truth when all they've got's the news."

That should be posted on the wall of proud editorial rooms, as a reminder that we aren't all that hot.

I rewrote the Liebling/Frazier drafts, added some of my own ideas— maybe Wolcott's?—and finished three parts by Sunday afternoon. One of the secretaries came in to type up clean copies.

Louis was delighted to get the copy Monday morning and disappeared into his office to read it. Or maybe have John read it; I am not sure Ruppel read anything.

Anyway, he told me that afternoon that he was very pleased and as a reward, he would work out an assignment for an original series for which I would get extra pay, à la Manning.

A revealing look at this affair came the next morning when I was in Louis' office at some kind of a meeting. Dick Chaplin, the associate publisher, walked in and announced he was now happy with the Time Inc. material.

"I never thought we could get that stuff into any shape to appear in the magazine," he said. "Now we can go ahead. A fine job."

Now I understood what had been bugging Louis. The publisher, Ed Anthony, and the rest of the Crowell-Collier brass, were nervous about this story concerning another publishing empire. They had apparently found both the Liebling and Frazier versions wanting and were unhappy about all the money spent on the subject.

As far as I know, it never was published. It probably was still in the *Collier's* inventory when the magazine folded on December 14, 1956, an event vividly recalled in Theodore L. White's book, *Death on the 40th Floor."*

Chapter 10

LOOK
Over to Madison Avenue

ONE DAY, I ran into Bill Lowe, a big, charming ex-Marine from a wealthy and very social family. After the war, he had moved to Paris as economics editor of the *Herald* and we had worked together congenially. He was now managing editor of LOOK, Mike Cowles' picture magazine. Bill said he wanted me to have lunch with Cowles. Okay, rich publishers are acceptable hosts.

Mike, a talented and likeable man, said he wanted to make LOOK more serious and had decided to add a section of foreign news. At that time, LOOK featured numerous layouts of Hollywood beauties and other slightly titillating stuff. It was thought of in the trade as a "barber shop book," one gazed at by men while they had their hair cut. (I found out later that Mike was anxious to upgrade the magazine because the automobile manufacturers in Detroit thought it was too racy for their advertising. How things have changed!)

LOOK, a bi-weekly, was printed at the huge R. R. Donnelly plant in Chicago. To shave costs, it had a very long deadline, six or seven weeks for many pages. Cowles had figured out that a four-page "wraparound" could be bound inside the front and back covers with a two-week deadline. Which would make it possible to publish stories from abroad on a reasonably tight schedule.

He proposed that I join LOOK as foreign editor in charge of this new section. We could hire another man to work in Europe. I liked the idea, but when Bill assured Mike I spoke French, I had to deny it and the deal was almost queered. But he finally said okay and we shook hands.

When the question came up about who would write this foreign news, I assured them I could procure a steady stream of top-quality pieces from the correspondents of the finest newspapers. From my years in Europe, I knew that $1 a word sounded like big money to reporters. Any of them. And at *Collier's* I had learned that was peanuts for a big magazine.

I proposed we hire Steve White as European editor. Lowe heartily seconded and Mike agreed.

Ruppel wasn't happy about it but not surprised by my defection.

It worked out just as planned. On September 27, 1950, the first LOOK Reports appeared on yellow paper bound inside the cover. The lead story was from Pusan, Korea, by none other than Homer Bigart, the *Herald Tribune*'s great star. He had been incredulous and delighted when I offered him $750 for that many words. I got the same reaction from George Axelsson, *The New York Times* man in Stockholm, Eric Downton, the *Times* correspondent in India, and Amos Landsman, the AP man in Formosa. Steve sent in a piece from Paris and I wrapped it up with a few paragrpahs on the back page explaining what we were doing.

The second issue, two weeks later, had pieces from Sidney Gruson, *The New York Times* man in Brussels, and Teddy White from Paris. Steve sent a piece from Berlin. Teddy did another piece in the third issue and we had contributions from Ned Russell and Don Cook of the *Herald Tribune*. All good stuff.

A few weeks later, the section was devoted to the problems of the atomic age and a little feature titled "LOOK Calls" posed the question, "What is likely to be the greatest benefit from the development of atomic energy?"

Dr. J. Robert Oppenheimer replied:

"Perhaps in the long run the technical contributions to science will turn out to be the greatest asset but in the nearer future, as in the past, I think and hope that the atomic bomb will serve by disccuraging the recourse to war as a means of settling international conflict."

Not the usual LOOK material. Just what Mike wanted.

After the Reports section was safely launched, I made plans for a swing around Europe with Steve White. A few days before I was scheduled to leave, I was lunching with John Crosby in Bleecks and told him my plan.

"I've never been to Europe. I wish I could go with you," he said.

"Why don't you just call Dave Parsons and get a ticket?" I replied. Dave, brother of Geoffrey, was the Pan American Airways press agent in New York.

So two days later, John and I were aboard one of the old Pan-Am flying boats with a bar downstairs in the hull. Slow but very comfortable.

In London, we went to the Dorchester, a grand hotel. The first thing John did was get on the phone and begin checking around to "see who's in town." He had never been to London before. The next thing I knew we had been invited to a cocktail party at a fine town house on Grosvenor Square. The party, it turned out, was being given by a potential investor in a movie to be called *The African Queen*. The producer was Sam Spiegel, in London to raise dough. With him was the star, Humphrey Bogart, who had brought along his wife, Lauren Bacall.

After cocktails, we all walked a few blocks to what our host said was a black market restaurant that could rustle up fine steaks. Five years after the war, life in London was still austere and food was rationed.

At dinner, I was seated next to an attractive lady who was Spiegel's date. I had brought along a supply of Uppman 23 cigars and before coffee arrived, I took one out of my cigar case and laid it on the table. When I turned to pick it up a few moments later, it had disappeared. There at the head of the table sat Spiegel smiling at me and lighting up my Havana. His girl had glommed it.

During the few days we spent in London, Crosby picked up a nifty blonde who announced she was going with him to tour Europe. She did.

Our next stop was Paris and the Plaza Athenée. Steve had a lovely office nearby which Fleur Cowles, Mike's wife, enjoyed during her visits to France. Fleur was the editor of another Cowles magazine called FLAIR, famous as the one with "the hole in the cover." It did literally have a hole, through which could be glimpsed a picture of a woman or a flower or something on the first inside page.

I had never been to Scandinavia, and Steve and I decided to go there. I would go on to Germany and Austria and meet Crosby in Rome.

The day before we were to leave for Copenhagen, we went out to the races at Longchamps. Walking through the restaurant under the stands, I heard someone call my name. It was Sam Spiegel, sitting alone at a table behind a bottle of champagne. He had the money.

We flew to Copenhagen and I found out what kind of food should be served on all airlines at all times: Delicious cold sandwiches, fish, cheese and delicacies, along with ice-cold acquavit and Tuborg beer.

During the flight, I asked Steve about the cities we were going to visit.

"Well, they call Copenhagen the Paris of the North because it is so beautiful," he said.

"Stockholm?"

"Stockholm is called the Venice of the North because it is laced with bays and waterways."

"Helsinki?"

"Helsinki," he said, "is the Tim Costellos of the North. Everyone is drunk all the time."

Copenhagen was indeed beautiful. We stayed at the Angleterre, which may be the finest hotel in the world, and one night we dined in the Tivoli gardens. Steve said he had made arrangements for us to visit the great physicist Niels Bohr at his home the next afternoon.

When we got into a taxi the next day, Steve directed the driver to the Carlsberg Brewery. He explained that years ago the brewing company had been willed to the Danish government. The will stipulated that a mansion in the middle of the brewery was to be made available as a home for the "greatest living Dane" as long as he lived. He got the house and a case of beer a week.

Bohr was an impressive, scholarly-looking old man who spoke English with difficulty. He showed us around the lovely mansion, which included a great "winter garden" conservatory.

Then our host proposed we go for a walk. He led us up a wide lawn to some stone benches along a tree line. There we sat and talked about the political situation in a world where the atomic bomb had arrived.

He had been deeply involved in developing it and, like many scientists whose work had contributed to the development of the terrible weapon, Bohr seemed sorry that the effort had succeeded. I thought maybe even a little guilty about his role.

After we left, I realized Bohr had deliberately led us away from the mansion. He probably thought it was bugged.

I found Steve's characterizations of Stockholm and Helsinki to be on the nose.

In Helsinki, I walked up to the door of the Russian embassy and asked to speak to someone about getting a visa to visit Moscow. They found a man who spoke a little English and he explained, haltingly, that they were not prepared to give visas to American editors. I still have never been to Moscow.

In Berlin, old friends, such as Drew Middleton of *The New York Times* and Joe Fleming, late of *Stars & Stripes* and now of the UPI, had stayed on after the war and they gave us some valuable fill-in. There was still a lot of rubble around the city but Unter den Linden was lined with smart luxury shops.

In the old Berlin tradition, the night life was lively, and one night I found myself in a little club playing the piano along with a German bass player, who followed me perfectly. He was delighted. It was the last time I remember playing before a hiatus of 30 years. Alas, all the songs I had in my head and fingers have now gone somewhere else.

Steve went back to Paris and I flew on to Vienna, where I had never been. Si Bourgin, yet another *Stripes* alumnus, was now running the USIA office in Austria and he showed me around the city.

When I got to Rome, Crosby was ensconced in the Hotel Excelsior complete with blonde, and we did quite a bit of pub crawling during the next few nights, especially enjoying the Hosteria del Orso.

Back at the Plaza Athenee in Paris, Steve and I went over our impressions of the trip and Europe in general. When I got back, I wrote a modest account for my own Reports section.

Steve and Crosby's friend escorted us out to Orly airport for the trip home. Then she returned to my suite in the Plaza Athenée where she and *another* fellow ordered up dinner and enjoyed the place. I had left the bill for Steve to pay from the LOOK office, which she apparently knew. A bimbo.

That September, we rented a house with my old Salt Lake friends, the Joneses, at Fire Island, a beach popular with many artists and writers. Fall is the best time there, the weather is good and the ocean still warm. It was nice but one day something happened that presaged a dark future for Jean. Shopping in a clothing store, she suddenly had an epileptic seizure. Kay Jones had been an Army nurse during the war and knew exactly what to do: Keep her from swallowing her tongue, calm her flailings as much as possible and wait for the seizure to pass. Unfortunately, the epilepsy contiued and she died in 1965.

Two good things happened. I persuaded John Lardner to write a column for the Reports section, which had changed from yellow to white glossy paper and was running more than foreign material. It was very classy stuff.

And Steve White came back to New York to work at various editorial tasks. Mike and Fleur Cowles had spent some time with him in Paris and thought he could contribute to improving the quality of writing in the magazine. We hired Bill Attwood to replace Steve in Europe. The team of Attwood, Freidin and Perlman had broken up and Bill was at loose ends.

After he had done two or three columns, I got a phone call one day from Lardner.

"What is someone doing to my column?" he asked.

I had, just by habit I guess, made some minuscule changes in his copy. He had spotted them immediately and let me know in no uncertain terms that Lardner copy was not to be tampered with. I didn't do it again.

Late that year, John discovered he had tuberculosis and was ordered to stay in bed for several months. The doctors said he must not do any work whatsoever. Several columnists, including John Crosby, offered to guest-write "New York, N.Y. by John Lardner" but Mike didn't like the idea. Steve wrote the column for a while but it was finally dropped. John recovered completely and went back to work at *Newsweek* and *The New Yorker* for the rest of the decade. He was very prolific and always did work too hard, harder than any other writer I knew.

One day, Mike Cowles and I were flying back from Washington together and he said casually, "Les, I would like you to be managing editor of LOOK." He explained that Woodrow Wirsig, would move over to run a pocket-size magazine called QUICK, another Cowles property, and that Bill Lowe would move up to executive editor.

Having absolutely no inkling of any such changes, I was astonished. I thanked Mike but said I was very happy with my job editing the Reports section and thought I should continue with it. He seemed surprised but made no other comment.

But he called me up to his office the next day and said, "When you take over as managing editor on Monday..."

Okay Mike," I said, "you win. I'll do the best I can." I did.

QUICK was an odd little weekly, sort of a poor man's *Reader's Digest,* filled with one or two paragraph items, some news, some features. Cowles began to put regional television programming inserts into it, then sold QUICK to the Annenberg interests in Philadelphia. It was renamed *TV Guide* and is today the nation's largest-selling magazine.

LOOK was a picture magazine, although in the Fifties, it ran more and more text articles. LOOK had a fine staff of photographers, who shot stories all over the world. The director of photography was Arthur Rothstein, famous for brilliantly recording scenes of the dust bowl during the Thirties for the WPA.

The content of LOOK grew principally out of suggestions submitted by the staff or proposed and discussed by the editorial board, which consisted of the Cowleses, Lowe, me, Assistant Managing Editor Bill Arthur, Art Director Merle Armitage, Leo Rosten, a well-known humorist who worked for Mike as "special editorial advisor," and sometimes S.O. Shapiro, the circulation director.

"Shap" had more influence on the editorial content than he should have because Mike believed firmly in his judgment about what covers and content would sell best on the newsstands.

After one period of indifferent sales, we editors were instructed by Mike, in writing, not to make hard plans for covers or major features without discussing them with Shap.

In addition to the photographers, there were excellent writers on the LOOK staff, including my old *Herald Tribune* rewrite buddy John Durston, Joe Roddy, Bill Houseman, Tom Morgan and others.

Bill Lowe, Bill Arthur and I would draw up proposals for an issue and go over them with Armitage and his assistants. They would then lay out a "dummy" of, say, 96 pages, filled with photographs shot by Rothstein's staff. The photographers always shot dozens of rolls of film on any assignment, just to make sure they didn't miss anything. The art directors would examine sheets of contact prints from the rolls and order scenes they liked enlarged. They then cropped and arranged the photographs to tell a "picture story."

If we indicated we wanted to use a certain text piece, say something by Tim Cohane, the sports editor, they would paste up dummy type and spot some illustrations through it.

The dummy pages, on cards, were then placed on racks running around all sides of a big conference room so we could walk around the room and get a perspective of the whole magazine. It was an excellent way to see how the balance worked between pictures and text.

Everybody had his say in the layout room. Sometimes we decided to cut a five-page story down to three. Sometimes, if the pictures were especially striking, we would have the number of pages increased.

Mike Cowles was a very astute businessman who published LOOK with a minimum of investment. He didn't buy physical properties but rented furniture and equipment and presses as needed. Maybe he didn't really think the magazine would last. He was constantly dissatisfied with the newsstand sales, which he believed could be pushed up by entertainment and personality features. So he approved such features, at the same time insisting that he wanted a magazine of high quality. I suspect what he really wanted was the reputation of a Henry Luce without having to invest millions in something like TIME.

Marvin Whatmore, the general manager who had come with Mike from the family business in Des Moines, was the finest business manager I ever saw in action.

LOOK was one of the mass "popular" magazines and its unabashed goal was to get as large a circulation as possible to sell as much advertising as possible. High editorial quality was sought and re-spected but the real name of the game was big numbers. The magazine was a mix of picture and text stories about entertainment, political and sports personalities, fashion, health and science features, sports and sometimes even very serious things like a series of reports from Adlai Stevenson during a world tour.

Sex appeal was part of the mix and we put Marilyn Monroe on the cover a lot. She was at her peak, a devastating beauty. The "text" magazines *Saturday Evening Post* and *Collier's* were having rough sledding, although *Reader's Digest* seemed immune to competition from pictures. But LIFE and LOOK were the strongest of the full size magazines and going up.

I put in 20 years with newspapers and magazines and another 25 with CBS News, the class act of television, and I have been asked repeatedly how I felt about working for LOOK. I liked it a lot.

Because I think *anything* can be news. For a magazine, stories about Miss Monroe are just as valid as those about the doings of presidents and senators and almost always more interesting. We were out to attract a large audience by putting out an attractive product. We did our best. And along the way published a lot of factual information valuable to our readers.

As I write, the great and allegedly powerful institution of television news is sliding faster and faster into "show business" to attract bigger audiences. For the sole reason that bigger audiences will make more money for the station and network owners. Just what we were doing 30 years ago.

It will be interesting to see if the present enormous television news organizations will wind up like the giant picture magazines. In 1954, LIFE had a circulation of 5,524,954 and LOOK 3,859,353. Those figures seemed enormous, absolutely guaranteeing a prosperous future. It was not to be.

They couldn't see it then, but publishers of the mass magazines were playing the wrong game. Their circulations were built on cheap newsstand prices—LOOK sold for 15 cents—and subscription prices so low they often turned out to be a loss for the publishers after huge promotion costs were paid. The money to operate came from advertising revenues which were, in a vicious cycle, dependent on big circulations.

They couldn't see that massive circulation promotions were buying not assets but liabilities. When a cut-rate promotion signed up say 25,000 subscribers for LOOK, it meant that the magazine was obligated to send each of those subscribers the magazine. And when the television networks soared to enormous circulation levels, big advertisers deserted the magazines, leaving them with circulation contracts they had to make good on without a similar base of advertising revenues. They went out of business.

I spent my years in the editorial areas of journalism and, characteristically, knew little about the business affairs of publishing or broadcasting. But it was clear to me early on that good management was as important to a publishing or broadcasting enterprise as good journalism.

And, as administrative head of the editorial department of LOOK with access to cost figures, I was fascinated to discover one day that the entire editorial budget to produce an issue, every salary, telephone, office expenses, travel—everything—added up to 15 percent of the advertising revenue sold for that issue. The company was in the printing and distribution business and didn't know it.

Chapter 11

Howard Robard Hughes, Jr.
The Most Glamorous Man

MIKE AND FLEUR Cowles invited us to dinner at their weekend house in Conneticut one Saturday in 1953. We arrived for cocktails and found among their house guests Irene Mayer Selznick, daugher of Louis B. Mayer and former wife of producer David Selznick.

Over cocktails Mike said, "We are always putting glamorous women on the cover of LOOK. Who is the most glamorous *man* in the country?"

"Howard Hughes," Mrs. Selznick said instantly.

She had grown up in the most rarified strata of Hollywood society and was a very savvy dame. I guessed she had a pretty good fix on that subject.

Other names were mentioned but there seemed to be general agreement that Hughes was the man. I only dimly remembered him as a famous aviator, movie producer and squire of many beautiful ladies.

When the subject was brought up at the next editorial board meeting, Leo Rosten pointed out that he had been a screenwriter in Hollywood and was therefore highly qualified to write about Mr. Hughes. Leo said he would get in touch with the man and see what kind of story could be done.

So Leo wrote a letter to Hughes, suggested they get together. The result was a phone call from a press agent saying Mr. Hughes had no interest whatsoever in any such project and was not available talk to Mr. Rosten. Leo was surprised and very displeased.

I then suggested that we put Steve White on the story. His title was assistant managing editor but he was available for miscellaneous writing chores.

Being a journalist instead of a Hollywood character, Steve started out practicing the reporters' trade. He looked up who had been close to Hughes and set out to talk to them, planning to wind up by interviewing the man himself.

Hughes retained a big New York public relations firm, Carl Byoir Associates. Not to get his name in the papers but to keep it out. And they were good at it. Most people who knew or had known Hughes simply referred Steve to the firm, saying they preferred not to talk about him. The word from Carl Byoir Associates was that Mr. Hughes did not talk to the press, he was too busy with his aviation and industrial businesses in California.

Hughes was a native Texan, the only son of "Big Howard," who had perfected—or at least got his hands on—a bit which could cut through hard rock fast to speed up oil drilling. The Hughes Tool Company, of Houston, owned the rights to the bit. The bits weren't sold, but leased out to drillers. The company was a fountain of money which young Howard spread around lavishly when he first went to Hollywood to make movies. He was the sole stockholder.

Steve set out to find and talk to whoever *would* discuss the elusive gentleman. Most who knew him wouldn't say a word, including his first wife, Ella Rice, who had remarried and lived in Houston. Other women he had dated over the years, such as Katharine Hepburn, also had nothing to say.

One person who would talk about Hughes was Jesse Jones, the crusty old Texas banker who had been chairman of the Reconstruction Finance Corporation. Jones liked him.

When Steve got to Los Angeles, he found that Hughes' headquarters were not in any office building but stashed in an old movie studio at 7000 Romaine Street, south of Hollywood Boulevard. It was nothing like a normal business setup.

"Romaine" housed what the staff called "Operations." It was presided over by a formidable lady named Nadine Henley, who started as Hughes' secretary and became the central figure in his organization. The chief officer was an accounting genius named Noah Dietrich who had come with Hughes from Texas years ago. (They later had a bitter falling out when Dietrich asked for a share of the business. Hughes had no use for partners or minority stockholders.)

Miss Henley had recruited a staff of young men to perform the daily work, which consisted solely of doing whatever Mr. Hughes desired. Anything. Anywhere. At any time. As fast as possible. They served as clerks, phone operators, messengers, drivers and—sort of— bodyguards. In his later, declining, years they apparently became his nurses.

Curiously, they were all Mormons. This had come about because when Henley set up the organization, the first man she hired, Bill Gay, was one. He proved to be very hard-working, polite, quite willing to be on duty day and night—and he didn't smoke. Hughes had trouble hearing and breathing because of injuries sustained when he crashed a plane on a Beverly Hills golf course and was almost killed. He liked people around him who did not smoke.

After Gay passed muster, Hughes suggested to Henley that she "get some more of these fellows." So she had Gay recruit other clean-cut young men from the Mormon community.

They were prepared to do anything. Procure hotel rooms, planes, cars, cash, girls, you name it. If Mr. Hughes wanted it, it would be done. The Boss, or The Man, as they called him, worked at night and slept, sometimes, during the day. They were ready for his summons day or night.

A telephone call for Hughes, from Europe or New York or Texas, went to the switchboard at 7000 Romaine. A man always answered and courteously took down the message. He passed it on to his fellow workers on duty with Hughes, wherever he might be. The Boss would decide whether to return the call or ignore it. Usually the latter.

At that time, Howard Hughes was one of the richest men in America—very likely *the* richest.

The Hughes Tool Company was a gusher of money. He hadn't visited it in 15 years.

The Hughes Aircraft Company in Culver City was one of the nation's largest manufacturers of electronic equipment. It had a backlog of orders for 600 million dollars worth of hardware, mostly from the government.

Hughes owned *75 percent* of TWA, one of the nation's largest airlines, then prospering.

He had the controlling interest in RKO.

He owned a large brewery, built at his orders on the grounds of the Hughes Tool Company just before prohibition was repealed.

And he owned huge tracts of land in Nevada and Los Angeles, one especially valuable piece between the LA Airport and his own private air strip in Culver City.

(During this exercise, we estimated he was worth at least 500 million dollars—an enormous sum at the time—and mentioned the figure to him. He just smiled.)

When Steve sought to contact the owner of all these goodies, he was automatically passed on to the Carl Byoir man assigned to the Hughes account in California. He was Bill Utley, a friendly type who liked to play at the Riviera Country Club and was delighted to entertain White there. But, Utley insisted, "just forget about seeing the man himself." Steve found out from other sources that Hughes had gone to Las Vegas and was living in the Flamingo Hotel. So Steve went there and made a routine call to the Hughes suite. He was told that no meeting would be possible.

So he bought a stack of newspapers and magazines and sat down in the small, stark lobby. (Casino hotels don't feature comfortable lobbies. They like people to spend their time at the gaming tables.) After he had been reading for a half hour, a bellboy approached and asked if he was Mr. White. Steve said yes and was informed that there was a telephone call for him.

The man on the other end of the line said Mr. Hughes would not see him. Steve said he knew that, but he planned to remain in the lobby and read. Another half hour brought another phone call. The voice said Mr. Hughes knew he was there, and it was making him uncomfortable.

"Tell Mr. Hughes that he shouldn't be uncomfortable," Steve said. "I'm just sitting here reading."

After this routine had been repeated several times, a new voice came on the phone, high-pitched and plaintive.

"This is Howard Hughes," the voice said, "why are you doing this to me? I'm not going to see you." Steve replied that he knew that, but he was only doing his job.

Then Mr. Hughes said it wouldn't change anything but he would meet Steve in the lounge in 10 minutes.

Thus began a series of meetings between Stephen White and Howard Hughes during which a lot of information about his habits, work and personality came to light. Hughes apparently recognized that Steve was not your average reporter interested in titillating stories about dames. Hughes was already beginning to insulate himself in a closed society of errand boys and yes-men. Steve had an intellect not to be found among Hughes' associates and I suspect Hughes found someone with brains congenial company. Anyway, they got on well.

Hughes casually told Steve one day that he should ask "the boys" for anything he wanted; they had been told to take care of him. From that time on, anything he needed was provided—and would be until The Boss told them to stop.

After a few weeks, Steve suggested that Bill Lowe come out and meet this chap we proposed to feature as the country's most glamorous man. Bill did go to LA and came back with glowing accounts of flying around with Hughes in his private plane. Bill said Hughes even let him take over the controls for a while when they were cruising through the Grand Canyon below the rim line.

Steve then urged me to come out and meet The Man, not to assist with the story but as a sort of junket. He said he could arrange a meeting and that I would have a good time. So I went to Beverly Hills, in November 1953. Steve told me to register at the Beverly Hills Hotel and call OLdfield 4-2500. I did just that and the man who answered said he would call me back. He did, with instructions to go out the back door of the hotel and walk over to Rodeo Drive.

I did as told and found at the curb of the dimly-lit street a nondescript Chevrolet sedan with a man at the steering wheel. He was Howard Robard Hughes, Jr. Hughes was tall, six feet three, I discovered later, and sort of huddled over the wheel. He said hello and we started to drive around aimlessly. We talked about the LOOK series and he apologized for not being more available. He said he just couldn't completely neglect his business. He didn't specify just what business he had in mind.

Finally, he pulled up in front of 8484 Sunset Boulevard, a two-story white building on the Sunset Strip between Hollywood and Beverly Hills. The inside turned out to be a very well furnished apartment.

Hughes introduced me to a large, florid man named Walter Kane, who he said was one of his friends and associates. Kane had been an agent in Hollywood for years. Hughes kept him in lavish hotel suites and Cadillacs to function as a sort of social secretary. Which, undoubtedly, sometimes involved obtaining for Hughes and anyone he designated the company of attractive ladies.

Kane and I had drinks but Hughes did not. A French couple, a cook and butler, were on hand to provide sustenance. The conversation was general. I didn't try to get information for our series; that was White's job. Hughes began to call me Les and said Walter and the Operations boys would provide anything I wanted. So I was now under the umbrella, too.

Howard was, as Mrs. Selznick had insisted, a fascinating man. He had a large head, high forehead, dark hair and eyes. His gaze was intense. His mind, it became obvious, worked very, very fast indeed. (I used to say White's mind could go around the block ten times while he was waiting for me to finish saying something; I later decided Howard's could go around the block 100 times.)

He habitually stooped, perhaps the result of having to bend over to hear people speak. He wore nondescript tan trousers, a white shirt with no tie and a plain brown jacket. His shoes were obviously English and cracked with age. Not sneakers. His voice had a trace of Texas accent and a high, whining quality.

This enormously rich man was accustomed to having whatever he wanted. He believed every thing and every man and every woman could be bought and that he had the necessary wherewithal.

Hughes had told Steve when they started that he wanted to review the LOOK articles before they were published. White explained such censorship was not possible but did agree that Hughes could check the manuscript for possible errors of fact. We didn't then understand how closely he would want to check and how much *Sturm und Drang* would result from that arrangement.

Steve had almost all his writing done by December and was in New York when I took another trip which brought me to Beverly Hills on New Year's Eve. The next morning, Walter Kane called and announced happily that he had two tickets to the Rose Bowl Game. He was quite disappointed when I told him I didn't care for football and saw no point in spending a day at the game. He was, of course, just doing his job.

Walter said The Boss was too busy to see me and proposed that we go down to Palm Springs. So we flew down in a Hughes plane and spent a few days at the Racquet Club. Then came word that Howard had received some of White's copy and wanted to talk to me about it. He was in Vegas, so I was flown up there in an A-4 dive bomber, which had been converted into a small civilian transport. Very fast trip.

By now, I knew Howard Hughes well enough to understand that he was obsessed with detail. The tiniest details of anything his mind was concentrated on at the moment. The design of an airplane cockpit. The dialogue in a movie script. The contures provided by an actress' brassiere. The earnings of Hughes Aircraft. Anything.

The trouble was that when his brain was concentrated on a certain thing, everything else in the empire had to be put on hold. No one else could make a single decision. This caused a lot of grief and unhappiness among people who tried to do business with him; their messages simply went unanswered no matter how important the matter.

Our project had been completely ignored for days and sometimes weeks at a time until his attention could be recaptured. It was now.

In Vegas, I was told to meet Howard at the Flamingo at 11 P.M. I found him in a small single room on the first floor. The only unusual feature was a black amplifying box underneath the telephone.

He had read some of the manuscript and wanted to talk about details. He had no objection to the description of him as a "lean, weary man, six feet three inches tall, dressed in dark nondescript trousers and a white shirt open at the throat, glumly eating steak and salad at a table in the bar of a gaudy hotel...looking as if he didn't have two silver dollars to rub against each other in his pocket."

Or the opening pages which listed the extent of his wealth and power, his major accomplishment...and some of his eccentricities.

But why, he asked plaintively, did we want to state that he "turned 48 only two months ago but has been accumulating wealth, power and beautiful ladies almost without cease since his early youth." Why the beautiful ladies? he wanted to know.

He didn't mind our recalling that his four-year marriage to Ella Rice Hughes ended in divorce after she couldn't stand living in Hollywood. But why did we have to say he regarded the divorce as "the most disgraceful event" of his life?

Because that is what he had told Steve, I replied.

Well, it didn't look good, he said.

Why did we have to say he "played furiously" in night clubs in earlier years and why did we call him a Playboy? Because he had been one, I answered.

When we got to the account of his designing a brassiere for Jane Russell to enhance her already ample bosom for his movie *The Outlaw,* he didn't suggest the story wasn't true. He just didn't think we had the perspective right.

"Goddammit Les," he said, "I never laid a hand on that girl." (Twenty years later she was still on the Hughes payroll.)

He didn't have any reaction to accounts of romances with Katharine Hepburn, Ginger Rogers or Billie Dove—and a dozen others—but why must we recall that he had been seeing Ruth Moffett when she was 15 years old and had "shown an interest in Mary Rogers, the 16-year-old daughter of Will Rogers?" Because it checked out, I replied.

He obviously felt he wasn't getting anywhere and picked up the phone. A few moments later, a man arrived who was introduced as Tom Slack, one of his Texas lawyers. Howard began to talk to the obviously startled Slack about the possibility of purchasing either LOOK or *Collier's.* I guess he thought he was putting some kind of pressure on me, how I can't imagine.

Sometime in the early hours, he asked me to excuse him and made another telephone call. This time it was evident he was talking to Jean Peters, the young actress who later became his second wife. And just listening to him talk on the phone made me realize—again—what a charmer he was. Once he concentrated, he came across so sincere, caring and loving that who could resist? He could be infuriating but also irresistible when he so chose.

When we got to the account of his role in designing the Lockheed Constellation, a four-engine propellor airplane far ahead of its time, I did agree we would reconsider the language. I got the impression he wanted *some* credit for the design but didn't want to claim the lions' share. I thought we could take his word on that. When he questioned some dollar figures, I agreed that we would try to check them again.

But his principal complaints were that we were making him look frivolous with phrases like "the life of a romantic playboy" and "he resents taking anyone into his counsel" and "one young lady after another."

"They are part of the story Howard," I insisted, beginning to lose patience with his niggling. Apparently sensing it, he suddenly said, "Let's go have some fun and get something to eat."

By now it was past 3 A.M., but when we walked out of the Flamingo, one of the "boys" was there with a Chevvie sedan which Howard drove down to the Strip to the Desert Inn. We went into the big showroom and were shown to a table down front. He ordered a steak and salad and watched the rest of the late show. His head had simply turned off what we had been talking about.

The third or fourth time I went to California for the "final" checking session, Steve was there. One night, we were sitting around 8484 Sunset with Walter Kane and some ladies he had invited. One was a strawberry blonde actress named Lucille Brewer who, I suspect, thought associating with Kane and Hughes would further her career. Two others were out-and-out tootsies.

Howard showed up and announced we were all going to Palm Springs. Right now. He would fly his own Convair and the rest of us would go in a converted B-20 bomber which was part of the Hughes fleet.

"Dietrich doesn't know I'm stealing his plane," he chuckled.

We got to Palm Springs and to the El Mirador Hotel, the big, sprawling place downtown. We did some partying that night, and even Howard had a glass or two of champagne.

Late the next morning, I was sitting by the big swimming pool with Steve when Howard walked up. I was surprised to see him in daylight.

"It's a beautiful Sunday morning," he said. "Let's go for a ride."

He drove us out to the airport and up to his Convair. There was a man in the cockpit, but he waved the guy into the cabin—which had seats for 65 passengers—and told me to take the co-pilot's seat.

I had never been in such a position and was fascinated to watch him go through the check list for takeoff. He was one of the world's greatest pilots and it was a great kick to watch him in action.

Airborne, he turned south toward Mexico. The Southern Pacific tracks were directly below us and he spotted a passenger train moving toward Palm Springs. He put the plane into a steep dive straight toward the engineer's cab. For some reason not satisfied with the maneuver, he circled and came around to buzz the train again head-on.

It was almost an exact replay of the opening scene of the movie *Bad Day at Black Rock*.

Howard obviously loved to be flying. He was happier than at any other time I had been with him.

For some reason I don't understand, he seemed to be able to hear better in the plane than on the ground and even tuned the radio to a music station.

I was booked to return to New York that night on the TWA overnight flight which had berths on board. But when we got back to the hotel, Howard proposed that I stick around for a few days. We were having fun, he said. But I had work to do and insisted on returning to New York. And Steve said he had no desire to stay in Palm Springs. Howard grumbled a bit but agreed to take us back to the LA airport.

He then asked one of the boys to get him a big plate of ice cream with chocolate sauce. His blood sugar was low and he wanted it up before flying, he explained. We all sat around the room and watched him eat it.

Lucille allowed as how she sure would like to go to New York. No problem, Howard said, she could go right along with me.

"But I can't go in these clothes," she cried. She was wearing shorts and probably had only them and one summer dress with her.

So the Hughes organization sprang into action. Bill Utley was told to get into her apartment, pack a bag for New York weather and get it out to the airport. He did.

When Kane, White, Lucille, the tootsies and I trooped aboard the Convair, a fourth lady joined us. "Howard's little girl," one of them sniffed. She was not introduced.

He invited me to take the co-pilot's seat again and when we flew over the mountains the Los Angeles basin was beautifully visible on the crystal clearnight. The valley was a sea of glittering lights.

"Let's do some sight-seeing," he said.

He got on the radio and told someone to hold the plane on the ground until he arrived. I guess they gave the passengers some cock-and-bull story about engine trouble.

Anyway, that plane sat there for an hour or so while we flew in circles around the sprawling city. Howard talked, rather eloquently, about how beautiful Southern California was, how much he liked it.

Finally, he landed and taxied up to the waiting Connie. Howard introduced me to the captain, who was waiting to greet him. The man seemed a bit nervous and said the weather report for New York was not good.

We stood around talking until Howard finally turned away and we got up the ramp. After the takeoff we had a couple of drinks and I went to sleep. In a berth. Miss Brewer had a seat.

When I woke and got dressed in the morning, the plane was bucking around in high winds. After I got seated, the stewardess announced, "Hold on, we're going for a ride!" And we did.

At one time, I looked out to see a runway directly below. The plane was on its starboard side bouncing around directly over the airport. Finally, the motors were turned up to full pitch and the plane flew to Boston. It came directly in for a landing, probably low on gas.

When the plane pulled up near the terminal building and the ramp was lowered, a load of exhausted, scared—and some sick—passengers filed out.

A man standing at the foot of the stairs asked if I was Mr. Midgley. When I said yes, he identified himself as the manager of the Boston airport.

"Howard Hughes called me," he said. "There is a limousine here waiting to take you to New York." Lucille and I finished the trip by car.

Back in New York, I continued working on the final version of the Hughes series, which we had decided would be published in three parts beginning about the first of March. The next big decision would be what picture to put on the cover. During that late-night session at the Flamingo, Howard had given me a somewhat formal portrait of him by Bachrach. It showed him facing directly into the camera, knees up, probably sitting on a stool. He was wearing a white shirt and a *tie!* I thought it was great and would be ideal for our cover. But for some reason he didn't like it, and since the picture was his property, we couldn't use it without his consent.

One day, to my surprise, Nadine Henley showed up in my office in New York. She was carrying a batch of pictures of The Boss, which she said he had approved. None of them was as good as the Bachrach portrait and, in the end, LOOK ended up using an old file photograph of him sitting in the cockpit of one of his racing planes wearing a leather flying helmet. Not the best choice, I thought then and ever since. That Bachrach photo has been on my office wall for 35 years.

Howard was still picking away at the copy, and Nadine and I had some discussion of details. But she was a shrewd lady and knew we were not going to twist editorial content around—even to please her powerful master.

Steve was completely finished with his part of the project and had decided to resign from LOOK and remain in California.

And in the middle of January, something happened that took me out of the picture too. I was fired.

When LOOK got started in 1936, Mike's principal editor was Dan Mich. He had left the Cowles organization several years before I arrived to become editor of the *Woman's Home Companion,* then a large-format, high quality magazine. But Mike always hankered to get him back, and at the end of 1953, they had come to an agreement that he would return as LOOK's executive editor.

A year or so earlier, Mike had become unhappy with the way Bill Lowe was operating and hired Dana Tasker, a veteran editorial executive at TIME and LIFE, as "editorial director." But Tasker turned out to be extremely difficult to work with and for because he insisted that LOOK wasn't doing things the way the Luce organization did. Which, in his opinion, was the only right way.

One morning, Mike called Tasker up to his office and told him Dan Mich was coming back as boss of the editorial department. Then he told Lowe goodbye. I was next. "Les," he said, "I want you to resign from LOOK. Dan Mich is coming back to run the editorial side and he has to have his own team."

I protested a little, pointing out that the goals he had set had been reached, that LOOK was moving up well in quality and circulation. He agreed but said his mind was made up; he wanted Dan back. He was generous enough, saying he would give me a year's salary, $20,000.

I always admired Mike and his abilities as a publisher, despite the final collapse of the big magazine. He did me a favor priceless to anyone working in the publishing business: He doubled my salary from 10 to 20 thousand dollars. That kind of jump means a big change in an editor's status and affects the rest of his working life.

Steve was in New York at the time and had come into the office without a clue as to what was happening. A group of us were chatting, commiserating, when my secretary came in to tell Steve that he had a telephone call from someone who would not give his name. Steve knew who it was.

Howard said he had heard from Dana Tasker that I was being fired and he didn't like it. After some conversation he told Steve to tell Mike that he would buy LOOK for $20 million. Steve told Howard that he certainly should not buy the magazine and that what was going on that day had nothing to do with the upcoming series about him. The upshot was that Steve told me about this development, which really didn't surprise me, knowing how weird Hughes could be. We agreed that it really was a bum idea. Steve said Howard wanted me to call and I went downstairs to use a pay phone.

Howard told me to come out to LA, he wanted to talk to me. I told him that I now had nothing whatsoever to do with the Hughes series and there was no point in any more discussions with me about it. He said he knew all that but he wanted to see me anyway.

Howard told me to register at the Beverly Wilshire—not the Beverly Hills—as "Mr. Highland" or some such moniker. I couldn't imagine why he wanted me to do this but he had an obsession with secrecy that grew, as we know now, into a terrible affliction. Why would anyone else have the slightest interest in any connection between me and Mr. Hughes? We had been meeting openly for months.

But I did as I was told. When I registered, they took me up to the penthouse, not a suite but one enormous room. It was odd, but very luxe. Probably usually used for cocktail parties.

I got together with Howard at 8484 Sunset on the evening of January 18. Steve was there and Walter Kane and a few of Walter's girls, all wearing "cocktail dresses." We had a drink or two and then Howard said, "Come with me" leading the way into a large bathroom, the first I had ever seen with wall to wall carpeting.

"I want you to come to work for me," he said. "One of these days I am going to get into publishing and I want you to look around and see what might be available. How much did Mike pay you?"

When I told him 20 thousand, he said he would pay the same. I didn't have anything else specific to do at the moment and thought working for this interesting and powerful man would be a lot of fun. So I said okay. I would be paid, Howard said, through Hughes Productions, which in course of time turned out to be an all-purpose company at 7000 Romaine used to pay odd kinds of bills, such as cash sums given to ladies stashed in expensive apartments for months at a time awaiting his call.

Steve had decided he wanted to try screenwriting and Howard arranged for him to join 20th Century-Fox. One studio owner always would do a little favor for another.

Two funny things happened that evening.

First, I happened to remark that it was my birthday.

"Howard, give him a million dollars!" one of the girls said instantly.

Almost everyone had left as midnight approached and Hughes was increasingly occupied with some papers that had been delivered by messenger an hour before. Squatting on a chair beside a big coffee table, he kept picking the papers up and putting them down. The messenger was waiting in the hall.

Finally, he took a pen and signed several of the papers.

"Well, I just gave away Hughes Aircraft. Mr. Hyland is the boss now," he said.

I guessed it to be the legal transfer of the great electronics company to a trusteeship, which would channel its profits into a medical foundation in Florida. The company had done spectacular work for the space program and still builds the most complicated satellites. Hughes owned all the stock but it would now legally be held by a foundation.

He apparently never again intervened personally in the affairs of Hughes Aircraft, and it prospered mightily.

I guess the papers were drawn up to be signed before midnight and—in true Hughes fashion—he procrastinated until the very last minute.

One of his old associates said Howard did everything as though he was going to live forever. It was true. He always knew he should make a valid will but he never got the job done.

The phony hotel reservation caused some mixups. Lowe and others tried to reach me from New York and were told that no one named Midgley was registered. One day, I needed money and realized that the hotel wouldn't cash my check. I called Nadine's office and explained the problem. Within an hour, one of the boys was at the door with an envelope containing $200 in cash. It was the beginning of a lot of cash transactions.

I went back to New York and rented a one-room furnished office on a floor of the Shelton Hotel which had been converted from hotel to office space. One room on the floor contained a telephone switchboard and mailboxes for the tenants' correspondence.

And twice a month, into my mailbox there came envelopes stamped "Special Delivery. Return Receipt Requested." Inside each one was a sheaf of $100 bills, my salary from Hughes Productions. No checks. Cash. It was the way they did business. The envelopes came from a man named Lee Currin, who had been described as "Hughes' money man."

Howard obviously knew something about human weakness because the proper amount of income tax was deducted from each semi-monthly payment. And at the end of the year, I got standard tax forms from the Hughes Tool Company in Houston. My salary was "on the books."

I had told Howard that if he really was interested in magazines—which I didn't believe—he should have his financial men look into *Collier's,* which was floundering. (It was, as it turned out, the first of the big magazines to go under.)

If he was interested in newspapers, I suggested he think about the *Herald Tribune* because of its fine reputation and potential to be revitalized. By now, Mrs. Reid had installed her youngest son, Brownie, as publisher, replacing his sibling Whitey. But the Reid family simply couldn't operate the paper successfully without Ogden's steady—even when in his cups—hand.

One day, Henley phoned and said I should go down to Wall Street and see a Mr. Somebody, a vice-president of the Irving Trust Company who handled Hughes financial business in New York. She said I was to introduce myself again as Mr. Highland. Weird.

So I went down to Irving Trust and called upon Mr. Somebody. I told him I was looking into the possibility of the sale of the *Herald Tribune* to Howard Hughes and had been instructed to come to him. He was visibly hostile.

"What on earth does Hughes want with the *Herald Tribune?*" he asked. "That's not his kind of thing."

"I don't know why he wants to do anything," I replied. "I was told to see you and ask if you would contact the Reids to see if they might sell the paper."

He said, with obvious distaste, that he would do so but indicated clearly he didn't think Howard was the right sort of fellow to be operating the *Tribune.* He told me to come back in a few days. Why the

Hughes organization had dealings with bankers who thought he was some kind of weirdo I couldn't understand.

When I went back, he said, with obvious relish, that the Reids "had absolutely no interest whatsoever" in selling the paper to Mr. Hughes.

One day, I decided to see if I could get a little more guidance from these strange people and flew out to Los Angeles on TWA. Steve met me at the airport, and we heard my name called over the paging system. But when I checked at the message desk, they knew nothing about a message or a page. I spent a few days with the Whites, visited the Fox lot and had dinner with Walter Kane, who was affable as ever. He said he just didn't know what the boss was up to. Walter was living high on the hog in one of the most beautiful suites at the Bel Air Hotel and drove around in yet another new Cadillac.

Finally, I decided to go back to New York. Just as I was walking through the gate—it was a gate in a wire fence then—a TWA man holding a phone stopped me.

It was Howard. He said he was sorry we hadn't gotten together. "Maybe my staff didn't tell you I was all tied up," he said. I explained I just couldn't go on doing nothing. He said he understood and wanted me to go on a vacation to Florida. He would arrange it.

I never saw him or talked to him again.

When I got back to New York, Nadine called and told me to contact a Hughes man who lived, and for all I know worked, at the New York Athletic Club. I did and he said he had made reservations for me, my wife and children to go to Daytona Beach, Florida, for a vacation. We did and had a fine time on a lovely beach.

It was evident that Hughes had merely done me a favor by putting me on his payroll. He had nothing to gain at the time; there was nothing I could do about the article in LOOK. When he said he was interested in owning publishing properties, he *might* have meant it. At the moment. But he simply had too many other things to do.

Hughes was an enigma, not only to a public titillated by his exploits but to those close to him—if anyone ever really was.

He was only 48 years old when we met and tirelessly active in various business affairs, flying airplanes, partying. But the seeds of what happened at his tragic end were visible even then, the paranoia, passion for secrecy, eccentric—to put it mildly—life style.

The "boys" who were with him in his final years probably know just what happened but they aren't talking. I suspect he simply insisted that they and his doctors give him whatever drugs he wanted and none could say him nay. He obeyed no man.

I am not a pilot nor an engineer and, God knows, not a financier, but even during our brief acquaintance, it was evident that Howard Hughes was a master at all of these trades. Plus being able to write and produce some great movies.

But in retrospect what I came to admire most about Howard was that he really was the man who "did it my way." And only his.

If he wanted something, he told people to get it. An airplane, air airline, a car, house, hotel, girls, you name it. He set up an efficient organization to do nothing except comply with his wishes. Nothing more; nothing less.

There was not much levity at Operations but the story was told that one day a man phoned and said he had to talk to Mr. Hughes, that it was important.

"Important to whom?" the man at the switchboard answered, getting a little out of line, "to you or to Mr. Hughes?"

There are dozens of stories about Hughes' eccentric behavior. My own favorite is this.

Howard used to go into a certain drug store in Los Angeles very often to make calls from a telephone booth. One day, the druggist complained he was tying up the phone, which was supposed to be for the use of his customers. The next day, two men from the telephone company showed up at the store.

"Mr. Hughes says you need another phone in here," they said, bringing one in through the door.

Although I never saw Howard again, I was in contact with his organization for years afterwards. Because he had given instructions about the payments, they continued to arrive for more than a dozen years until I finally wrote him a formal note requesting that they be discontinued and mailed it to Nadine. He had long since disappeared from public view.

Near the end of the Fifties, he spent much of one year in Boston, apparently at the Massachusetts General Hospital for reasons unknown, then took a *train* to Las Vegas. There he bought a whole group of hotels and casinos. Chester Davis, a tough New York lawyer who had won a big Supreme Court suit brought by TWA against Hughes, was now his chief lawyer, although Davis never met him in the flesh.

Davis, Bill Gay and Nadine organized the Hughes properties under the name of the Summa Corporation. Chief of operations in Nevada was an engaging former FBI agent named Robert Mayheu, who also never met Hughes, although he ran a lot of million dollar deals for him. Bob finally fell out of favor with the Operations groups and was squeezed out by Bill Gay, Raymond Holliday, one of Hughes' few associates from Texas, and Chester Davis.

I admired Davis' work and asked if he would be my lawyer. He happily agreed and so functioned for years. Without sending me any bills.

After Betty Furness and I were married in 1967, we made several visits to Las Vegas and were entertained by none other than Walter Kane, now director of entertainment for all the Hughes hotels. He had risen, with Hughes' help, from being a minor agent to the most powerful booker of big-name talent in the biggest gold mine entertainers had ever seen.

And I saw Nadine Henley many times, both in Nevada and during her infrequent trips to New York.

I had two minor business contacts with the Hughes group in later years.

When the *Herald Tribune* merged with the remnants of the *New York Journal* and the *World-Telegram* into what would prove to be a failing attempt to publish in the afternoon, the *Paris Herald Tribune* remained the property of Jock Whitney. Since it was common knowledge that Walter Thayer, Whitney's general manager, had disapproved of Whitney becoming involved with newspapers, I thought Thayer might now be interested in disposing of the Paris property. I suggested to Nadine that it would be an excellent thing for Howard to own and she got back to me with instructions to talk to Thayer about it. I did and got a reception almost identical to that from Mr. Irving Trust Company years before. Thayer wanted nothing to do with the eccentric Mr. Hughes.

And after Clifford Irving published what he claimed was a first-person account of Howard Hughes' life, done with his cooperation, a big flap ensued about the authenticity of the book. My bosses at CBS

News, along with everyone else in the news business, wanted to interview the elusive Mr. Hughes. I went out to Summa headquarters, then in Encino, California, to see if anything could be arranged. Bill Gay and Nadine and I had lunch and talked about it but nothing happened. I got an inkling from what they said that Irving's material might have been swiped from a book ghost-written for Noah Dietrich and in the end that proved to be true.

The Hughes organization finally arranged a "telephone press conference" during which Howard denied he ever met Irving or had anything to do with the book. At least the voice sounded like Mr. Hughes to me. Who knows?

Besides some lovely memories, I have three artifacts of Howard.

One is the Bachrach picture. Another is the simplest kind of Christmas card with a small Santa on the front. Inside are the words "Merry Christmas, Jean and Howard Hughes." It was postmarked the morning of December 22, Beverly Hills, Calif. and bore—of course— an airmail stamp. Eight cents. My guess is that Jean was telling people who knew Howard that they really were man and wife. Why me? Who knows?

The third thing is something else.

Almost a year after Betty—who dated Howard when she was a very young Hollywood starlet—and I were married, I got a call from Nadine Henley.

"You have been married almost a year," she said, "and the boss wants to know what you would like for a wedding present."

Some question. Half of Los Angeles?

"An old pool table," I said. Why I don't know; I am no pool player.

"That's a great idea," she said.

Nothing happened for months, which didn't surprise me one bit. But one day, a billiard supply house in Yonkers called to say they had received a pool table from California which was consigned to us in Hartsdale. But, they said, they could only deliver it to the street in front of our driveway.

"Better check back with the shippers," I said.

A few days later, they arrived and installed it. The grandchildren love to play on it.

The Last Word on the Page

A FEW MONTHS after making the deal with Howard, I ran into Joe Barry, a G.I. who had stayed in Paris after the war and had become involved with the literary scene there. Joe said he was an associate editor for, of all things, *House Beautiful,* a large, very stylish magazine published by the Hearst Corporation for upscale—hopefully rich— homeowners.

When I told him I was under-employed, he urged me to talk to his boss, Elizabeth Gordon, the editor of *House Beautiful.* Having nothing to lose, I went to see her. She turned out to be a well-dressed middle- aged lady who had propelled herself up the Hearst ladder with a combination of charm, hard work and making sure she had first class people working for her. That's why Joe was there.

The upshot was that I got involved in editing the kind of publication I had never worked for and never even read.

Until I began at *Collier's,* my experience had been confined to newspapers, a lot of them. Being deeply interested in the basics of news content, I was intrigued to discover that writing, editing copy and designing pages for large magazines was really the same thing as doing that work for daily newspapers. Only the format and deadlines were different.

The *news* for *Collier's* was "fact" articles on current topics, such as the Korean war, profiles of prominent or intrinsically interesting people, some fiction and humor.

The *news* for LOOK was lots of pictures of glamorous Hollywood types in slightly risque poses or situations, how-to spreads on fashion, beauty, cooking and sports. Plus, increasingly, serious fact articles on national and world politics and what was going on in Washington.

The *news* for *House Beautiful*, I discovered, was how to remodel a whole house—into something beautiful. Or make a kitchen more workable and pleasant to spend time in. Or how to plan and lay down flagstone walk and a lovely stone wall. Plus some text articles on cooking, wines, buying the right new furniture, and so forth.

Miss Gordon was sometimes called a dragon by her staff, but the stuff they got together for her was first class, well written by guys like Barry and presented in high style by fine art directors.

NOT the news as seen from the bull pen at *The New York Times*, but news nevertheless.

I did some heavy rewrite and laid out some pages for two issues, after which Miss Gordon and I agreed that this particular corner of journalism was not for me.

It was my last adventure with the word on the page.

BOOK II

The Word Flies Through the Air

Chapter 12

Television News

WHAT I HAD NOW was a double salary, for a year at least, and very little work to do.

I was lying on a dock at Lake George a few months later when Elmer Lower, vice president of public affairs for CBS News, called. Elmer had been chief of the photo bureau of the Associated Press during the war, with an office upstairs in the Herald building.

"What are you doing?" he asked.

"Nothing."

"Come on down here and get into television," he said.

So I drove to New York and went to see Elmer in the CBS building, right across Madison Avenue from LOOK. At least the neighborhood was familiar. He wanted me to join a group assigned to produce pilots for an early morning show on CBS television. For two years, the "Today" show on NBC had completely dominated the hours from 7 to 9 A.M. Nothing CBS did had made even a slight dent in the NBC ratings. Irving Gitlin, a senior producer of great reputation, had been given a budget of several million dollars and told to develop a show to compete with NBC.

I knew nothing about television and didn't even own a set. But I did know a lot about news editing and photo journalism. Elmer proposed that I sign on as a writer and I agreed. There was another writer on the project, a very skillful one indeed, who did know his way around television because for several years he had written amusing ad libs for Arthur Godfrey. He was Andy Rooney.

Having no idea how television news worked, I began again to exercise my old habit of watching what went on and listening to people who knew how it worked.

Our first effort was something called FYI (For Your Information). The director was Av Westin, a young man of great energy and talent. The on-air hosts were Chuck Romine and Bill Leonard, years later president of CBS News. Among the reporters were Bud Palmer, Frank Reynolds and a woman named Noel Mills, in from a Philadelphia station for a shot at the big time.

During one of the segments, Reynolds delivered some "hard news"—dummied up for a pilot—then Av cut to Noel, who said she wanted to demonstrate a new vacuum cleaner called the Roll Easy. You didn't have to lift it, it rolled along. The trouble was she couldn't get it to roll on camera. Back to Philadelphia.

The CBS brass looked at a kinescope of the pilot and waved us all back to the drawing board.

The next go-around had a new star, Will Rogers, Jr., who looked and sounded just like his famous father. Andy and Rogers worked especially well together and the project was perking along when I got another phone call, from John Day, the CBS News vice president for "hard" news.

In addition to a 15-minute report of the news of the day on the network, Day had another regularly scheduled show, a half-hour on Sunday afternoon presided over by Eric Sevareid, a handsome broadcaster of great reputation.

There was another production group within CBS News. It turned out "See It Now." Edward R. Murrow was the star and Fred W. Friendly the producer. I presume Friendly reported to Lower in principle but in practice Murrow and Friendly went their own way. Murrow had been very close to William S. Paley, the CBS chairman, during the war when Ed was making his famous radio broadcasts about the bombing of London and Paley was an army officer. Murrow and Paley shared much of their social life including a very grand mistress.

Day told me that Ernie Leiser, who was now producing the Sevareid half-hour, wanted to go back to Germany as a correspondent.

"You are a newsman," he said, "you shouldn't be working for Gitlin, you should be working for me." He wanted me to take over from Ernie as Sevareid's producer.

(Yes, the same Andy and the same Ernie from Paris days.)

I accepted John's offer, knowing I would be more comfortable working with topical news than with features designed to appeal to housewives. All I knew about producing had come from watching the FYI pilot being put together but, like the young Bugeja in Paris, I didn't see anything particularly difficult about it.

So I went down to the dingy offices of CBS television news in the north block of the Grand Central Terminal Building. The main newsroom was there and the staff that turned out the Sevareid show was set up across the hall.

Breaking news was scarce on Sunday, so Ernie had hired Newt Mitzman to produce "backgrounders," film reports on topical subjects which would run longer than the few minutes allotted to straight news. To fill out more of the half-hour, he had his film editors, Mitch Rudick and Howie Lester, assemble a "newsreel" of film routinely provided by the CBS News organization. Joe Zigman was in charge of film editing. Because Sevareid had trouble reading in "synch" with film, the announcer, Harry Kramer, did the voice over. Which he loved.

Ernie also had a very fine writer who stitched the show together. He was John Sharnik, yet another old friend from the *Stars & Stripes* in Paris.

Since I was starting at the top and was supposed to know how everything worked, I followed Leiser everywhere he went for the next two weeks. Watching how he laid out the contents of the show in a "lineup," how he worked with the film editors, how he conferred with John on copy. I said nothing. Just watched and listened.

How we worked and the black and white results were primitive by today's standards. TV news only got underway at the end of the 1940s and was still being "invented" in the early '50s.

Some of the early shows were sponsored, but many were not, including Sevareid's Sunday News. It was designated as "sustaining." Because the news department sustained it, I guess.

Eric, who lived and worked in Washington, came to New York on Saturday, and talked over the show with Ernie and John. On Sunday morning, the film would be given a final viewing and the copy a final reading. Then, around 3 P.M., everyone would troop down the dirty old marble halls and across a catwalk high above the great waiting room of Grand Central to CBS Studio 41.

Now the show was under the control of Vern Diamond, the television director, who called up the film and cued Eric in proper sequence. The staff knew how to do their work and, as noted, I didn't see anything particularly difficult about it. So Ernie went to Germany and I became a television producer.

That's what *they* called the job. Actually, of course, we were editors, just like those working on newspapers and magazines. But when news moved onto television after the war, job descriptions were borrowed from the TV entertainment area which had adopted the movies' nomenclature of "producer," "director" and so forth. And all of this was set in concrete with monumentally bad judgment by network business affairs administrators who themselves had grand ideas of becoming moguls, just like in the movies.

It was immediately apparent to me that "show business" was part of what we were doing, although John Day and Sig Mickelsen, the president of CBS News, were indignant at any such suggestion. They insisted stoutly that we were in the news business, just like *The New York Times* and TIME magazine.

Well, not quite. Even a tyro could discern that this was a visual medium, like the picture magazines but more effective because these pictures walked and talked. Just like the movies.

If we could get a little sex appeal or music or humor into a show, we knew instinctively that our chances of getting people to watch would increase. It was not openly discussed but Don Hewitt, then producer of the daily "Evening News With Douglas Edwards," got the same kind of stuff into his 15 minutes. For the same reason. Now he does it with sounding brass on "60 Minutes."

But this was a good thing we were doing, good journalism. We tried hard to give our audience information that they "should" know. And if we entertained them along the way, why not?

Chapter 13

Big Stuff on the Tube

CBS NEWS WAS responsible for the 15-minute network show each evening, the Sunday half-hour, some on-and-off participation in the floundering early morning show, plus emergency broadcasting when big news broke. And every four years, the division geared up for really big coverage of the presidential campaigns, conventions and elections. In addition to this network fare, CBS News was then in charge of local news programming on the five stations owned and operated by the company. The "O & Os" now run their own independent news operations.

Besides the Murrow/Friendly "See It Now," there was a half-hour weekly series, "The Twentieth Century," produced by Bud Benjamin and starring Walter Cronkite. There were other documentaries, religious programs on Sunday morning and a few other shows under "public affairs."

Everything was primitive by today's standards. The studio cameras sent out black and white images. The meager amount of newsfilm available was shot with .16mm film cameras, which had replaced cumbersome .35mm movie-type machines. (Although some shows like "See It Now" used the bigger cameras because they produced better quality pictures.)

Live pictures and film could be sent out on air or over telephone lines to headquarters in New York from major centers like Washington, but film of foreign news developments was flown in by plane. It usually ended up on air the day after an event, introduced with phrases like "this film just received in New York."

There were no satellites, no videotape machines, no color and only crude graphics.

The Sevareid show staff was an ideal unit to rush into action when big news broke, and we began to get more and more such assignments. A really big one came when Russian troops and tanks rolled into Budapest in October 1956, to put down an open insurrection by the Hungarians against their Communist masters.

Leiser had gone to Budapest with a film crew as the Russians advanced and they were in the middle of the fighting. Sound and fury on film...just what TV pants for!

And at just the same time, British and Israeli armies were invading Egypt in effort to open the Suez canal, which had been closed by the Egyptian government. The Eisenhower administration had warned the British and Israelis not to invade. When they went ahead anyway, the most powerful diplomatic and economic pressures were brought to bear and the British and Israelis backed down.

This was big stuff indeed, and John Day told me in the middle of one week to get together an hour and a half show, covering both stories, for the following Sunday afternoon.

I chose the title "World in Crisis" and got Howard K. Smith assigned as the studio reporter. Howard had been a correspondent in Europe for years with much experience in both Hungary and the Middle East. And he is a fine writer.

We knew from film already arriving in New York that Ernie would provide sensational pictures of battles in the streets of Budapest and we could get other eyewitness reports from surrounding countries as Hungarians by the thousand fled across their own borders.

Vern Diamond, although assigned to direct news, was a showman at heart. (For many years he directed the Rose Bowl parade in Pasadena and was often assigned to the Miss America pageant in Atlantic City).

Music, even on film, was frowned on in straight news broadcasts and it was unthinkable in a news studio, but Vern and I figured we could get away with some for this big special.

So he hired Tony Mottola, one of the greatest pop guitarists, and told him to bring along a couple of other guitar players. Tony was a pro. We told him what we were doing, let him watch a rough rehearsal and said it was in his hands.

I thought it was going to be great. But John Day came to the studio that afternoon and brought along his wife, Vivien, to watch from the control room. During the last part of the rehearsal, he sought me out, obviously distressed.

"Vivien says we shouldn't have guitars," he said. "For Hungarians it should be violins.

Vivien, it seemed, was Hungarian.

"Sorry, John, it's too late" was all I could say.

The Days might have been upset, but Tony was swell. And so was the whole show.

We had booked Studio 42, one of CBS' largest, and Vern had ordered a huge map of Eastern Europe and the Middle East painted on the floor. He mounted cameras on high pedestals, so when Howard started to talk about Budapest, he walked across to it on the map. The cameras put both him and the map on the screen. When the story moved to Suez, Howard stepped over to that area. Vern got cameras high enough in this big barn of a studio to make it look like a movie set. We loved it.

Maybe the title producer was okay!

But the heart of the show was, of course, the great scenes of battle in Budapest, with everything, including rocks, thrown by Hungarians at Russian tanks. To no avail. And before the tanks arrived, heroic statues of Josef Stalin, no less, were pulled from their marble pedestals to crash in the streets. On camera.

The show won a Peabody Award, my first of six.

In October 1957, the Russians sent Sputnik, the first artificial satellite, into orbit around the earth and by so doing shook up the American political, scientific and education establishments. And gave me the chance to do a really BIG job of what even I could call investigative journalism and television production.

Sputnik was a nasty shock because we had built the first atomic bomb and most Americans assumed their country was the world leader in science and technology. But Sputnik proved the Russians had moved ahead in the technique of building very big and powerful rockets, capable of lifting objects into space at speed and altitude that would turn them into artificial moons. The US space program, bogged down in rivalry between the Army and the Air Force, did not then have rockets capable of such a feat.

My bosses at CBS News decided this called for a major investigation and a full and frank report to the American people. I was told to run it. I had excellent assistance. Alexander Kendrick, a fine reporter with worldwide experience, was available. Don Hewitt agreed to help as director and co-producer. And Steve White, who knew more about science than any reporter around, joined us as associate producer and writer. As a matter of fact, it was Steve and one of his weekend guests who fired me up for this project.

The news of Sputnik broke on a Sunday with radio reports about it, and I got a call from Steve, who lived about 20 miles north in Westchester county. He said Sammy Eilenberg, chairman of the mathematics department at Columbia University, was his house guest and was bubbling with delight and information about the Earth's new "moon."

"We're coming right down to talk to you," Steve announced.

A half-hour later, in walked Steve and a short, bald, bright-eyed man he introduced as Professor Eilenberg. Who asked for a piece of paper and a pencil and began explaining how the satellite worked.

"It's going at 18,000 miles an hour," he said, "at an altitude of 560 miles above the earth. It is not being propelled, like an airplane. It is constantly falling, falling around the earth, pulled by the force of gravity, just like Newton's apple. But it will always keep going around, kept from flying out into space by the pull of the earth's gravity. Just like the real moon."

My daughters, 11 and nine, stood around the table and listened with fascinated attention. Sammy was giving us a lesson in astronomy and physics and mathematics, about which I was as ignorant as the children. He made it clear and compelling. The girls never forgot him and his discourse that Sunday. A great teacher.

Up to now, almost all my work at CBS had been to do with what I call "processing" news. By that, I meant putting stories into proper form for television.

The same event, for example, would be treated in one way by a daily newspaper, another by a magazine and yet another by television.

For the daily newspaper it would be: Lead overall story on what had happened, comments from leading scientists, reaction from Washington and other capitals, interviews with American scientists and manufacturers trying to build a satellite and lift it into orbit with a rocket, opinions from military men about what this might mean to the nation's security.

For a magazine, the processing would be similar but, hopefully, more complete with better perspective after more intensive research permitted by later deadlines. And far better graphic displays.

For television, news "producers" would try to acquire all the above information but would be forced to keep the number of words to a minimum, use every scrap of good film they could find and devise graphic illustrations to tell some of the story. Because television is a visual medium.

But what we set out to do with this story was quite different.

Don Hewitt lived in suburban Connecticut. He suggested we assemble there for a deli lunch. So Alex and Steve and I and others involved went there for a planning session. We were very lucky to have Don. He tended to put on an "Aw shucks, fellows, I don't understand this big stuff" act. But I had known, since he was head copy boy at the *Herald Tribune,* that Don has a very sharp mind and great natural talent.

I decided to call the show "Where We Stand." It would be nothing less than a report to the nation on where it stood in rocketry, civil defense, military power and education, especially scientific and technical education.

To do this, we would have to go beyond what had happened—and in this case what had failed to happen—physically. We would have to conduct a thorough investigation into the faltering American space program. And beyond that, try to come to rational conclusions about what Sputnik was telling us about the state of our science and the state of scientific education in our schools.

And try to answer the question, "Why were the Russians ahead of the proud United States of America?"

And—possibly most important—what were the military implications? Did this thing flying around the Earth and sending back information pose a threat to national security?

Alex would go out as field reporter with camera crews. Walter Cronkite and Howard K. Smith would share the studio work, Walter concentrating on the scientific areas and Howard the military and political implications of Sputnik. But first we needed basic information. Just what *was* the story?

Steve and I decided to go to California to look at the Apollo rocket program. Apollo, being built by Convair in San Diego, was touted as being the country's best bet to get into space soon.

Enroute we stopped in Sunnyvale, just south of San Francisco, to talk to one of Steve's friends, Louis Ridenour, a brilliant physicist who was in charge of research and development at Lockheed. Louis, whom I had met previously in New York, had several thousand people working for him. We didn't know it but a lot of them were turning out the hush-hush spy plane U-2.

Although most of what he did was highly classified, Ridenour trusted Steve and me and was surprisingly frank with us. Maybe even a bit indiscreet. He outlined the state of the art in rockets and missiles and listed the major problems of the American development program. He was very, very knowledgeable.

At one point in the conversation, I remarked that all the analytical stories I had read in the newspapers indicated that an intercontinental ballistic missile could not be shot down once it was launched toward a target, say Washington.

"Not so," said Ridenour, "you can intercept a ballistic missile with another ballistic missile."

"But you would have only a few minutes," I said. "How would you know when a Russian rocket was fired?"

"A satellite above Russia or the Atlantic would tell me precisely when the rocket went off and I could then fire an anti-ballistic missile to intercept it."

"So *that's* what satellites are for!"

"One of the things," Louis said.

Being a journalist makes you eligible for constant education.

Steve and I went on to Convair to talk to the men working on the Apollo. They explained some of their problems and hopes, and we made arrangements for Kendrick and crew to come to the plant. They did and got some fine film of rocket testing and other parts of the space program. We discovered that America did have a satellite ready to go but it was waiting for a rocket to hoist it aloft. But it was even smaller than the Sputnik which had been derided in Washington as a "basketball." Even President Eisenhower said he didn't see much future for these things.

When Alex was working on civil defense aspects of our story, he managed to get some humor into it. Interviewing the director of civil defense in a small town in New Jersey, he asked if the man had an emergency supply of food for the people who lived there, plus perhaps thousands of others who might be fleeing through his town from New York in the event of a nuclear attack.

"Oh yes," he answered, "we have a good supply of food."

"Where is it?" Alex asked.

Right there at the A & P," the man said, waving down the street.

And at a high school in Southern California, one with a superior rating, a student told Alex he was not taking any science or mathematics courses because it was his senior year and they were not required.

"You know, it's playtime," he said.

"Well, what are you taking?" Alex asked.

"Well, co-ed cooking," was the answer.

"What good will that do you?"

"Well you know, when I'm out of school I might want to cook something to eat and I would like to know how to do it."

He said he was planning to be an engineer.

Alex reported in his final script that the Russians were turning out far more scientists and engineers than the American educational system, and the development of new technical capacity must start at the school level.

One day, Kendrick and I were told we had been booked to attend a meeting of something called "Excom"—short for executive committee—in Mr. Paley's office. The committee included the top executives of CBS, not only news but also entertainment, finance, law, public relations, etc. In theory, it was the final authority on policy planning. Except, of course, no committee but only the chairman, William S. Paley, actually had the last word in everything involving CBS.

It turned out that this top brass had heard something about "Where We Stand" and wanted Alex and me to tell them what we were doing.

I am not good at selling myself or my work and Alex is not much better at it. We tried to explain we were going to report on the whole range of America's rocket program, military position, civil defense, education and so forth. The measure of how we got across came when Mr. Paley remarked, "I wish we hadn't talked about this as our biggest ever reporting effort."

"So do I, Mr. Paley," I replied.

I never did believe in building up what you were going to do in advance, much preferring to let the results speak for themselves.

When we were just starting the project, White had proposed that we engage Professor I.I. Rabi of Columbia University as a consultant and advisor. Rabi had won a Nobel Prize for his work with the sonic resonance aspects of radar. He was one of the giants of American science. He inspired and encouraged many young men who became the nation's finest physicists after World War II. During that war, he had worked on the atomic bomb at Los Alamos and was very close to men like Robert Oppenheimer, Jerrold Zacharias and Jerome Weisner.

Rabi was deeply interested in the subject and readily agreed to help us. His advice was invaluable because it kept us on the right track as far as scientific facts were concerned. He was a marvelous companion and we had many hours of stimulating conversation. When I brought up the subject of a fee, he said to forget it. But when I found he didn't own a television set, I offered to send one up to his Riverside Drive apartment. That he did accept.

Finally, our air date, Sunday, January 5, 1958, rolled around, three months after Sputnik went aloft. We had commercials in this show because Sig Mickelson, the news division president, had decided to call it a "special edition" of Cronkite's "20th Century" series.

Don had found an old movie theater on upper Second Avenue which CBS Entertainment had converted to a studio. It had a huge floor and the control room occupied what had once been the theater balcony.

Don had set designers build big globes painted to represent the Earth, Mars, Saturn and other planets. The globes were hung from the ceiling on wires, scattered around the studio. Walter sat on a stool next to the globe of Earth, which he could turn by hand to indicate where the

USA was in relation to other nations, especially, of course, Russia. The whole set was lighted dramatically and worked—we thought—kind of like Hollywood.

Don is a great journalist but also a showman, and after a rehearsal, had checked out the timing of the segments and everything seemed to be in order. He stood up as air time approached and began pacing the control room, firing up his crew and the cast on the floor with commands and encouraging words.

During the show, he was superb, cueing the live reports from the floor and calling up the film, still photos and graphics. Accompanied when appropriate by the actual sound of the beeps Sputnik was sending back to Earth. He had thought all this up himself and told our primitive art department what kind of drawings to make so he could turn them into animations with his live cameras.

I had invited Rabi to watch the show from the control room and when it was over he said to Don, "Congratulations, Mr. Toscanini." Don asked me later what that meant. "It meant Rabi thinks you are a great director," I told him.

Frank Stanton, president of CBS Inc., came to the studio that afternoon to watch us put on the show and he was delighted by it. "This," he said, "is just what we should be doing." (When I left CBS 23 years later, he sent me a note recalling, among other things, this early success.) So Mr. Paley's reservations were laid to rest.

Frank is one of the great men of television. He was a constant strong supporter of the news division during all the years he was president.

The show business in "Where We Stand" was both fun and impressive—we were just getting our feet wet—but what really mattered was, of course, the content.

The lineup for the show was 1) Opening; 2) Satellites; 3) Rockets & Missiles; 4) Arms and Arms Systems; 5) Defenses; 6) Economics; 7) Education; 8) Summation; 9) Closing. Sound like enough subject material for one broadcast?

Included in Cronkite's opening copy were these words:

In the competition for leadership in space, in the race run by rocket, where is the finish line? Do we end up in a nuclear war? Or do we try to live in the constant fear of one? Scientists and military men have told CBS News what that prospect really means:

Perhaps a quarter of our population dead in the first hours of a nuclear holocaust. Our biggest cities gone...Leveled by the bomb.

The survivors condemned to radioactive danger—not just for the hours of an attack but for days, possibly weeks, afterwards. Food, water—the air itself—poison to the touch.

And to do more than wait in constant readiness would be so costly—in dollars and discipline—that it would change this country into something totally different from the one we are now trying to defend.

The challenge...and how we measure up to it...this is the subject of our next 90 minutes as...CBS News reports to the nation: "Where We Stand."

In the next hour and half, we did cover all those subjects, with field reporting by CBS correspondents and interviews with movers and shakers in all the fields.

Howard K. Smith delivered the summation:

Here are the conclusions that CBS News believes can be drawn:

We see that for the first time our country is not first in strength. We have fallen behind in the field of missiles. We may fall behind in over-all strength if our pace and some of our attitudes are not changed. The challenge of Sputnik—of course Sputnik is only a symbol of this challenge—is a challenge to our way of life and to our very survival.

We must, therefore, do at least these concrete things:

First, we must spend whatever is necessary in effort and money to achieve and maintain military parity with Russia.

Second, we must re-examine our whole educational system. Knowledge—and not mere "social adjustment"—must be restored as a purpose of education.

Third, as there *is* a possibility of war we must decide what to do about the shelter program, and...

Fourth, while building our strength, we must recognize that this is a means and not an end. This end is peace and we should be prepared to use every reasonable opportunity to negotiate for disarmament. . . .

Howard's final words were:

Our leaders have the grave and continuing duty to tell us the facts. We must be educated to danger. It is only then that we can meet it.

We must reward intelligence and learning, honor creativity, respect integrity.

We must be prepared to make sacrifices—to pay higher taxes, to face controls—if necessary to achieve our goals.

We may have to change the whole climate of American society. In a sense we must restore some of the attitudes and values of our Founding Fathers.

We believe that the right mood for the present is not one of pessimism or fear. The challenge is clear, and the very nature of the new fantastic weapons that bring on the challenge is itself a promise that the reward of strength and peace can be greater than anything the world has yet known.

Strong stuff from a medium that was too often scorned for being soft. A *television* report to the nation in January 1958.

1958!

Because I had seen the most prosperous fiction magazines put out of business by "fact" magazines like TIME, *Newsweek,* LIFE and LOOK, I always maintained that the same thing inevitably would happen in the world of television. I expected that "fact" broadcasting would, over the years, replace much of the entertainment schedule.

It hasn't yet.

Today, the most successful "fact" show is "60 Minutes," on every week and in some years rated Number One in popularity of *all* broadcast shows. And all the networks now produce a half-hour of evening news seven days a week, instead of the 15-minute shows of the

Fifties. Plus the excellent "Sunday Morning With Charles Kuralt" and the Sunday morning interview shows on all networks.

But otherwise, the picture is not so bright. In recent years, each of the three networks put on about 10 documentary broadcasts each year and their number is steadily declining. Most entertainment shows attract bigger audiences and thus more money. The network moguls of today are interested in money, not in an informed public.

During the year which began with "Where We Stand," my little unit alone produced 13 one-hour or half-hour shows about major news developments, plus four reports on Middle East crises and six shorter reports on moon shots and space probes. That was in addition to the "See It Now" and "The Twentieth Century" series and many traditional documentaries done by network film producers.

After Sputnik, everyone was interested in outer space, and Hewitt and I teamed up again to turn out an hour we called "Ceiling Unlimited," a look at how men might build and inhabit space stations in the future. Just to see what it might be worth, we shot this one in .35 mm film. Not worth it.

In July, we did an hour called "The Ruble War" about economic competition with the Russians. The Cold War was big then, but something as dense as economics in prime time?

We ended the year with "The Face of Red China," a film documentary about a vast country usually off limits to western reporters and cameramen.

The film was extraordinary. Ernie Leiser heard that Rolf Gilhausen, one of the best photographers on the staff of the German picture magazine *Der Stern,* had obtained permission to work in China. In addition to shooting still pictures, he had taken along a small film camera. Ernie screened Gilhausen's film of life and work in Chinese cities and on farms and factories from Shanghai to Manchuria. It was the time of Mao's "great leap forward." Ernie was highly enthusiastic about the film and bought the rights for $5,000. Peanuts.

"The Face of Red China" was narrated by Walter Cronkite. The associate producer-director was Av Westin. Another associate producer was Alice Weel, a talented writer for the daily news show who was married to my old friend Homer Bigart.

The show won an Emmy Award, my first of three. It was unearned. The credit should have gone to Rolf Gilhausen. But I took it. With thanks.

We thought 1958 had been a big year, but 1959 really was a blockbuster. During the first seven months, we turned out 16 shows on subjects ranging from Castro's Cuba to statehood for Hawaii, Iraq, Sudan, the St. Lawrence Seaway, the Vienna Youth Festival (featuring an attractive young American delegate named Gloria Steinhem talking enthusiastically about how the CIA supported such activities) and Vice President Richard Nixon's visit to Russia during which he had the famous "kitchen debate" with Chairman Nikita Khrushchev.

The last two were broadcast the *same night,* August 9, Steinem from 6 to 6:30 and Nixon from 7:30 to 8 P.M.

The Nixon show had a curious history, including the fact that it wound up being narrated mostly by the Vice President himself.

Nixon had been invited to an international trade fair in Moscow and western news cameras, not often allowed in the USSR, were permitted to cover the visit. Cameras were set up at the American exhibit which included such consumer goods as stoves and washing machines. When Nixon and Khrushchev toured the fair together, they got into a heated discussion after the Vice President told the Chairman that, unlike the Russians, almost every American home had such things. Khrushchev indignantly retorted, "We also have these things."

This "kitchen debate" sequence was an excellent piece of film and we had another one, of a visit by Mrs. Nixon to a school in Moscow. It occurred to me that we might be able to get Mr. Nixon to give a first-person account of the incident to use with the film and Mrs. Nixon to do the same with the school visit. Bill Small, chief of the Washington bureau, requested that they participate. The answer from the Vice President's office was that he would but Mrs. Nixon declined.

Our air date was on Sunday, and Mr. Nixon agreed to come to the CBS News Washington office at 2020 M Street the day before to view the film and do the narration.

Vern Diamond, the director, booked a studio and a set including a desk at which we planned to have the Vice President sit as he viewed the film and made his comments as it ran. Standard practice for correspondents narrating film was to show it to them in advance, time each sequence with a stop watch and have a script written to lengths which matched the film. It is not easy, even experienced correspondents sometimes find it hard to match voice and film. And we were, of course, asking Mr. Nixon to ad lib.

After he arrived, we showed him the film on a monitor. During the first part of the debate, Khrushchev was bare-headed but later he was seen wearing a hat. The cameramen had not shot a scene of him putting it on. Our film editors would never permit a "jump cut," having a hat appear out of nowhere and had inserted a "cutaway" scene to make the transition smooth, during which some of the actual sound track was deleted.

Mr. Nixon watched the film with interest, but then remarked that some language had been dropped from the sequence. We explained the hat problem, but he said he would rather have a hat jumping out of nowhere than lose some of the words. I agreed we would restore them.

When I escorted Mr. Nixon to the studio, he said he would rather perch informally on the edge of the desk than sit behind it. We did it his way. Vern rolled the film and Mr. Nixon explained "voice over" what was going on. He did quite well, falling behind a couple of times when the scenes he was watching brought recollections of things not visible to the audience.

Finally, we had a usable take but he was dissatisfied with some of his lines and asked that they be deleted.

"You can edit this, can't you?" he asked.

"Yes, we can," I told him.

That was risky. I shouldn't have said it because we had recorded him on the new technique of videotape and editing it was dicey.

Videotape was one of the technical advances that changed the whole system of reporting news and sports events. The machines recorded images from electronic cameras that were so excellent it was almost impossible even for experts to tell whether a scene was being broadcast live or from a piece of tape. And the tape could be played back instantly, without any kind of processing. But, at the beginning, we had to select a length of tape and run it without any editing because when the tape was physically cut, the picture "broke up" or "rolled over" into a series of jagged streaks when a splice rolled past the picture head on the playback machine.

But the tape editors—who we later found to be wonderful allies of the news department—already were trying to make cuts work. The solution, they decided, was to make a pattern of electronic impulses on the tape match up exactly on either side of a splice.

They knew that when iron filings the size of bits of ground pepper were sprinkled on a piece of tape they instantly arranged themselves in the magnetic pattern already on the tape. If they could make the patterns match exactly on either side of a splice, they reasoned, there would be no disturbance of the picture. So they sprinkled filings on tape and looked at the patterns through magnifying glasses. When the patterns matched, the splices did run through without breakup. It was tedious, and splice after splice didn't work. But some of the technicians got very skillful at it and we finally could do rough editing.

After Nixon left, Vern and I got onto a plane and back to New York as fast as we could. We worked far into the night stitching the show together. The Vice President looked very good. I have never been a Nixon partisan, but he was unfailingly courteous and helpful during this enterprise.

Later that month, I was vacationing at Lake George when John Sharnik called to say the unit had been assigned to produce a half-hour special about President Eisenhower's trip to Germany. It would be titled "Eyewitness to History" and sponsored by the Firestone Tire & Rubber Company. This was the first show in what would become a weekly series in prime time covering "the big news of the week." The television equivalent of the "cover story" in TIME or *Newsweek*.

This series was my most successful work in television and certainly the most fun. And by proving that big news stories could be covered both fast and in some depth, it was the precursor of the daily half hour news shows which arrived in 1963.

The involvement of the Firestone company was interesting. "The Firestone Hour," devoted entirely to classical and semi-classical music, was an early institution on radio and then television. It had ardent supporters but not enough of them to suit the networks' entertainment bosses. They figured good music turned off audiences.

Harvey Firestone's mother had written the theme music for "The Firestone Hour" and he wanted to continue it. No dice, the networks wouldn't even take his money.

Frustrated, Firestone had been looking for something the networks *would* broadcast under its name. John Karol in the CBS sales department suggested the company sponsor a show about President Eisenhower's trip. Firestone liked the idea of being the President's sponsor and liked the show. Others followed, covering Ike's visits to England and later to Europe and Asia. Finally, in September 1960, the series went on the air in a regular time slot, 10:30 P.M. on Friday.

But before that came about, we had a major test of videotape. Nikita Khrushchev made a grand tour of the United States in September, and CBS News stretched its muscle to cover him with video cameras. We produced 10 shows during the tour, including several one-hour reports.

Hewitt went on the tour as producer-director and I stayed in the attic above Grand Central Terminal where the first Ampex editing machines had been installed. We bought telephone company lines linking Don's cameras with the machines. He would shoot, say, Khrushchev waving an ear of corn on the Garst farm in Iowa and feed it to me, suggesting when to start and stop recording. With no time to spend trying to edit with the help of iron filings, we went for chunks of the action.

The Chairman went to Washington, New York, the Midwest, California and Pittsburgh before departing. In Hollywood, he visited a sound stage where a film version of the Broadway musical *Can-Can* was being shot. He and Mrs. Khrushchev watched the dancers kick their legs high and wide. We didn't detect any reaction on his part then, but the next day in San Francisco, he made some very sharp comments about the decadence of countries which permitted suggestive sex exhibitions. Did Mrs. K. have some words with him overnight?

Khrushchev's visit was an historical event, both for the governments involved and for us. He was a natural ham and gave us great performances. Leaving a farmhouse before lunch, he was given a thick sandwich to eat in the limousine. As he entered the car he waved it aloft saying, "One for the road."

When it was all over, I told Sig Mickelson, the news president, that the stack of video tapes we had accumulated during the Khrushchev tour were documents which must be preserved. Nothing like this had been done before, and historians of the future would want this great resource. He agreed.

But a few days later, he called me to say, "We can't save the tapes. We can't afford it."

I was appalled. But I knew that tape could be and was used over and over and the re-use saved a lot of money. That, plus the cost of storing and indexing, undoubtedly led the network to veto any storage archives. It was years later before adequate libraries were established and much valuable material had been destroyed.

The beginning of 1960 brought more Eisenhower trips to foreign capitals, this time in South America, and more "Eyewitness to History" shows.

And in May, there was a serious confrontation in Paris between Eisenhower and Khrushchev when the Russian abruptly cancelled a scheduled summit conference and bitterly denounced the United States for spying. A U-2 plane had been shot down over the USSR and the pilot captured. The President of the United States sat and listened to the abuse. Ike took full responsibility, but there is still a big question about who actually ordered Gary Powers' flight to coincide with the meeting in Paris. Many believe the President was set up by people in his own government. I was in Paris, producing in the field.

Nice month to be in Paris.

But not everything was rosy.

That summer, Dick Hottelet and I took a camera crew to Brazil and spent two weeks flying from Sao Paulo in the south to Brasilia, where a new capital city was being built in the wilderness, and on north to the old cities of the Amazon. We got a lot of good stuff which I took back to New York and edited as a one-hour show. Only to discover that while we had been gone, James T. Aubrey had become president of the television network. Jim told Mickelson he had no interest whatever in Brazil. The show never got on the air.

Chapter 14

Eyewitness

A Cover Story Every Friday

MICKELSON AND I made a trip to Dayton, Ohio, in the summer of 1960 in the CBS company plane, a DC-3, my all-time favorite aircraft. Sig asked for the plane because Dayton was one of those "you can't get there from here" places. We went to visit the Firestone headquarters to propose that the company sponsor "Eyewitness to History" as a weekly half-hour show. Jim Aubrey, president of the television network, had, surprisingly, agreed to give us the 10:30 P.M. spot on Friday *if* the tire company would buy it. They did.

And they agreed to pay for the air time plus $25,000 a week production costs. A marvelous deal for CBS News.

On the flight back, Sig, in a state of euphoria, told the steward to break out the booze. I told him that as far as I was concerned, the sale meant that the CBS News organization had $25,000 more a week to spend covering news; I saw the "Eyewitness" unit operating inside the news department. He was delighted.

My two energetic and talented field producers, Phil Scheffler and Bernie Birnbaum, wanted to set up a separate operation, "just like Murrow and Friendly." My answer was that we were going to stay quietly inside the news organization and "operate like fish in the sea. It is going to be our strength, not our weakness." One of the wisest decisions I ever made. Ever.

Cronkite had been anchor man on the first series of "Eyewitness" shows; he and I had traveled to Rome with a film crew when Ike visited Italy. But Walter was involved with other things like "The Twentieth Century" and especially with really major news projects, like elections. Mickelson proposed that Charles Kuralt, a young writer and reporter from North Carolina, take over the weekly show. Sig thought Charlie had the intellect—and the voice—to become a second Murrow. Which he and everyone else was looking for. I had already worked with Charlie and found it a joy. He was not only one of the finest writers at CBS—now *the* finest—but savvy about how shows were put together. Which makes a producer's job far easier and more productive. Too many good-looking and ambitious correspondents had no idea of how the whole thing worked.

Our unit was very well suited for this enterprise. My co-producer was John Sharnik, whose writing skills and good judgment had been apparent since Paris days. Scheffler and Birnbaum were the best field producers in television news, and I could borrow others if they were needed. Jane Bartels, an alumnus of TIME magazine, was our researcher. Film editors were Jerry McCarthy, Dave McCruden, Ken Dalglish and Joe Rogers. Many of our shows were literally created in the screening room where everybody had a say in how we could make it work. The film editors were very much part of the team and we listened carefully to and respected their opinions. A pretty and sharp-witted young lady named Hinda Glasser had become my secretary on the recommendation of Don Hewitt, and we had an office boy, Charlie Rozzi. Very important, an office boy. Vern Diamond would direct in the studio.

This bunch already had done nine or 10 television "cover stories" on an intermittent schedule. Now we would have to come up with one every Friday night, whether or not big news broke. We had one great advantage: Everybody knew what he or she was doing and why. We had been together long enough to "talk shorthand." We didn't have formal meetings. (I always disliked large staffs. If there are a lot of people around, you have to talk to them.)

Our editorial planning was a miniature version of that done by the weekly news magazines. I would start by looking at the news futures calendar to see if there were any obvious subjects in the coming week or two. For example, the weekly "Eyewitness to History" series kicked off on September 23. The date coincided with a meeting of the United Nations Security Council during which a clash between the United States and the USSR was expected. That did occur and was the subject of our report.

The second show, on September 30, was about troubles in the Congo, and the third was, somewhat to my surprise, about the World Series. I am not a sports fan but John and Phil are and they persuaded me to go for it. Baseball was a good choice, because it signaled that "Eyewitness" was not going to be concerned with only news of stuff like government and politics. Our "big news" did indeed turn out from time to time to be that of music and fashion and fads.

The next three weeks were devoted to the presidential campaign, which was nearing its climax, a very close victory for Kennedy over Nixon. In November and again in December, we reported on the integration crisis in the New Orleans school system.

While we worked on a show for Friday's deadline each week, I always had to look down the road. Because if a foreign story looked good, Phil and/or Bernie needed a couple of days to get on the scene.

Our modus operandi was to have an "Eyewitness" film crew work on a breaking story to get more than the regular new crews were able to cover. Walter Dombrow, a talented free-lance cameraman, became almost a full time "Eyewitness" contributor and gave us excellent pictures to complement the newsfilm. Walter later became one of the stars of the "60 Minutes" team.

We had complete access to routinely assigned CBS News coverage, and because the evening news show was only 15 minutes, excellent film shot for it was often never seen until we put it into an extended "Eyewitness" package.

The routine was to decide Monday morning what would go on the air on Friday. In principle. In actual practice, we started many times with a story early in the week only to switch to an entirely different subject midweek or sometimes the day of air. Because we were, first and last, in the news business.

A really spectacular switch of subjects came after we had been on for three months. For Friday, December 16, I had decided to go for the selection of Jack Kennedy's cabinet. The President-elect had been having meetings all week at his house in Georgetown and would emerge from his front door from time to time to introduce to the press a new cabinet member standing on the steps beside him.

A heavy snow had fallen, amazing Washingtonians, who never believe snow will come down in *their* city. All week long, a crowd of reporters assembled in the slush outside Kennedy's door waiting for news.

Instead of using film for this scene, I had decided to use video tape, and a big remote tape truck was parked at the curb containing recorders and a control room. A television remote truck is highly visible and Jack Kennedy knew what we were doing. He also knew we had a half-hour of time on Friday night. So he was—sort of—cooperating with us.

Vern, Bernie and Phil were in the truck directing the cameras shooting the comings and goings of candidates for the cabinet and pictures of such big-shot advisors as W. Averell Harriman and Dean Acheson going in and out of the Kennedy house. We had an open telephone line from the truck to the video tape roost in Grand Central so I could see from New York what the cameras saw in Georgetown.

"Bernie, the door is painted green isn't it?" I asked him on Thursday. Puzzled, he said he didn't know. "Just tell me it's green," I said. "Okay, it's green," he answered.

I wanted it to be green because I was planning to start with a montage of people coming and going through the door, speeded up to look like a Charlie Chaplin commedy sequence. Over which we would play Jim Lowe's current song hit which went, "Green door, what's that goin' on in there...."

The truck was in place in the snow on Friday morning and I was in the video bay watching the live feed when Jack came out to announce that the new attorney general would be his brother, Bobby. Good stuff.

But suddenly, bulletins from the newsroom began coming over big speakers mounted above the tape machines. Two airliners, one United Airlines, the other TWA, had collided over Manhattan and one of them had crashed into a street in Brooklyn.

I was holding a phone open to the truck and told them to put Vern on the line. I said "Listen to this," and held the phone up to the speakers, which continued to blare out news of the air disaster.

When I put the phone back to my ear, all he said was, "Do you want us to leave right now or tape for a while?" He knew the answer before I said it, and he and Bernie fled the truck and rushed for the Washington airport.

The "big news of this week" that night was the air crash. The Kennedy tapes never were broadcast. No green door. Too bad.

(Shades of the past: I got a call the next Monday from Nadine Henley. She said The Boss was deeply upset and wondered if we knew any more about the crash than what had been on the air. I was able to tell her the FAA investigators wouldn't confirm it for publication but they thought United had run into his plane. She was very grateful. I don't remember if that was indeed the final determination.)

"Eyewitness" covered the world. We did a show in late February about fighting in the Congo and the next week our story was about the look of spring fashions in the salons of Paris. Produced by Av Westin, then running the Paris bureau.

Space, Cuba, Laos, Jackie Kennedy's solo trip to Europe and India, the UN, civil defense and fall-out shelters, the Berlin Wall, a revolt in Santo Domingo, protests about nuclear submarines off Scotland—all were subjects for half-hour productions. The very last one that year had an ominous title: "Diem's War—Or Ours?"

Sound prophetic?

In addition to being a major product of the news department, "Eyewitness," much to the surprise of Jim Aubrey's executives, turned out to be a commercial success. They always scoffed at news as loss leaders, insisting only entertainment—however shoddy—could make money by appealing to mass audiences.

The operation was very economical. Firestone opted off the show after a year or so but the budget was continued at $25,000 a week. The show always was in the black, sometimes piling up $100,000 or so in unused dollar allocations. This was very useful, because on occasions when I wanted to go for an expensive television remote crew instead of film. Jim Connors, the business manager, always said to go ahead, we had plenty of money in the bank.

And the show won a basic audience share of 25. This means that, according to the Nielson gods, 25 percent of the sets turned on at 10:30 Friday night were tuned to a news show, "Eyewitness." A 25 is not blockbusting but very satisfactory, especially for a continuing weekly show.

And, we were delighted to discover, the share remained the same no matter what we covered. A show about Marilyn Monroe's death got a 25. But so did one about the international balance of payments. How about *that* for an audience grabber?

The conclusion was inescapable: People tuned in to watch "Eyewitness" as a weekly habit, not knowing what we were going to do but confident from past experience it would be something they would want to see. "60 Minutes" has that cachet today.

But the television network bosses were not satisfied. Although his boys had never been able to do better in our Friday night period, Aubrey wanted the time back. So Jim began a rough anti-Kuralt campaign, complaining to Mickelson over and over that Charlie came across as "low key, slow, not what you want." He was so persistent that Sig finally caved in and told me we would have to put Walter Cronkite in the studio anchor spot. I protested that Charlie was doing just fine, but it was no use.

Not that I had anything against Walter. He was CBS News' finest broadcaster and a consummate professional. We had done many fast-breaking shows together. But it was a bad thing to do to Kuralt after he had worked so well and so hard.

Sig apparently knew what he was doing, because as soon as Cronkite went on, the Aubrey pressure abruptly ceased. I suspect Jim just didn't want to start up with Cronkite. Even then, he was a power to be reckoned with.

After a few months, Walter got a first-hand taste of how "Eyewitness" operated in the field. Although he loved to do it, his busy schedule usually prevented him from getting out to cover stories first-hand. But this time, he and producer Sandy Socolow had gone to Israel to cover the opening of the Eichmann trial. They finished filming Thursday and started home with a stopover in Rome. As he walked through the airport there, Walter saw an Italian newspaper headline announcing that Yuri Gagarin, a Russian, had orbited the Earth, the first man to do so. Walter says he knew instantly that all the film from Israel was down the drain and our show the next night would be about Gagarin. He was right.

So you won't think "Eyewitness" was a rush job, not serious abut background documentation: Phil Scheffler recalls that he and Walter Dombrow went all the way to Buenos Aires to do a segment on how Eichmann was captured by Israeli agents. That, too, never saw the light of the flickering screen.

Our willingness—and ability—to change subjects became something of a minor legend around CBS. At a Christmas reception he gave for the whole company, Mr. Paley stopped me in the receiving line.

"I want to come down and watch you guys change your show in a hurry," he said.

I assured him he would be most welcome. He never came, but then we never alerted him. A nice thing to say. He always was on hand during convention and election coverage.

In February 1961, a major change occurred at CBS News. Sig Mickelson was replaced as president by Richard S. Salant, an attorney on the company's legal staff who was close to Frank Stanton and had been active in policy and planning areas. Salant told us he was not a journalist, that we knew what we were doing, and to carry on. His role, he said, was to help us. Dick turned out to be the best president CBS News ever had, always supportive and unobtrusive. But he had a sharp eye, and if something wrong or not in the best of taste got on the air, he was quick to spot it and call on offenders to straighten up.

That September, I managed to get the title changed to just plain "Eyewitness." Not so pretentious without the "to History."

In the spring of 1962, Charles Collingwood succeeded Cronkite, who had taken over the job of anchoring the daily evening news from Douglas Edwards. Collingwood was an excellent choice. He was a correspondent with years of experience around the world and in Washington and a fine writer. He still wore beautiful clothes tailored in London—but not a uniform of pinks.

A story broke in West Texas that spring that looked just right for us. A promoter named Billy Sol Estes had been charged with selling cotton farmers huge amounts of liquid fertilizer equipment on highly speculative loans. Many of the farmers were in hock far over their heads.

On Monday, I sent both Scheffler and Birnbaum to Dallas with two film crews and told them to get a young correspondent named Dan Rather to help with the story. Rather's good work covering a big hurricane for the CBS Dallas affiliate station had won him a spot on the network news staff. I had the usual hassle with the news desk about taking Rather off his regular beat for a few days but they finally agreed.

Phil and Bernie and Dan whipped around West Texas for three days and then came back to New York to work on the final editing. Film shot Tuesday and Wednesday had been shipped already and we knew we had a good show.

Phil now claims that when they shipped me film, they carefully held out the sexiest scene or interview or whatever and put it in a can marked "reel 1." Because, they say, they knew I would look at that reel first "and know we had a show." Well, maybe.

Anyway they arrived late Thursday with the final reels. They had swell stuff, especially farmers ruefully describing Billie Sol's hard sell. But they still admired his gall.

Dan did the "voice over" for the film and came on live with Collingwood at the close to talk about this charming Texas con man.

At 11 o'clock, we all trooped, as usual, across Vanderbilt Avenue to the Pentagon Bar. Dan looked a little dazed.

"Good show, huh?" I asked him.

"Sure was. I never thought you could do it," was his answer.

He really was astonished to see what our group could film, edit and put on air in a few days. It was television working like he had never seen before.

Because "Eyewitness" covered almost everything anywhere, we sometimes ran into conflicts with other CBS News enterprises.

One day, I got a call from Blair Clark, who had succeeded John Day as news director, asking me to come up to his office at 485 Madison. When I arrived, there sat Fred Friendly and his assistant, Palmer Williams. Fred was objecting, loudly and vigorously, to our plans to cover—that week—a story his people had been working on for months. I don't remember what the story was, something like school integration.

While Blair looked on unhappily, Fred told me at length what his people had been doing and how dismayed he had been when they discovered we were on the same story.

He finally said, "Well, what are you going to do this Friday?"

When I told him we would go right ahead as planned, he looked at Williams. "Palmer!" he said, and they both stood up and strode out of the office. Blair was very unhappy to have trouble with Mr. Friendly, but he didn't instruct me to switch subjects.

We had fun that June going to Mexico City to cover a state visit by Jack Kennedy. Bobby Wussler, who was in charge of covering big live events like conventions and elections and presidential tours, had booked television cameras and tape crews to go to Mexico, and he agreed to let us use the equipment to have Collingwood anchor from the scene. Bernie and I went along to produce. The first problem was that there was no coaxial cable linking Mexico and the US. The tape would have to be physically taken across the border to go on the network. The Mexican air force offered to have a military jet fly it to Brownsville, Texas, where it could be punched into the network from the control room of a CBS affiliate.

Wussler made a deal to use the editing rooms of Televisiona, the biggest broadcasting organization, and brought videotape editors from New York. The very best was a large, friendly black man named Harold Bailey who was the acknowledged whiz at assembling tape with razor blades. When we walked into the tape facility at Televisiona, Harold was a bit chagrined to find pretty young Mexican girls perched on stools in front of Ampex editing machines, obviously skilled at the technology. They giggled at him.

We had problems with Televisiona officials when they saw that our tape contained scenes not totally complimentary to Mexican society, especially some of overcrowding and poverty. But Charles, who had a house in Puerta Vallarta, knew the country well and managed to persuade them we meant well.

The taping worked, the jet plane flew to Brownsville on Friday evening, the show went on the air.

One Monday in August, we got the news flash that Marilyn Monroe had died in Los Angeles. I moved the whole operation that day to the big CBS production center in Hollywood, where we could get scenes from her movies and interview people like director George Cukor and actors who had worked with her.

When the publicity people in New York asked what the title of the show was I replied, "Who Killed Marilyn Monroe?"

When that title was announced, *Daily Variety,* published in Hollywood and fiercely protective of the film industry's reputation, printed a harsh story asking how we knew who had killed her and suggesting we were going to smear the Hollywood community. (The "who" I had in mind was, of course, her crazy mixed-up life and the strange business she was in.)

Blair Clark called in alarm and said we should use another title. So it became "Marilyn Monroe. Why?" We tried to answer the question, but it hasn't been done yet.

The series sailed along with a show about the America's Cup race off Newport, which got Sheffler hooked on boats. It was visually beautiful and contained a scene of Jack and Jackie Kennedy in full fig talking intimately at a formal dinner that is the epitome of all the images of Camelot.

Then on to elections; Pope John XXIII's Vatican Council; "Bad Day for Green Bay," on pro football; "Our War in Vietnam;" and, of all things, "The New Beat," about the Brazilian craze for the music called Bossa Nova: Charlie Kuralt was the CBS correspondent in Rio de Janeiro.

Interruption:

Apparently not having enough to do with just a weekly series, I was asked to plan a very large expansion of the daily news coverage of the CBS-owned station in New York when the city's newspapers were shut down by a strike. As noted, at that time the network ran O & O news operations. Clark and Salant, wisely, wanted CBS to fill the void left by the absence of newspapers.

I proposed: 1) The half-hour local evening news show be expanded to one hour, which could be done without too much sweat by anchor man Ron Cochran and the staff then producing it; 2) A new half-hour show at mid-day featuring Cochran and Jean Parr, a six-foot blonde who had done many shows on WCBS, and, most important, 3) A *two-hour* show to be put on at 10 A.M. every Sunday Morning which would attempt to fill the void left by the absence of the fat Sunday papers.

Salant and Clark approved all of the above *and* asked Collingwood to anchor and me to produce the Sunday shows.

Charles and I were ambitious. We decided we would include the principal elements of a Sunday newspaper, world and national news, sports, finance, theater and movies, and even editorial comment. Covering the news was no problem, but CBS didn't have any specialists in the other fields. So I proposed that we simply recruit the big byline writers of *The New York Times* and the *Herald Tribune* and put them on camera. Blair didn't think the newspapers would permit it. He was wrong.

My first call was to Red Smith at his home in Stamford to ask if he would come on the show. He said sure. I got the same answer from Judith Crist, the *Tribune* movie critic, and its financial editor, Norman Stabler.

Some of the *Times* people I contacted were reluctant to appear but when Ivan Veit, the paper's promotion director, heard what we were doing, he had word passed down by the highest *Times* brass that the paper would like its people to cooperate with any requests from CBS. Veit wanted, of course, to keep the *Times'* stars in the public eye.

Collingwood, with his long experience as a foreign and Washington correspondent and his expertise in the arts, was the perfect choice for the job. It was just the kind of show Vern Diamond loved, and he ordered up a lavish set in one of the biggest studios.

Red Smith dutifully showed up at 8 A.M. on the first Sunday, moaning about a hangover and announcing that he would never do this for anyone else. Good to have old friends.

Because of the *Times'* corporate interest, I think every writer we asked for appeared, including its editorial star, James Reston, who read his Sunday column before our cameras.

We really did manage to put on a television version of a big Sunday newspaper and it was a great success; the public liked it and so did we.

By the first week in January, the shows were running smoothly and Blair told me to turn the project over to Bill Leonard, who had been a correspondent and producer on WCBS, and carry on with only "Eyewitness."

In the spring of 1963, Collingwood and I went together to Guinea to do a show about now Ambassador William Attwood and how he and his wife Sim were doing in the never-ending contest against Communist infiltration.

Pope John XXIII died that summer and we buried him with plenty of soaring organ music from St. Peter's Basilica, courtesy of the Italian state network RAI.

On July 26, our subject was "The Test Ban Treaty," and on August 2, it was "Korea: The War That Didn't End."

If Korea didn't end, "Eyewitness" did. With that show.

What happened was that Messrs. Paley and Stanton had finally decided—after years of pleading by CBS News—to expand the evening news from 15 to 30 minutes.

I had heard rumblings about the expansion but nothing official until one day in July when Blair Clark called and said a half-hour "CBS Evening News With Walter Cronkite" would go on air the first week in September. The "Eyewitness" time period, he said, would revert to the entertainment division. It was intimated, but not said right out loud, that the give-back was part of the deal to get the extra 15 minutes for Cronkite.

Collingwood was very unhappy, understandably. He had done a fine job, got an excellent fee for doing it, the show fitted his style perfectly and had been a great showcase for him.

Curiously, Sharnik and I were not all that sorry to see the enterprise come to an end. I have been told that the managing editor's job at TIME changed hands every few years because the incumbent simply ran out of steam. I suspect it was the same for us; it had been fun but we had done it. Good-bye.

Clark's assistant news director was none other than Ernie Leiser, back from Germany. To my surprise and pleasure, Ernie had proved to be an excellent news executive. The operation had moved from the old Grand Central building to better quarters in the adjoining Graybar building, still physically connected to the terminal and the studios.

Ernie told me and the "Eyewitness" staff that they needed our help to produce pieces for the expanded show, pieces which would have the same high quality as "Eyewitness." They were concerned about not having enough newsfilm every night. They needn't have worried. After the half hour got going, it became evident tht CBS' organization produced every day far more news than could be squeezed into a half-hour. The half-empty glass filled up instantly. They simply didn't need "back of the book" material.

Don very generously billed me as co-producer but there can be only one hand on the helm. The hand was his.

Our first half-hour, at 7 P.M. September 7, 1963, featured a long interview with President Kennedy, taped on his lawn at Hyannisport. Walter flew to Hyannis to do the interview and Don went along to direct it. He fed the tape to me to edit in New York.

It got our new enterprise off to a smashing start. It even turned out to be part of history because the President said then, flat out, that the war was a struggle the Vietnamese people themselves would have to fight and win. America would help its allies, he said, but the war was essentially theirs. And the South Vietnamese were *not* winning, he added. This particular statement was repeated in retrospective programs for years to come.

It has been quoted often by Kennedy supporters as proof that he had become disenchanted with the war and probably would have cut our military operations there after the presidential elections a year hence. I doubt it. Jack and Bobby Kennedy really believed, in the words of his inaugural address, that we should go any place, at any time, bear any burden, to further the cause of freedom. No one knows what they *might* have done but the evidence is clear that they started the nation down the path to a quagmire in Vietnam.

Chapter 15

The Scary World of Instant News Specials

WHEN, FAIRLY SOON, it became evident that the evening news really didn't need our services, the old "Eyewitness" unit became a "fire department," on standby to produce "instant specials" on big breaking news stories.

Just that kind of story broke when elements of the South Vietnamese army rebelled against President Ngo Dinh Diem and his brother Ngo Dinh Nhu. An attack on the presidential palace in Saigon caused the brothers to flee via an underground tunnel. They hid in the Chinese section of Cholon until assured of safe passage. Then they surrendered—only to be murdered while in custody.

The "Midgley unit" produced a half-hour show covering that event, and not long after, I wrote the following document principally, I guess, as an *aide-mémoire*, so I would not forget the names of those who put the show on air against frightening deadlines. It explains in detail how that kind of work *was* done.

Reading it today still scares me.

169

DEATH OF A REGIME
A Biography of One CBS News Extra

This story began on Friday, November 1, 1963, when the Vietnamese army (ARVN) rebelled against the Diem regime. Ernest Leiser, CBS News manager for television, and I considered the possibility of a news extra that night. But when we saw what was going into the evening news broadcast, and lacking any fresh film from the scene, we decided to wait. Our best bet was Sunday.

Correspondent Peter Kalischer and cameraman Juergen Neumann had been working on the story for weeks and we knew they would come up with fine stuff. The trouble was we had no way to talk to them.

Early Saturday morning, Kalischer got through with a message to CBS Radio. He had "thousands of feet of film and sound tape," including the final battle at Diem's palace.

The film, he said, was aboard Pan American Flight #1. Which went from Los Angeles to New York—the long way around. We couldn't figure out how he had done it, since Flight #1 didn't stop at Saigon. He must have gotten it to Hong Kong or Bangkok.

All day Saturday, Leiser and I talked constantly with Ralph Paskman, assignment editor, Art Kane, technical manager, Casey Davidson, who ran the film department, and Bill Covell's traffic staff.

We were not sure there was *any* CBS film on the flight, but I started the production machine rolling. #1 was scheduled to land in New York at 9:10 P.M. Sunday. The best time for a news extra that night was 10:30 P.M.

That made it very tight, but barely possible. A look at the schedule showed another flight, #119, leaving Teheran about an hour after #1 was to arrive. And #119, via Rome and Paris, was due to get here at 6 P.M. Obvious solution: Get the film transferred from plane to plane, picking up three hours.

I telephoned David Parsons, public relations boss at Pan American, and asked him to 1) have his operations staff all along the route of #1 try to verify if there was any package aboard labeled CBS, and 2) if so, have the stuff transferred. He said they would do everything possible.

But I kept trying other things. I asked if a relay satellite pass was scheduled for Sunday. Maybe we could offload the film somewhere along the line, process it and bounce it into New York with the speed of light instead of the speed of jets.

But this was Saturday, and the problems of getting agreement from NASA, plus firing up ground stations in Europe and here, was almost impossible on such short notice. And there would be an additional drawback: At that time anything sent via satellite had to be shared with a pool. Our film would thereby be handed celestially to NBC and ABC. Not our idea of heaven.

While hoping to make the trans-shipment and get our precious film by 6:00, I made alternative plans. Leiser proposed sending two portable units to Idlewild Airport, to process and convert film directly to video tape machines linked to the control room at Grand Central. I felt that if the trans-shipment was made, four hours would be enough to get the film into Manhattan. Kane was inclined to agree with me. But Leiser pointed out the machines would not only be protection against late delivery, but could handle at least some of the footage without bringing it into town. (As it turned out, this decision was critical.)

Constant communication was maintained with Pan American who, sad to say, could not verify, either in Calcutta or Karachi, that they were indeed carrying a package for us on #1.

I closed out very late that night by organizing the crew: Correspondent Douglas Edwards, director Vince Walters, assistant directors Barry Burman and Joel Banow, writers Peter Herford, Ronald Bonn and John Sumner, researcher Jane Bartels, production supervisor Gerald Slater, film editors Mitchell Rudick, Len Raff, Robert Rocks and Thomas Phillips. My assistant Hinda Glasser, secretary Roby O'Connor and the control room and studio technicians were notified to be on the job Sunday.

Most important, given the tough time schedule, was the setup at Idlewild. Producers Alice Weel Bigart and William Crawford, who came up from Washington, were made responsible for that segment.

At 2:30 A.M. Sunday, the phone woke me with good news. Roger Johnson, Pan American duty officer, said CBS did indeed have a package aboard #1. It had been taken off and put aboard

#119. Both flights were running on time. There were no documents or anything else to tell us what was in the package.

I waited until 8 A.M. to notify the news desk. Leiser called a few minutes later and we agreed the project was on.

Principal elements were to be:

1. The film Kalischer had described.

2. The situation in Washington, where White House and State Department staffs were hard at work trying to figure out what would happen with Diem gone.

3. An interview with Mme Nhu, shot Saturday in Los Angeles. The fabled "dragon lady" was a widow now.

4. A pictorial history of the Diem regime.

This fourth segment had been put into work Saturday night. Producer Bernard Birnbaum and film editor Rudick were screening and editing thousands of feet of film shot by CBS in Vietnam over the years, to provide the story of Diem's rise. (Bernie had been in Saigon himself the previous year to shoot an "Eyewitness" report and had become friendly with the dead president.) In this film, they found a scene of Diem in his office with Duong Van Minh, who was now the new president.

I drove to the office to check on the critical shipment. That morning, we received Kalischer's first cable in two days, with information about the content. He had managed to catch an Air Thai plane to Bangkok to get the stuff on Pan American #1. By late morning, #119 was reported to be on time. We seemed to be in business.

Then in the middle of the afternoon, a routine check with Pan American told us that a small accident, involving the craft of another airline, had blocked the runway at Orly, Paris. Our flight was delayed "a couple of hours." So now we faced the prospect of processing and attempting to do justice by 3,300 feet of film and sound tape even faster than planned.

The mill ground along. Marvin Kalb made his State Department rounds in Washington. The pictorial history was finished, scripted and Edwards read it during a video tape transfer to permit safer handling on air. The excellent Mme. Nhu interview also was put on tape.

Then word came that #119 had at least taken off and was due at Idlewild—wheels down—at 9:10 P.M. So the job was: Get the package off the plane, over to where we were set up in the International Arrivals building, processed, viewed, edited and scripted in an hour.

Then we got a small break. A telephone operator called me to say Kalischer was right then recording in our radio newsroom and wanted to talk to me. I agreed.

Kalischer gave me detailed descriptions of what was on the film and where. Invaluable information such as, "In package number 3 is the battle scene," "In number 7 is the aftermath footage."

He had marked the most important with bands of red tape—making good use of same at last. This meant Crawford could find the best stuff fast. Then Kalischer recorded a late news voice spot for the program, describing Saigon at the moment. The audio quality was not good but it added up-to-the-minute excitement.

To cope with the possible problem of adding a voice to film we hadn't seen, I asked the master radio anchor man Bob Trout to go to Idlewild as soon as possible.

There Crawford reported everything was ready to go. All facilities were checked out.

Old 119s wheels touched down at 9:12 P.M. and were "blocked" at 9:17. The forward hatch was opened and the pouch on the runway in a minute. Covell grabbed two cans of film marked CBS and tossed them to Vito Lopresi, who jumped into the panel truck waiting beside the plane.

Crawford scanned the script sheets and determined the order of processing in one minute. Seventeen seconds in an elevator got the first film to the technicians. Back at the home ranch in Graybar, the phone rang at 9:30 and I heard Crawford's voice: "The film is on the machine."

Twenty minutes later, Bill and Alice said they had seen excellent footage. At 10:10, Leiser made final confirmation to the television network that we would go on the air. They had, of course, something on tape standing by, just in case.

So, at 10:30, "Death of a Regime" went out to a waiting audience from Studio 41, third floor, Grand Central Terminal. The opening section was voiced by Trout. The battle scene began with Kalischer's voice, then Trout picked up. The scenes of Saigon after the battle were handled the same way.

While we were on the air, about half-way through, Alice told me on the control room phone that Bill had a good eight minutes of scenes of the city in turmoil, not four as assigned on my lineup. So I eliminated the radio voice report from Kalischer and let the Saigon scenes run on.

We got on and off on time. The acid test.

All this involved what was usually promoted as "the full facilities of CBS News." Well, it involved the full facilities of CBS News all right. And it involved the full talents of scores of people, all of whom should be listed here. They gave their very best to a very tough job. Who can ask for anything more?

For those of us in the trade, this is quite a story to tell. But think of the stories Peter Kalischer and Juergen Neumann, who did *their* work on the dangerous streets of Saigon, have to tell!

To quote some forgotten reviewer, "It was indeed television news at its best."

—LESLIE MIDGLEY

All that *Sturm und Drang* would be completely avoided today by using the marvelous satellite machines. But we *did* get the big story on the air in prime time. The networks can't seem to manage that now.

We didn't know it then, but it subsequently became clear that the murders of President Diem and his brother Nhu had been committed with the approval, at least implied, of the American military commanders in Saigon and the American Embassy. Diem had appealed to the Ambassador for protection and mistakenly thought he was safe.

And we didn't know then that the murder of another President was coming. Later that same month.

Chapter 16

John Fitzgerald Kennedy
A Perfect President for TV

SOME REPORTERS who cover the White House become intimate with Presidents. Those with swollen egos claim they have advised Chief Executives on matters of high-level policy. Being a middle-level editor in New York, I didn't know Jack Kennedy; my view of him was the same as the television audience. But for a dozen years, I had a lot to do with the Kennedy saga on television.

I did meet him once, in 1960, when he was fighting hard to beat Hubert Humphrey in the Wisconsin primary. Humphrey, from next-door Minnesota, had a natural edge in the upper midwest, but the Kennedys were out to win.

I had been sent to Milwaukee to produce, with Sam Zelman, a special broadcast reporting the Wisconsin results. We spent the day before elections setting up in the CBS affiliate's studio. Late that night I got out of a taxi to find our researcher, Jane Bartels, earnestly lecturing a tall, smiling young man on the hotel steps. He was John Kennedy, amused and listening. She introduced me.

The next morning, I got a message that Robert Kennedy wanted to see me. At Kennedy headquarters, he greeted me very frostily, then

175

said that a Louis Harris analysis, broadcast on CBS a few days earlier, did not parse with the findings of his own polls. Unless CBS put a "correction" on the air disavowing the Harris conclusions, "The Senator will not appear on your show tonight no matter what happens," Bobby said. He came across like a small man trying to act tough.

I told him such a decision could not be mine. I would put it up to my boss, Sig Mickelson, who was enroute to Milwaukee. But, I told Bobby, don't hold your breath for any retractions.

I called Sig and told him about the ultimatum. He said to forget about any disavowals of Lou Harris.

Well, Jack won. And Jack came to our studio and appeared on our special. So did Hubert, one of Sig's old friends. He had been hit by a steamroller. The Kennedys went on to clinch the nomination in West Virginia the following week. Then they beat Nixon. By a perhaps tainted whisker.

Jack was a glittering natural for television, handsome, quick and clever. He obviously enjoyed bantering with, and usually besting, reporters at his press conferences in the State Department auditorium. Earlier Presidents had forbidden direct quotations without express permission. Kennedy went right on the record—on camera. Live give-and-take on television was a something he knew how to use and he enjoyed the exchange.

He had been, for three years, a consistent star on "Eyewitness": Making major speeches, visiting an aircraft carrier off California, planting a tree in Ottawa (during which he damaged his bad back), proclaiming "Ich Bin Ein Berliner" at the Wall, defeated (the Bay of Pigs), victorious (the Cuban missile crisis), watching the Americas Cup race, visiting Mexico, meeting Nikita Khrushchev.

Then.

On Friday, November 22, 1963, I was eating lunch in a booth at Tim Costello's saloon on Third Avenue, one block east of the Graybar Building. Dick Barkle, a press agent for American Airlines, came over to say his office had heard from Dallas that shots had been fired at President Kennedy while he was in a motorcade. The President had gone to Texas to give political support to Vice President Lyndon Johnson and Governor John Connally.

Wide use of videotape for news coverage began with Khruschev's visit to the U.S. in 1959. Walter Cronkite, Midgley and a tape technician watch the Soviet Premier speaking at the UN. (CBS Photography)

Mitchell Rudick, film editor, Leslie Midgley, producer, and Walter Cronkite, correspondent, discussing the merits of pictures they had squinted at on a Movieola, an early film editing device. (CBS Photography)

The newsroom in which the half-hour "CBS Evening News With Walter Cronkite" was put together each day--and which became a studio for its broadcast each night. Discussing details are Hinda Glasser, administrative assistant, Don Hewitt, executive producer, Ernest Leiser, assistant general manager for television news, Midgley and Cronkite. (CBS Photography)

President Eisenhower's visit to Rome was covered for an early "Eyewitness to History" segment in 1959. On location were Cronkite, Midgley and Don Hewitt, producer/director. (CBS Photography)

On location in Binh Dinh province, Vietnam, in 1966, to prepare "The Other War," a one-hour prime time report on the state of economic development in the war-torn country. Major Be, a dedicated Vietnamese officer, with Correspondent Charles Collingwood, Midgley and Vietnamese peasant workers.

In the working newsroom of "The CBS Evening News With Walter Cronkite" in 1968 are Executive Producer Midgley, Cronkite and Producer Sanford Socolow. They are intently watching monitors showing material being fed from distant points for use in the show. (CBS Photography)

Midgley and Hewitt absorbed in a story being fed over telephone lines and/or satellites for the "Evening News."

Title for a CBS News investigation of the Warren Report's account of the assassination of President John F. Kennedy, broadcast for an hour on four successive nights in 1967.
(© CBS Inc.)

Lee Harvey Oswald in the Dallas Police headquarters late at night after his arrest for the Officer Tippitt murder. (CBS Photography)

Cronkite on the set of the Warren Report series on the second night. He confirms that CBS News had concluded that Oswald did shoot the President.
(© CBS Inc.)

Correspondent Dan Rather sighting through the scope of a Mannlicher-Carcano rifle similar to the one owned by Lee Harvey Oswald. Dan is seated in the window from which Oswald fired, according to Warren Commission findings. (CBS Photography)

Film shot through the telescopic sight of Lee Harvey Oswald's *own rifle* during a recreation set up by the FBI.

A scene from "The Face of Red China," broadcast in 1958. The film was shot by German cameraman Rolf Gillhausen, one of the first foreigners allowed into China. The show won an Emmy. (© CBS Inc.)

Mme. Nhu, President Ngo Dinh Diem's sister-in-law, widely known as "The Dragon Lady," as she appeared in an "Eyewitness" show in December 1961. (© CBS Inc.)

"Morley Safer's Vietnam: A Personal Report" appeared as a one-hour special in April 1967. Included was this scene of an American GI setting a Vietnamese dwelling on fire with his Zippo lighter. It became a powerful icon to those opposed to the war. (© CBS Inc.)

Planning details of a 1973 one-hour special, "The Senate and the Watergate Affair," are Leslie Midgley, executive producer, and Correspondent Roger Mudd. This show won an Emmy award. (CBS Photography)

Charles Kuralt on the set of a special broadcast on the occasion of the death of John Wayne in 1979. (© CBS Inc.)

Jack Benny died during Christmas week in 1979 and a one-hour tribute to him was put together in three days. Kuralt wrote the script and was anchor man. (© CBS Inc.)

The Emmy award for "The Senate and the Watergate Affair" was happily received by Midgley and his wife, Betty Furness. (CBS Photography)

I thanked Dick and told my companions I was going to finish this lunch because if the story turned out to be true, meals would be scarce for some time.

Ernie Leiser stopped me at the newsroom door.

"We have no obit at all," he said. "It's your baby."

I caught up quickly with the bulletins. The President and Governor Connally had been shot while driving through Dealey Plaza. They had been rushed to Parkland Hospital in the President's limousine. The extent of their injuries was not yet known.

The place was in an uproar as technicians rushed to get Cronkite on the air from a desk in the newsroom. Within a half hour, he was broadcasting bulletins and talking with Rather in Dallas and correspondents in Washington.

When the bulletin came that the President was dead, Walter momentarily lost some of his famous composure. He did, in fact, choke up.

Hewitt was in charge of the live coverage from his office just off the newsroom, feeding the network a steady flow of reports from New York, Dallas and Washington. Information was scarce but Rather did a fine job with what he could get.

Late that afternoon, a man named Lee Harvey Oswald, who worked in the Texas Schoolbook Depository at one corner of Dealey Plaza, was arrested on charges of shooting a Dallas police officer. The Dallas authorities said they believed he also had shot the President and Governor Connally from a window on the sixth floor of the book building. This kind of bulletin news kept coming in bits and pieces from the guys frantically working in Dallas.

Ernie said I would take over from Don in the evening with a review of Jack Kennedy's life and career. Harry Reasoner would be the anchor. Everyone fell to, searching for film, stills, videotape, *anything* to flesh out a coherent story of the dead President's family, youth, war service, political life and thousand-day presidency.

We planned, of course, to interrupt this review with any news breaking from Dallas and Washington, where the President's body had been flown. Our "obituary" went on the air at 8:35 and continued for more than three hours.

Reasoner did a masterful job. Alice Weel Bigart whipped out some excellent script but almost everything Harry said that night he filled out from Alice's notes or simply ad-libbed. Highlights were the campaign, the Inaugural speech, the Bay of Pigs, the Cuban missile crisis, Kennedy's travels, press conferences and addresses to Congress.

Frank Stanton arrived during the afternoon and stayed. Once late that night, I wondered aloud how long we should stay on the air and heard a voice behind me say, "Les, stay on just as long as you want." The boss had spoken.

Around midnight, there was a general planning session. The news department had been told to fill *all* the time on the network, day and night, until the President had been buried, which was expected to be on Monday. There would be no commercial announcements whatsoever during the next three days. The time was all ours. (We found out later that the bosses at NBC were very unhappy to hear that Stanton had ordered such a massive pre-emption. But they had no option except to do the same thing, losing great amounts of advertising revenue.)

We split up the producer's job, with Don in charge during the daytime hours and me at night. The whole news department went into frantic overdrive.

Don filled the next day with breaking news from Texas, where Oswald was being questioned, and Washington, where the President lay in state in the White House. There were reports of reaction from around the country and the world.

On Saturday night, we were on the air from 8:30 to 11 P.M. with "A Day to Mourn," Collingwood anchoring.

I stayed in a hotel Friday and Saturday nights. On Sunday morning, I decided to drive home to Crestwood to change clothes. On the way, I stopped at a local grocery store to pick up some food.

"I hear they just shot Oswald," was the greeting from the proprietor's wife.

I got back in the car and drove to the office.

Collingwood did a fine job again on Sunday, and on Monday night we put on "The Four Dark Days—From Dallas to Arlington," for three and one-half hours.

It reviewed the tragedy, from Kennedy's laughing appearancce at a Fort Worth breakfast on Friday morning through the shootings, the death of the President, the swearing-in of Lyndon Johnson, the return of the dead President to Washington, the dramatic lying-in-state beneath the Capitol dome, and the funeral procession of mourners on foot.

And the strange and totally unexpected murder of Oswald Sunday morning in the basement of the Dallas Police headquarters by a sleazy night club operator named Jack Ruby.

I believe it was Stanton who remarked afterward, "Television news will never be the same."

TV news did come of age during those four dark days in November. The enormous technical power of television to bring vivid, shocking scenes of history into their homes brought the people of America together, sharing at the same moment a great emotional experience in a way never before possible.

But the story was by no means finished. It had not been established exactly who had killed the President. The prime suspect was himself dead and the man who killed *him* insisted there had been no conspiracy.

If there had been a conspiracy, who might have been involved? The Soviets? Castro? Criminals? Right-wing hate merchants who had warned Kennedy not to visit Texas?

Immediately after the assassination, President Johnson appointed a commission of seven prominent Americans to investigate the murder. Their principal charge was to discover if people other than Lee Harvey Oswald had been involved. The President insisted that Chief Justice Earl Warren be the commission chairman.

The Chief Justice got a staff of lawyers together and started to work. He assigned, unfortunately, J. Edgar Hoover's Federal Bureau of Investigation to do the field work. The FBI investigation was unbelievably sloppy, we found out in later years.

It took just 13 months before the Warren Commission Report was released. And it was the fountain of many more hours of television reporting and broadcasting by CBS News.

Chapter 17

Vietnam
Eleven Long Years

ONE EVENING IN February 1964, word circulated that Dick Salant was out as president of CBS News and Fred W. Friendly was in. Salant had been an excellent president and loved the job. The newsroom speculation was that Friendly, unhappy with not getting the time slots he wanted for "CBS Reports," simply wanted to be president.

I left the office and walked over to Costello's. Sitting in a booth were my good friends John Lardner and Walt Kelly. I didn't even hint about leaving CBS but John, who was very sensitive, said, "Listen, Les, don't do anything rash. Fred isn't all that bad. Stick around and see how it works out." He had discerned my mood was one of resignation. Resignation from CBS News.

After a couple of drinks, I walked back to Grand Central and caught a train for Crestwood. I was in bed and the lights were out when the phone rang. It was Fred.

"Don't resign," he said abruptly. "I want to see you in my office tomorrow morning."

So he, too, had figured out that our past differences might make it hard to work together.

The next morning, Fred said he was well aware we had had problems, but he liked my work very much and wanted me to continue as a producer for CBS.

"Look," he said. "You can do anything you want. What would you like to do?"

"I'd like to go to Vietnam," I answered.

"Go ahead," he said.

So I did, to produce what we agreed would be a one-hour documentary. I proposed that Charles Collingwood, then chief European correspondent based in London, go with us to Vietnam to work on the show. Charles had traveled and worked in Asia. And he was one of the finest writers on the CBS roster. Fred agreed.

Collingwood said he would fly there from London. I left a few days later and was joined in Los Angeles by Wade Bingham, a cameraman who had contributed great stuff to "CBS Reports." Wade was an old hand at working in Asia.

The Caravelle Hotel in Saigon was headquarters for most television and print reporters covering Vietnam. The CBS News office was in a big corner suite, complete with news tickers and a teletype machine. There was a terrace bar on the roof, where nightly gossip sessions flourished.

Peter Kalischer, the CBS correspondent in residence, had been in Asia so long he was apparently immune to the constant threat of diarrhea and ate anything he fancied, even exotic finger food from native stands along the sidewalk. We newcomers were more careful.

Pete did most of the early combat coverage for the evening news show. Bernard Kalb, based in Hong Kong, came to Saigon frequently, usually to report on political and economic affairs.

For our special, Collingwood would be the principal reporter and Kalischer and Kalb would contribute pieces.

Charles had stopped in Paris to interview Mme. Nhu, the widow of President Diem's brother.

She gave him a long, fiery harangue during which she denounced the American Ambassador, Henry Cabot Lodge, as "the executioner of Vietnam."

"You Americans!" she said scornfully, "You are set up for atomic war but you know nothing, nothing! about subversive war." She went on to observe that the mother of the current president, General Kahn, "is only—what do you say—a barmaid?" Good stuff.

When we all sat down in the Caravelle office, Kalb and Kalischer asked a familiar question.

"What do you guys want? What do you plan to do?"

"That's what *you* have to tell *us*," I answered. "You know what the story is here. We don't. What should we do?"

That answer always seemed to surprise correspondents used to receiving cables from New York instructing them to report on such and such. Which they almost always knew, or soon discovered, had appeared in *The New York Times*. It was one of the major frustrations of television reporters abroad. Their own judgments about news always seemed to rank behind those of the *Times* and the *Washington Post.*

Having by now produced several hundred television programs, I knew the way to go about it was to "make the lineup." That is, decide what the principal elements of a story were and then line them up in logical order.

Following the guidance of Kalb and Kalischer we settled on some elements:

American Green Berets "advising" South Vietnamese troops in the field. (Kalischer)

The "strategic hamlet" program with which the Kahn regime hoped to protect peasants from both physical and political pressure from the Viet Cong. (Kalb)

An interview with General Nguyen Kahn about how he expected to succeed in defeating the enemy when his predecessors had failed. (Kalischer)

An interview with Ambassador Lodge about what kind of a timetable he envisioned for victory by South Vietnam. (Collingwood)

An interview with Robert A. McNamara, the Secretary of Defense. (Collingwood)

And, of course, the jazzy Mme. Nhu stuff.

We spent two weeks working in Vietnam with this plan before I returned to New York to start editing.

Kalischer said that for his Green Beret segment we should go up to the Montagnard country, in the mountains of northwest Vietnam. So at dawn one morning, Pete and I and his cameraman, Juergen Neumann, took off from Ton San Nhut airport in an Air America plane for the trip north. Air America was a small but busy airline, operated by the CIA. A kind of shuttle service, very useful for getting around fast and free.

The Special Forces camp we visited was in a valley filled with rubber plantations. It was surrounded by mountains and looked, to me, very much like the film of Dien Bien Phu, where the French army lost *its* final battle for Vietnam. When I asked one of the Green Berets if the surrounding mountains didn't make the place vunerable to attack, he said, "Well, you do have to worry about that."

Four Americans were stationed there, working with 100 ARVN (Army of the Republic of Viet Nam) troops. When Pete interviewed the commander on camera, it was revealed that there had been five of them until the previous week, when one had been killed by a sniper.

I also went with Peter when he did a second piece on Special Forces, in the Delta area south of Saigon. One advisor, the father of four, had been wounded twice but went right on working with the peasants in their fields.

"We've got to get the support of the little fella," he said. "They can only be persuaded by seeing that you will protect them . . . it is the little fellow out here who will decide this war."

When Bernie Kalb did his report on the admittedly-failing "strategic hamlet" program, a Green Beret explained that the Viet Cong came to such a hamlet at night and ordered the head of a family to pull down the house he had built with government assistance then leave the area. At the point of a gun.

"What would you do?" he asked Bernie.

General Kahn told Peter he would succeed because he would have new programs the people would support.

Kalischer, who was vastly more experienced in Vietnam than most of the American military, pointed out to Collingwood that the US now had 15,000 advisors in the country, but only 3,000 of them were in the field. The others were all in rear echelons.

He went on to say that air power was being used indiscriminately to bomb villages only suspected of harboring Viet Cong, and when the villages went up in flames, the bombing created more anti-government fighters than it killed.

But, Peter insisted, "America is fighting a cheap war here. There have been only 750 casualties in three years." And American expenditure was *only* $1,500,000 a *day*, he added.

I got a look at what was called the Viet Cong when Peter called my room early one morning and said the ARVN had taken some prisoners in a village about halfway to the Delta. Army press agents had laid on a plane if correspondents wanted to go there. We did.

We were shown a group of 40 or 50 little brown men—and a few women—squatting on the ground with their hands tied behind them. They certainly didn't look like soldiers to me. They looked like poor farmers in rags with impassive faces, resigned to being peered at by big white men. One of the American information officers insisted that they were dangerous types who did indeed commit all kinds of outrages.

He was carrying a rifle I had never seen before. It was the first model of the M-16 a lightweight carbine that fired bursts like a machine gun. It became the standard weapon of the US forces in Vietnam, although CBS News carried several reports about jamming and other problems with the weapon.

My most vivid memory—and as the years went by it seemed more and more tragic—of my first visit to this exotic land concerns a public ceremony arranged as a farewell to Defense Secretary Robert A. McNamara, who had been in Saigon while we were there.

The PR office told us to go to a square about halfway between downtown Saigon and the airport. Cameras would be welcome.

As we watched, trucks filled with men, women and children pulled up. The people were off-loaded and marshalled behind sawhorses along a road leading to a speakers' stand at the end of the square.

When jeeps arrived bearing McNamara, General Kahn, Ambassador Lodge and General Maxwell Taylor, the President's personal military advisor, McNamara did something surprising. He told the driver to stop, jumped out of the jeep and began to walk down the line, smiling, laughing and shaking hands just like Jack Kennedy working an airport fence. I turned to Keyes Beech, correspondent for the *Chicago Daily News*.

"This guy is running for something," I said.

"Godammit, you're right," he said, taking out his notebook and pencil.

McNamara took the microphone and announced that his government had total confidence in General Kahn's ability to rally his people and win the war.

He ended by raising both hands high over his head and shouting, *"Vietnam muon nam"* (cheers). *"Vietnam muon nam"* (louder cheers). *"Vietnam muon nam"* (wild cheering from the throng).

McNamara took General Kahn's right hand and General Taylor moved forward and grasped his left. All three then raised their arms aloft in the symbol of unity which marks the end of the American political conventions. The crowd roared.

After the big shots left in their jeeps, trucks returned and the captive audience of men, women and children was taken away.

After we got back, Collingwood interviewed McNamara in his office in Washington. The Secretary assured Charles that *this* general, Kahn, was not corrupt and would use American aid wisely.

Kahn was gone in a few months.

(I always did personally hold with Senator Wayne Morse of Oregon who maintained, loudly and constantly, that we had no business in Vietnam and that our operations there were illegal. Our own laws, he pointed out, dictated that only Congress could declare war. It never had done so in the matter of Vietnam. I said then and I still say that tragic affair could not properly be called a "war.")

Our air date was April 1, just two weeks after McNamara's appearance before the captive audience in Saigon. Birnbaum and I worked day and night with our film editors to get the show ready.

When we had assembled a rough cut, I had a screening for Friendly. This was common practice for documentaries and I had no quarrel with it. Had I been president of the news department, I certainly would have wanted to know—in advance—what was going to be shown and said on the air. That was not, of course, practical in the case of the "Evening News" and we had been spared any such review during the years of weekly "Eyewitness" shows.

Fred was delighted with the show.

"Les," he said, "Would you mind calling this a 'CBS Reports'?" I was amazed. "CBS Reports" was his own thing, from the Murrow days.

"I would be honored," was my answer. So "Vietnam... The Deadly Decision" went on the air to the sonorous music of Aaron Copland's "Appalachian Spring" and with the zooming titles of "CBS Reports."

Jack Gould wrote in *The New York Times*: "This was a painstaking and detailed account of a war that appears to have no early end in sight and still lacks the full support of the Vietnamese farmers...

"CBS Reports minced no words. It asserted flatly that the war was not being won and that there was no guarantee it can be. Its conclusion was that the United States had best prepare for continuing economic burdens and casualties for years to come."

Right on, Jack.

In 1964, Saigon was nothing like it became later under the deluge of Americans. It was a beautiful city of broad avenues, laid out by French planners in the manner of the boulevards of Paris. The avenues were lined, not with the chestnut trees of Paris, but with lush oriental trees and plants. Lovely villas stood in walled gardens.

Very few Americans were visible on the streets except for journalists around the Caravelle and the Continental Palace, an old French colonial hotel which faced the Caravelle across the broad square. At the end of the square was an opera house which had been converted into the National Assembly. At least the building had been converted; the assembly was helpless against military rulers.

Southeast Asia is a beautiful part of the world, and because we were able to get a stunning look at its green mountains and lush valleys from helicopters, Vietnam seemed the loveliest place of all. The wide valleys, filled with rice fields, were crisscrossed by rivers and small streams which glittered like silver threads in the sunshine.

Towering in billows miles high above the green mountains, the clouds of Vietnam were constantly changing lovely sights. After visiting Africa and South America, in the same latitude as Vietnam, I decided there is some special quality to the cloud skies above that particular latitude.

The thatched roof villages looked like they had been built for a movie set. The small brown people working in the rice fields ran laughing after their cattle when we disturbed them and the enchanting children crowded around to stare at these big white-skinned people pointing their cameras this way and that. And the young girls in their aodais—slit skirts—seemed to float down Saigon streets or through rural villages.

At that time, the landscape seen from above was one of broad rice fields with a canopy of lush green covering hills and high mountains. But there was a hint of bad things to come.

One of my early flights north of Saigon was in a Bison two-engine aircraft, which has a big ramp at the rear of the cargo bay. The ramp can be lowered to permit trucks and jeeps to be driven aboard—or paratroops to jump out in the air. When I clambered up the ramp, almost the entire bay of this plane was filled with what looked like a huge oil tank. Canvas passenger seats lined the sides.

I sat down next to an airborne colonel and asked what the tank was for.

"Well, we aren't supposed to talk about that," he said, "but look out under the wing."

Pipes extended out from the fuselage under each wing and nozzles were set at short intervals along the pipes. Ready to spray the poison which would, in only a few years, make huge areas of this green land look like it had been struck by a plague of death.

How the colonel answered my question indicated clearly that *someone*, at least, had qualms about what this plane was doing in the skies above Vietnam. The qualms didn't prevail.

My own conclusion, as I left Ton San Nhut that very first time, was that the United States should bring an aircraft carrier up the Saigon river, load every—EVERY—American in the country aboard and sail away.

It was not hindsight.

My unit did 16 other shows in 1964, and the situation in Vietnam compelled our attention again and again.

In the fall, Collingwood wrote an excellent outline about the long history of conflicts in Vietnam and how America became involved beginning with the Eisenhower administration. It was the basis for a fine hour and Charles and Bernie went back to Saigon to work with Kalischer. The result was a powerful show in January called "Vietnam—How We Got In—Can We Get Out?"

I was too busy with other projects to go then, although I really wanted to get back to Vietnam. It was a fascinating place. But there would be, I suspected, other opportunities for oriental travel.

The "Can We Get Out?" show began with the statement: "The French fought in Vietnam for eight years, four billion dollars, 92,000 dead. The United States has been in Vietnam for 10 years, six billion dollars, 248 dead so far."

248! A decade later it was 58,000.

Collingwood began his script with the words, "The United States has been on the losing side in Vietnam from the beginning. We were on the losing side when we went in. We still are . . . We went in without any clear idea of where it was going to lead us. We went in piecemeal and a long time ago. Four Presidents have accepted and extended our commitment."

He then went into an excellent film treatment of the history of conflict in Vietnam, involving both the French and the USA. The package reprised President Kennedy's statement in 1963 that "In the final analysis, it is their war to win or lose." It continued with the Johnson Administration's strong commitment to Nguyen Kahn and his subsequent fall.

Kalischer interviewed the new ambassador, General Maxwell Taylor, South Vietnam's titular president Huong, and Buddhist leaders who openly opposed a government led by generals, sometimes to the point of setting fire to themselves in the streets.

The final segment was a discussion of the Vietnamese dilemma by Senators Mike Monroney and Wayne Morse, refereed by Eric Sevareid. Monroney insisted this country must continue aid to South Vietnam in its own national interest. Morse vehemently argued the time had come for a negotiated settlement. Anything else, he said, was extremely dangerous.

Collingwood said in his closing: "It is quite clear that we cannot continue doing what we're doing now for very much longer. We must either do more or we must do less—and we're just beginning to consider the alternatives. It's pretty late in the day . . .

"At the beginning of this program we asked, 'Can We Get Out?' I should tell you that no one knows how. But neither does anyone know how we can stay in indefinitely. We might as well realize that we've run out of good solutions for Vietnam. That's why Lyndon Johnson, the fourth President to face decisions on Vietnam, faces today the toughest ones of all."

(Johnson did. The following summer United States Marines waded ashore at Da Nang and the United States was in all the way.)

In April, the President ordered continuous bombing of North Vietnam under the authority of the infamous Tonkin Gulf Resolution and we were back with a half hour: "Air War North."

A month later, we followed up with an hour, "The Hawks and the

Doves," a heated debate between legislators about what was going on in Vietnam.

After United States forces were formally committed to Vietnam, we decided another hour special was called for. Birnbaum and Collingwood flew to Saigon, and I started after them via Anchorage and Tokyo.

I was asleep in the Okura Hotel in Tokyo when the phone rang in the middle of the night.

"Les, this is Gordon Manning" a voice said. "Your wife is dead. She drowned in Lake George today."

"No," I said.

"It's true. She's dead."

All Gordon knew was that she had been found floating face down in the lake and had been there too long to be revived. My daughters, Leslie and Andrea, and son Jeddy, were at the lake with her but not present when the accident happened. All their lives they had had standing instructions to call my office in an emergency. One of the fringe benefits of working for a news organization.

The CBS bureau got me on the first plane to San Francisco and New York. Once home, I found that my brother Grant had taken over and made preliminary arrangements. Jean had been born a Catholic, and her mother and sister would have liked a church service. The local priest was reluctant to conduct one because we had not been married in the church, but he finally presided over a brief service.

On the long flight home, I decided to sell the Lake George house and find another place for summer vacations. I didn't think the kids, all teenagers, would want to continue to live right at the place where their mother had died.

But, greatly to my surprise, the morning after the funeral service they all said, "When are we going back up to the lake?" I was astonished and asked if that really was what they wanted to do. They said yes and we went.

I did not get to Vietnam that year.

The show I was going to Saigon to work on appeared in September. It was "Vietnam . . . A Day of War." As the title suggests, it was all shot on the same day, August 25, 1965. There were already 100,000 US troops all over South Vietnam.

We had 15 cameramen and soundmen assigned that day. Collingwood spent the day with General William C. Westmoreland. Peter Kalischer and Morley Safer went out with patrols in the jungle and Delta. Murray Fromson was aboard the aircraft carrier Oriskany off the coast and Bernie Kalb was at the big air base at Khe San. It was indeed a look at "a day of war."

We ended that year with two shows. The first, on Christmas day, was two hours of news highlights of the year. They were indeed highlights: The Americanization of the war in Vietnam, Winston Churchill's funeral, the visit of the Pope to New York, police brutality in Selma, Alabama, and, as they say, much, much more.

And three days later, Kuralt/Birnbaum came up with one of their great half hours, "Christmas in Vietnam." It concentrated on one patrol in the jungle during which a sergeant was painfully wounded and included scenes of his wife and five children enduring the holiday in California without him.

It was a cruel and true look at the Vietnam folly and a warning of things to come. But nobody seemed to be paying attention to "the most powerful news media of all—television."

That November, Betsy Cronkite called to invite me to a birthday party for Walter at their brownstone in 84th Street. She sat me next to a very well-known lady named Betty Furness, whom I had seen occasionally at Television Academy events when she was president of the New York chapter. She was pretty and charming and I took her home to her apartment in 86th Street. I asked around and discovered she had been a widow for years. We had a couple of dates, and in January, she invited me to a party in her apartment to celebrate her 50th birthday. We were, it appeared, going to be the same age for two weeks every year.

The next month, she invited me to another party at her place, but I called and told her housekeeper, Alice Miller, I couldn't come because I was going to Vietnam. "That's a good reason," she said.

In February 1966, Collingwood and I proposed that we return to Vietnam and look not at the "war" in the jungle and the delta and the bombing from carriers at sea, but at what—if anything—was being done to help the people of Vietnam to have more food and safer places to live.

The day before I planned to leave, I called on Fred in his office and found him distraught. The Senate was holding hearings on Vietnam and NBC was carrying them live. CBS was showing reruns of "I Love Lucy."

Fred said the problem was that he had been told he no longer could deal directly with William S. Paley and Frank Stanton in scheduling matters. He was, instead, to confer with Jack Schneider, the executive vice president of CBS Inc. Jack had made the decision to run "Lucy" instead of the hearings and Fred had no avenue of appeal.

"I've got to resign, haven't I?" he asked. "I can't do this job without access to the top. Schneider's just out to make a buck and a reputation as a money-maker."

I gave him a pep talk about the great job he had done for two years, saying Paley and Stanton always had been staunch supporters of news and would see the light. (I was not dissembling; despite our past differences, Fred had been extremely supportive of the work of the Special Projects Unit.)

But he was desolate and suggested that I cancel or at least postpone my trip to see how this crisis was resolved. I told him all my travel plans were made and I really should go. He reluctantly agreed, saying he would much prefer to have me stick around.

When I got to Saigon, there was a notice tacked to the office bulletin board announcing that Richard S. Salant had replaced Fred W. Friendly as president of CBS News.

Fred always has maintained that he resigned over a matter of principle, in protest against the network's decision to program entertainment when it should have been serving the nation by carrying the Senate hearings. But in reality, he resigned because he could not bring himself to report to Schneider.

And Fred may have a point. Salant told me years later he had returned only as "acting president" pending an agreement that he could consult directly with Frank Stanton on matter of high policy. Within a few months, he got a favorable decision and reverted to a full presidency.

Getting organized for the new show, we once again asked CBS people on the scene what the story was. They were very much aware that no matter what came over the wires from New York about broad coverage of the whole picture of Vietnam, including politics and economics, what really got on the "Evening News" was "bang, bang"—action from the battle fronts. So they thought the most acceptable thing would be another report on whether the military effort was succeeding or failing.

But Charles and I were determined to explore a different aspect of Vietnam. Bob Allison, then bureau chief in Saigon, and Kalischer told us the Americans were now pushing yet another aid program for the 80 percent of the Vietnamese who lived in the countryside. These peasants knew little or nothing about the government in Saigon and only wanted peace so they could raise rice and feed their families. This year's economic aid program featured what were called "Rural Construction Teams," government troops, trained by the CIA, who would be prepared to fight if necessary but whose stated mission was to work in the fields alongside the peasants.

It seemed, a year after the first US Marines had waded ashore at Da Nang, that General Westmoreland and his men finally realized they were not going to defeat the elusive Viet Cong guerrillas in the field and had better look for ways to strengthen the Saigon government's popular support.

The CIA was running a very large training school for rural defense "teams." There were 5,000 men in each class and each class lasted 13 weeks. Twenty thousand men a year went through the operation; Collingwood said it was the biggest operation the CIA ever handled. "Bigger than the training for the Bay of Pigs and, one hopes, more successful."

They were taught how to use weapons, how to organize demonstrations, how to conduct village elections. The Vietnamese in charge of the operation seemed to us wholly dedicated, convinced that they were helping to create a new society in their native land.

Henry Cabot Lodge, the American Ambassador, told Charles in an interview for our show: "We can beat up North Vietnamese regiments for the next 20 years and it will not end the war unless we and the Vietnamese are able to build simple but solid political institutions under which a proper police force can function and a climate is created in which economic and social revolution freedom are possible."

(I had called on Lodge before Collingwood got to Saigon to set up the interview. My own opinion after we talked about Vietnam was that most of what he said about it was nonsense.)

Knowledgeable sources in the AID organization and the CIA advised us that a good place to show this program in action would be Binh Dinh province, in central Vietnam on the coast around the city of Qui Nhon.

When we met one morning at Ton San Nhut airport to catch a ride north on Air America, I found our cameraman, Jimmy Wilson, and soundman, Bob Funk, both wearing .45 automatics and combat scabbard knives. When I suggested, somewhat naively, I guess, that correspondents were supposed to go unarmed, they indicated very clearly that there was no way they were going into Binh Dinh without guns.

Accompanying us were three of the most dedicated people I met in Vietnam, a Major Be who was in charge of the program, and Everett Baumgardner and Frank Scotten, Americans with the Agency for International Development (AID).

They took us to hamlet called Tinh Giang, one of 972 in South Vietnam designated as targets for what was variously known as "pacification," "rural construction" or "revolutionary development."

We filmed the building of a new bridge which would permit better access to the village and a dam which would provide irrigation water for rice. Also a school built by the reconstruction team.

Major Be and Scotten eloquently described on camera the situation in the village and expressed their high hopes that the project would succeed.

But during one of the first days we were filming, white clouds from phosphorous bombs appeared on the lovely mountains above the valley and Frank told us a division of Korean troops—with a reputation as the toughest and most brutal military organization on "our" side—was stationed nearby. To keep the Viet Cong out.

In conclusion, Collingwood wrote and filmed one of his eloquent assessments. This program, he said, looked a lot like the "fortified villages" and "new life hamlets" of the late President Diem's regime. But it's worth trying, he said. "It can succeed and should succeed. If it fails, it would be more than the failure of just another program of rural construction, because we're beginning to run out of time. If this fails, there may not be time enough or appetite enough to try again. It is still true that neither military victory nor a negotiated peace can solve the problems of Vietnam that so many Americans have come over here to solve unless there is also a national rebirth."

Well, the "war" went on for another eight years. And when I was in Vietnam for the last time, I asked Ev Baumgardner what had happened to our village of Tinh Giang in the province of Binh Dinh.

Ev was married to a Vietnamese and had spent many years trying valiantly to make the country work.

"Back in Viet Cong hands," he said sorrowfully.

So much for national rebirth.

Over the years, correspondents stationed there had chummy relations with Vietnamese who worked for them, chauffeurs, porters and hotel servants. And by the late Sixties, some of the finest camera work done for CBS was by Vietnamese. But the reporters didn't really know and understand the Vietnamese people. And most of the military had no use for them at all, commonly referring to them as "slopes" and "geeks."

I always had an uneasy feeling when we interviewed a politician who spoke English that he might not truly represent what his people felt and thought privately about the Americans. We accepted, as a matter of course, that they hated the French, their former colonial masters, but Americans always think their motives are so pure everyone should welcome them with open arms.

One of the most candid opinions I heard about Americans came from the dashing air marshal, Nguyen Cao Ky, later vice president, then briefly president of South Vietnam.

"Look," he said, "you Americans are not over here to help the Vietnamese people. You are over here for what you conceive to be your own interests. We are not fools."

That from a highly educated and capable man who watched the USA pour millions of dollars into his small country every day. And provided the jet fighters he flew with such gusto. The peasants just wanted to be left alone in peace.

Eric Sevareid spent several weeks in Vietnam in the spring of 1966 and in June we put together a half-hour entitled "Vietnam: Eric Sevareid's Personal Report." It was unusual because instead of combat film, a lot of it was Eric delivering, in his sometimes halting but literate and thoughtful manner, his own opinions and conclusions. They were dark.

Lyndon Johnson decided to go to Asia himself to see how things were going. The announced plans were for him to go to New Zealand, Australia, the Philippines, Thailand, and Malaysia, but we got a leak from the White House there might be a quick detour to Vietnam.

Bobby Wussler's troops, old hands at presidential journeys, would go along on the trip. I was asked to draw up a schedule of special broadcasts and proposed eight half-hours. To save time trans-shipping film in California, we moved the whole operation to LA to work out of the CBS Television City at Fairfax and Beverly.

We couldn't fit into the cramped CBS News office there, but when I told the production people what we were up to, they said to take over one of the big studios. They would build us a newsroom on the stage. What they have in Hollywood is stagehands. They built, overnight, a set which worked fine. Our film editors were off to one side, writers were on the stage near Collingwood's anchor desk, the rest of us had desks and phones and monitors, all the paraphrenalia of television production. In some ways, it was better than our office in New York.

The shows were timely and informative, Charles did his usual suave and professional job and the reporters on the junket, Dan Rather, Eric Sevareid and Marvin Kalb, were first rate. And Johnson cooperated by indeed going to Vietnam, to the heavily-protected naval base at Cam Rahn Bay, where he exorted a captive audience of GIs to "bring me home the coonskin."

Because of the time difference between the coasts, several of our shows were done on weekends from 4 to 4:30 P.M. in LA, to be on in New York from 7 to 7:30. We went to work at dawn but had time to relax poolside in the afternoon. One of the shows was expanded to an hour and went out at 7 P.M. LA time for a 10:00 airing in the east.

After we had done three or four shows, the Television City manager said he needed our set for another production—the next day. I was dismayed but he said it was no problem. When we came in the next morning everything was in place, in mirror image, next door.

I had discovered years before, during the days and nights with Howard Hughes, the pleasures of the beautiful Bel Air Hotel. And especially Room 100, a very large, comfortable room looking out through a garden to the swimming pool. I managed to book it for this jaunt.

So I suggested to Miss Furness that she come along to Bel Air for a couple of weeks. She said sure. Starting at age 16, when she began acting in the movies, she had spent years in Hollywood and had many good friends there, such as Charlie and Anne Lederer. I had been camping out occasionally in her apartment in 86th Street and figured I would return the favor. Still too old-fashioned to simply register her in Room 100, I booked her another one nearby. It was a waste of money; that room was used as a closet for her clothes.

She was a joy to have along and was extremely interested in watching us put on a show every other day. She was then in an interim period in her career, trying to get into television news and being turned down because the bosses said she was too strongly identified with the advertising image she had developed for a sponsor, Westinghouse. It took her another seven years and some surprising twists of fortune before she landed solidly in TV news.

We kept marching along the Vietnam trail the next year, beginning with "Air War in the North," produced by Phil Scheffler, with Bill Stout as the principal correspondent.

In April came "Morley Safer's Vietnam ... A Personal Report." I was on the credit list for this show as executive producer but actually had very little to do with it, being totally occupied with a four-hour series on the Warren Report. Morley wrote and produced it himself. But I looked at the final version in the screening room with pride and pleasure, because it told the truth about Vietnam.

It was titled a personal report and was just that. Morley had been in Vietnam on and off for several years and was one of the finest reporters ever to work there. He went into the jungle with the "grunts" and shared their fear, boredom and revulsion about what they were doing. But he was also a sophisticated observer of the political and social scene who viewed the corrupt generals and their wives with great distaste.

As part of his regular work, Morley had previously reported and his cameraman had filmed a scene which lingered in the consciousness of the American public and quite probably had something to do with the belated public realization that the whole thing was a mistake. US troops had moved into a village which was supposed to be harboring some Viet Cong. When they found only women, children and old men in reed huts, they ordered everybody out. One of the soldiers snapped open his Zippo cigarette lighter and set fire to a thatched roof. Soon the whole village was burning while the peasants ran around crying and trying to put out the fires.

Friendly has said for years he believes that scene was one of the most memorable of the whole Vietnam adventure and may have started a wave of public disillusionment with it.

In addition to his willingness to do hard and dangerous work, Safer had another great advantage over almost all his colleagues. He had been a producer in Canada so he knew how pictures and words went together properly. Too many "correspondents," sad to say, have only a vague idea of how television really works. Their overriding desire is to "get on camera" to become famous and therefore rich.

Most of the film for Morley's report had been shot by Ha Thuc Can, a Vietnamese who weighed about 90 pounds. He was brave and skillful in combat and worth his weight in lovely footage. And—very important—he spoke French and Vietnamese.

Safer had been given a special dispensation: During this hour, he could express his own opinions instead of delivering an "objective" report. The hour was bitter and caustic.

"The smell of green plastic and death is all part of Vietnam," Morley mused, "all mixed up with beer and sweat and cheap perfume."

One telling scene was the annual meeting of the Saigon horticultural society. The script: "Vietnam is like a lunatic asylum. The social condition is acute schizophrenia...it's like an old colonial garden party. Heavy French women, hated colonialists in their 1938 print dresses. Twittering Vietnamese flowers; the high-born ladies of Vietnam would find it declassé to roll bandages...Generals' wives are in the property business. Their language is Vietnamese, their taste French, their hobby horticulture, their bank accounts Swiss."

Over film of a smiling, exquisite Mme. Ky, the first lady of the nation, Safer said, "Her main resource is her beauty. Eyes freshly rounded, bridge of nose slightly raised. Clever, those Japanese surgeons."

Not your usual voice-over script.

His conclusion: The politicians "found a nice, safe place for a nice small war. Both sides evoke holy phrases about 'this sacred ground,' big shot politician rhetoric. On both sides."

Great stuff.

But nothing happened. General Westmoreland told President Johnson he needed more soldiers. Johnson refused to call up the reserves—that would be too much like a real war—so he gave the general youngsters who didn't have the money to go to college and be exempted from the draft.

Chapter 18

The Warren
Report
Who Killed Kennedy?

WHILE BUSY IN 1964 with Vietnam reporting, those of us who had been deeply involved in the Kennedy assassination story kept an eye on the Warren Commission working in Washington. Johnson was very anxious to get a report out quickly. "Assassinations buffs" started making speeches and writing aritcles maintaining there had indeed been a conspiracy and Johnson himself may have been a part of it. Not a pleasant position for anyone taking over for a glamourous, murdered President.

I made several trips to Washington and met some members of the Commission staff, Norman Redlich, later Corporation Counsel for the city of New York, Joseph Ball, the attorney in charge, and Wesley Liebeler, who was assigned to write most of what would be the official account of the crime. They said they needed more time but that the heat was on to get out a report by the end of the summer.

We knew from Eddie Barker, the news director of the CBS affiliate in Dallas, that Commission staff members had been in Texas interviewing witnesses to the crime or persons who might have information pertinent to it. Some witnesses had been brought to Washington for further questioning. The committee staffers wouldn't tell us what the witnesses had said, but they did give us their names.

I suggested to Friendly that we begin compiling our own "report," interviewing the principal witnesses on film, getting our own versions of the stories they were telling the Warren Commission. Then, I said, we would be ready with the whole story—in television terms—when the commission report was made public. Fred approved the enterprise.

Bernie Birnbaum, associate producer Jane Bartels and the Walter Dombrow film crew lived in Dallas for months that summer getting— with Barker's invaluable help—first person assassination stories on film.

We knew the President's whereabouts on that fateful day and also where Lee Harvey Oswald had come and gone. Dombrow set out to retrace their movements with his camera in "subjective" style. The camera was driven along the motorcade route and past the Book Depository Building so we could show how the surroundings might have looked to the President.

Walter then retraced Oswald's movements leaving his boarding house in the morning carrying "curtain rods" wrapped in paper, riding to work with Wesley Frazier, working on the sixth floor of the book depository, running down the steps after the shooting, taking a bus and a taxi back to his rooming house in Oak Cliff to get a revolver, being intercepted by and shooting Officer J.D. Tippit. And finally being captured in the Texas Theater, a movie house, by Officer Nick McDonald. What Dombrow got was background footage for what could have been made into a movie. In a sense it was.

Eddie Barker interviewed more than two dozen witnesses. Their stories were, as they say, fascinating.

Roy Truly, manager of the book depository, told how he came to hire Oswald and how he identified him as an employee to police officer M.L. Baker moments after the shooting. After which Oswald hurried out of the building.

Garland Slack and Malcolm Price said they had seen Oswald practicing at a rifle range. Slack said Oswald fired fast.

Mrs. Ruth Paine, who spoke Russian, told how she befriended the Oswalds, especially Marina, who could barely speak English.

Earlene Roberts, Oswald's landlady, said he rushed into and out of the house after news of the shooting was broadcast.

Governor John Connally, who was riding beside the President, told us—and has always since maintained—that he heard the first shot that hit the President and therefore never could believe that the same bullet hit him.

Marina Oswald said she feared "Lee did it."

His mother, Marguerite, told us "the government" was responsible.

Bonnie Rae Williams, Hank Norman and James Jarman told the Warren staff—and us—they had been watching the motorcade from a fifth floor window of the book depository and heard shots and shell casings falling to the floor above them.

Motorcyle patrolman J. W. Foster, who had been in the motorcade, said he thought the shots came from behind.

Mary Moorman took the President's picture just as he fell.

Bus driver Cecil McWatters described how Oswald boarded his bus, then left when it was stopped in traffic.

William Whaley told how he drove Oswald to the Oak Cliff rooming house in his taxi.

Mrs. Helen Markham said she saw Oswald shoot Officer Tippit.

Ted Callaway described how Oswald walked away holding a pistol after the Tippit shooting.

Johnny Brewer, a shoe store clerk, said he watched Oswald go into the Texas Theater and called police.

Officer Nick McDonald described how he arrested Oswald in the theater.

Dallas police chief Jesse Curry recalled how Oswald behaved in custody.

Lacking subpoena powers, we could not talk to Jack Ruby in jail or Jacqueline Kennedy. But almost everyone who figured in the later outpouring of books and articles about the Kennedy assassination was on our film.

It was a gold mine.

And we got a break. As part of its investigation, the FBI drove a car through Dealey Plaza at the same speed as the Presidential motorcade had been proceeding. Apparently not possessing a film camera, they hired an artist and cameraman from Eddie's station, KRLD-TV, to record the re-enactment from the sixth floor window. They even had him film *through the sight of Oswald's own rifle scope.* The station somehow found an extra copy of that film for us. More gold.

We heard in August that the Commission would issue a report at the end of September despite the staff's pleas for more time.

I proposed we put on a two-hour show, the first 90 minutes to be our own version of what had happened in Dallas on November 22 and the last half-hour devoted to comparing the Commission's official account with our own.

Finally word came that the report would be made public at 6:30 P.M., Sunday, September 27. The timing was perfect because the network would give us two hours on the air then.

We could get copies of the report's summary volume a few days before on a "hold for release" basis, which would give us time to compare the stories of the witnesses in our version with those in the report. (We had been tipped off that the Commission did not accept as valid the recollections of some witnesses.)

During the winter of 1964, CBS News had moved from the Graybar Building at Grand Central to a sprawling production center at 57th Street and 11th Avenue in what had been a milk distribution warehouse.

I booked the biggest studio in the center and Vern Diamond ordered two podiums placed on either side of a giant screen into which he could start film rolling before taking it "full screen." The podiums were for Walter Cronkite and Dan Rather, who would alternate in anchor roles.

Just as we were about to go on the air live, Vern called out on the studio speaker to warn Cronkite and Rather that the big teleprompters in the studio were not functioning.

Moaning, Walter reached in his pocket and put on horn-rimmed glasses. Without the prompters, which were faced with magnifying lenses, he could not read the script. Luckily the gadgets started to work in a few minutes and he took off the glasses.

The show worked beautifully.

The script explained that the Warren Report would be made public in 90 minutes, but before then we would reveal what the Commission had been told by its principal sources. Our FBI film from the window set the location dramatically and we were off into the first-person accounts.

When we got to the point where Garland Slack and Malcolm Price recounted seeing Oswald at a rifle range, the control room phone rang. Friendly wanted to know why their stories had been included, since the advance copy of the report had alerted us that the Commission decided they were mistaken.

I told Fred that when we got to the final half-hour, we would recap Slack and Price and report the Commission's decision. It only lent credence to what we were doing, I insisted. Friendly was unhappy but we were on the air live and nothing could be done.

(A few days later, Fred showed me a letter from Katharine Graham, the publisher of the *Washington Post* and owner of the CBS affiliate station in Washington. Mrs. Graham said she loved the show and especially that part where the stories of two men at a rifle range were rejected by the commission. "I guess I was wrong," Fred said.)

Our months of work in Dallas paid off handsomely. NBC and ABC put on shows at the 6:30 release time, but by then, we had told the whole story—in dramatic detail. We got only one squawk. Washington bureau chief Bill Small called to say some Commission staffers were miffed because we had shown a shelf of books, the official publication of the whole report, at 5 P.M. That, they said, was a violation of the release agreement. Tough.

Publicity-wise, it was a triumph.

Jack Gould in *The New York Times*: "In many ways the program was a remarkable documentary."

The *Daily News*' Matt Messina: "A remarkable job of TV reporting...One quibble, why did CBS-TV devote time to interviews with witnesses who claimed Lee Harvey Oswald practiced at a rifle range when the Warren Report, as admitted by Cronkite, discounted the testimony?" (He must have talked to Fred.)

Journal American: "Brilliant TV journalism."

John Horn, *Herald Tribune*: "Producer Leslie Midgley laid out his material in an absorbing, swelling crescendo." (That's the stuff, John!)

This was the first of what turned out to be a long series of CBS News examinations of the Kennedy/Warren story.

We returned to it in 1967 with a major investigation broadcast over four consecutive hours. In 1973, we put together a one-hour commemorative show. And in 1975, we were back with a series on "American Assassins," which included two more hours about Kennedy/Oswald.

The Kennedy assassination story posed problems from the beginning and still does. I worked on it many times over the years—the CBS effort in this field was by far the most thorough of any news organization—and still find it hard to accept as fact that Lee Harvey Oswald did this terrible thing all alone. From the start, we had to be very careful. In 1964, the night of the release of the Warren Report, Walter's closing was:

"There will forever be questions. Even a Commission of seven distinguished Americans does not have the power under our legal system to find Oswald guilty."

"That would have been the job of 12 ordinary men" And since he was killed before a trial, Cronkite concluded: "We are the jury. All of us, here in America and in the world."

Good stuff. Written by Steve White, working with us as a writer/producer.

Two years later, we began to talk about going back to the Kennedy assassination story. Not because any new evidence had surfaced but because, instead of fading away, the murder had become the focus of an increasing number of books, magazine articles and public debates, especially on college campuses. A Gallup Poll showed that six out of 10 Americans did not believe the Warren Report's finding that Oswald had acted alone. Most believed there had been some kind of conspiracy.

Mark Lane had written *Rush to Judgment*, which became a best seller. His contention was that the Warren Commission had not been trying to find out the truth behind the assassination but in reality was appointed to conceal it. He was certain others besides Oswald had fired shots.

Lane was not alone. Harold Weisberg had written *Whitewash*, which echoed Lane's theories. Edward Jay Epstein's *Inquest* was less hysterical in tone and seemed to have some plausible points. Other "assassination buffs" were Sam Anson, Leo Sauvage, Joachim Joesten and William Turner. Sylvia Meagher was a diligent researcher who spent years cross-indexing the entire Warren Report of 26 volumes.

These books and magazine articles and interviews by the "buffs" fed a growing skepticism about the trustworthiness of the government itself, a skepticism steadily increasing as the Vietnam war heated up in the mid-Sixties. Many Americans did not trust their leaders.

Dick Salant, by now back as president of CBS News, doubted that an organization lacking legal powers and resources for full-scale investigation of such a crime should undertake one. (He was, after all, a lawyer.) But, Dick said, we should go ahead with preliminary research.

Gordon Manning—over from *Collier's* and *Newsweek*—was now director of news and he was gung-ho for the project. He suggested we organize a debate during which members of the Warren Commission or members of its staff would argue the case with some of their critics. I maintained that was not enough. We should mount a major investigation to find out if the Commission had indeed failed to discover and report the truth.

Associate producers Jane Bartels, Walter Lister and Robert Richter began preliminary research. Jane had spent months in Dallas in 1964, so she was particularly qualified for this project.

As we got into the subject, it became more and more apparent there were a lot of loose ends the Warren Commission had not tied up.

At the end of November, I sent Salant a six-page memo.

"CBS should conduct its own investigation," I wrote, "not to do a duplicate police job on the murder but to examine areas of the Report which have been questioned, not only by kooks and opportunists, but by responsible people, some of whom were involved personally."

I proposed that we address ourselves to "the great questions" which had been raised about the Report, concentrating on the big one: Was Oswald the sole assassin? If he were not, the whole Report was blown.

"Involved in this is a key point," I wrote.

"Were Governor Connally and President Kennedy hit by the same bullet? If they were not, the shots could not have been fired by Oswald alone. Another rifleman must have been firing—in a conspiracy."

"Areas of doubt" I listed as:

1. How good had been the interpretation of film evidence about the bullets known to have been fired?

2. Why had there been confusion about the initial findings of doctors at Parkland Hospital and those at Bethesda Naval Hospital, where the autopsy was performed Saturday night?

3. Did Oswald have any connection with the CIA? The FBI?

4. Was Oswald correctly identified as Officer Tippit's murderer?

5. If there any reason to believe that Oswald and Ruby knew each other? Did they know Officer Tippit?

6. How exactly did Ruby get into the Dallas police station to shoot Oswald?

My original proposal was that we address these questions in the first hour of a series of three prime time broadcasts.

The second hour would take up stories of the "discounted witnesses," people whose eyewitness accounts of the murder seemed to have been overlooked or under-investigated by the FBI. (By now, it had become evident that the Warren Commission had made a serious mistake in permitting the FBI to conduct its investigation.)

The third hour I proposed to devote to a discussion by qualified experts which would, hopefully, culminate in some kind of acceptable verdict about the Warren Report.

(That was the original plan, which was greatly altered and expanded as our research indicated some of the questions were not really relevant and we found more profitable avenues to explore.)

The next day, Salant wrote a memo to Jack Schneider, who had succeeded Jim Aubrey as boss of the network, describing what we were planning and asking that we be given three hours on consecutive nights at the end of March 1967. (It turned out to be four hours in June.)

As the investigation proceeded during the fall, it became apparent that we could get some new and very likely exciting insights by actually conducting our own tests, even if they had to be somewhat crude by scientific standards.

One of the tests should be to determine how fast Oswald's rifle could be fired. The Commission's conclusions about the timing of the shots came from a "clock," a .16mm film of the assassination shot by Abraham Zapruder. This film showed the President and the Governor reacting to the shots and was the only actual record of the assassination.

The film had been purchased from Mr. Zapruder by Time, Inc., and in November, LIFE magazine published a series of frames from it, showing in shocking detail the bloody results of the rifle fire. The magazine also published an interview with Governor Connally in which he said again he never would accept the Warren Commission's conclusion that he and the President had been struck by the same bullet.

LIFE, whose editors were not kooks, called for a reopening of the investigation.

The pictures caught the attention of Professor Luis Alvarez of the University of California, one of the nation's foremost physicists and a man of great curiosity and inventive turn of mind. It occurred to Alvarez that photo analysis might reveal evidence of shock waves reacting on the Zapruder camera.

He suspected that when shots were fired, Mr. Zapruder's hands involuntarily shook a tiny bit as a result of the noise. Perhaps a series of these movements could be timed to coincide with the theoretical sequence of Oswald's shots. If so, another "clock" could be established. (The basic clock was, of course, the camera, which was presumed to be running at a constant speed.)

Dr. Alvarez wrote to Salant, and Manning and I went to Berkeley to talk to him. His theory was intriguing, although Alvarez decided later that shock waves could not be traced from the Zapruder film. But the very suggestion that useful *physical* tests might be conducted encouraged us to try some.

Alvarez sent us to Charles Wyckoff, a Boston photo consultant. He was extremely interested in the matter, and Gordon and I met him at the National Archives, where some photos and slides were available for examination. We retained Wyckoff to work for CBS.

Since the very best piece of physical evidence was the Zapruder film, CBS requested permission from Time, Inc. to conduct a new study of it. The general manager flatly refused, writing us that the film was "an invaluable asset of Time, Inc."

But the notion of running some tests with guns and cameras and film was increasingly interesting. We possessed neither the legal powers of the Commission or the laboratory facilities of the FBI. But we already knew that those facilities had been used very badly.

For example, the FBI had conducted tests with Oswald's own rifle by having agents fire it at a stationary target closer than the distance between Oswald's window and the President's car. This test was crucial. It was supposed to answer the basic question of whether Oswald *could or could not* have fired three shots in the 5.6 seconds the Zapruder film indicated he did. Firing at a closer range—giving the marksman a better chance to hit the target—and at a stationary object, when the President had in fact been a moving target, was inexcusable.

What other sloppy and questionable testing had been done, we asked each other. Even *we* could do better. So we set out to do it.

Although Dick Salant habitually let his staff alone to do their work, this Warren Report inquiry was extremely interesting to him, and he became more involved in it than in any other production. And his observations were both perceptive and helpful. He said much later that he owed me an apology for constantly writing memos raising detailed questions about our work and our script. He owed me no such thing. His interest in and concern for the quality and accuracy of what we did was invaluable to the final draft and conclusions. We owe *him* a debt of thanks.

For example, early on, he perceived that perhaps the most thorny question concerned what became known as "the single bullet theory." Especially the famous—or infamous—"although" sentence in the Warren Report which reads: "Although it is not necessary to any essential findings of the Commission to determine just which shot hit Governor Connally, there is very persuasive evidence from the experts to indicate the same bullet which pierced the President's throat also caused Governor Connally's wounds."

Dick sent me a memo seven months before the shows were broadcast saying, "I find this ambiguous," adding, "It seems to me that the meaning of the 'although' sentence is absolutely critical and I, for one, am not at all sure what it intends to say. How do you interpret it?"

I replied in part:

"As I understand this matter, the Commission decided there could not have been four shots if Oswald were the sole rifleman. This was determined after experts tested the speed at which the Carcano could be fired. (This was before I realized the calibre of those "experts.")

"Since it was determined that one bullet went wild and struck the curb, only two shots remain. Since we know one struck the President in the head, only one *must* have hit both Kennedy and Connally...

"My interpretation is that the 'although' sentence was put in the Report anticipating Governor Connally's dissent, since he maintained without exception that he was hit by a bullet fired *after* the one which struck Kennedy. If he is correct, there were four bullets and Oswald couldn't have done it alone."

(Months later, our conclusion in the broadcasts was, "Despite its own words, the single bullet theory is essential to the Commission's findings.")

We didn't have subpoena or other governmental powers and were not a scientific organization. We couldn't do *everything*. But.

We could go back to Dallas and re-interview all the witnesses and cops involved.

The Archives wouldn't loan us Oswald's gun, but we could buy Mannlicher-Carcano rifles of the same design and find out just how fast they could be fired.

We couldn't get the Zapruder film from Time, Inc., but some rough bootleg copies of it were around Dallas. Wyckoff could study them.

Maybe he also could test Zapruder's Bell & Howell camera to see just how fast it ran.

The doctors who treated the President at Parkland Hospital and those who conducted the autopsy in Washington might be able to confirm whether all the wounds were made by shots from behind. (One of the buffs' principal contentions was that some shots had been fired at the President from in front.)

In addition to the buffs, there were serious critics of the Warren Report, notably Dr. Cyril Wecht, a well-known forensic pathologist and coroner of Allegheny County, Pennsylvania. He thought shots had come from in front of the car. He was eager to be interviewed.

One of the most troubling questions was the condition of the bullet the Commission decided struck both Kennedy and Connally. According to the Report, this single bullet, designated Exhibit 399, passed through Kennedy's neck and Connally's chest, broke a bone in the

Governor's wrist and struck him in the leg. It was later found by chance on the floor of the presidential limousine outside Parkland Hospital. It was almost intact. How could that be?

Maybe firing tests could determine how much bullets were damaged when they struck targets similar to human bodies.

Photographs and X-rays taken of Kennedy's body during the autopsy might have cleared up a lot of questions. They had been given to Bobby Kennedy. He officially turned them over to the National Archives in 1966, with the provision that they not be made public for five years.

There was work to be done.

What we planned that fall of 1966 was an investigation unprecedented in the history of CBS News.

A fine staff was available. Birnbaum and Bartels were by now veterans at working the story in Dallas. Eddie Barker enthusiastically agreed to join the team. He was something of a celebrity in Dallas and enormously helpful arranging and conducting interviews.

I borrowed other producers.

Walter Lister was assigned the job of getting the Mannlicher-Carcanos tested and checking condition of bullets fired from them.

Robert Richter would sort out the various "critics" of the Report and set up interviews with some.

Sam Roberts would be a utility field producer.

Ronn Bonn and Clinton McCarty were primarily writers.

And, once more, Steve White had signed on as a producer/writer to give the script some class.

Early on, I conceived the shows as posing a series of questions and answers. That also seemed to be a good plan for conducting the investigation. So we started seeking answers to *the* questions.

Routine requests went to the FBI and the CIA. Both said they would provide nothing beyond what was in the Warren Commission Report.

Wyckoff started studying the Zapruder frames.

Bartels discovered that the Zapruder camera was in Chicago. The Bell & Howell Company had given him a film projector in exchange for it. A company spokesman said they were "testing" it but was vague about what kind of tests. When she flew out to Chicago and went to Bell & Howell, she was told that the company had *that very day* donated it to the Archives. So Wyckoff had to use other cameras of the same model.

(Bell & Howell later announced that their tests showed the camera was probably running at 18.3 frames per second, a speed already accepted by the FBI. Wyckoff found his test cameras ran both faster and slower. The camera speed is crucial for timing the number of seconds between evidence of shots found on the Zapruder film.)

One Sunday in January, the BBC broadcast four and one-half hours about the Warren Report controversy. I flew to London and watched a long, footless debate, involving Mark Lane and others, about the merits and sins of the Commission. Nothing in it for us.

Weeks and months passed as we sought out witnesses and experts. When the work was done, 64 people had been interviewed on camera and hundreds more for background. Reaction to requests for interviews was varied.

Governor and Mrs. Connally were reluctant but did agree. Domingo Benevides, a controversial witness to the shooting of Officer Tippit, had refused in 1964 but now said yes. Dr. Wecht couldn't wait to get on camera. Constable Seymour Weitzman, who had originally mistakenly identified Oswald's rifle as a Mauser, was not happy about going on television to correct himself, but he did.

Mark Lane, William Turner and Edward Epstein were ready to talk. Commander James J. Humes, the chief autopsy surgeon, had refused through the years to talk publicly about the case, but he agreed to do so now after we got clearance from Attorney General Ramsey Clark. (But Clark turned me down when I went to his office to ask for access to the autopsy report and films and slides sealed in the Archives.)

We wanted Chief Justice Warren, but he declined. John J. McCloy, a prominent Commission member, reluctantly consented to be interviewed by Cronkite.

Meanwhile, Lister was working on the physical evidence. He had a tower and a target track constructed at a ballistics laboratory in Maryland matching exactly the heights and distances in Dealey Plaza. The target track was angled to match the angle of Elm Street. He got 11 volunteer marksmen to fire a Mannlicher-Carcano fitted with the same four-power sight found on Oswald's rifle. Each fired clips of three bullets at a target towed down the track at the same speed the Presidential limousine was traveling.

Walter also set up tests to determine how damaged bullets would be if they were fired into gelatin blocks simulating human tissue. Charlie Wyckoff ran off his camera tests in Boston and Rather interviewed him about the results.

As the film flowed into New York to be screened and edited, patterns for the broadcasts began to take shape. The "questions" format would work very well.

We had one problem late in the game. Dick Richter had been tipped off by one of the buffs that District Attorney Jim Garrison was preparing to indict men he claimed had plotted the assassination in New Orleans. Richter went to see Garrison, and since Mike Wallace happened to be in Louisiana at the time, he went along to listen to Garrison's story.

Our problem was that if Garrison's evidence turned out to be valid—however far-fetched his story sounded—his inquiry, not one by CBS News, would be the big story. And if Garrison actually got indictments, the matter would be before the courts and it would be legally and ethically difficult for us to go ahead.

Bill Leonard, now the vice-president in charge of documentaries, and I met with Garrison in New Orleans in May. We agreed he was a screwball and that we should go ahead.

As we got closer to an air date, two things emerged as vital for effective and dramatic television production.

The first was to obtain permission from the owners of the Texas Schoolbook Depository to film or tape inside it. It was a private company and they had refused all such requests since the assassination.

The second was to get the Dallas police to let us re-enact the motorcade with cameras stationed on the sixth floor looking down on it. This would put Dan Rather and Eddie Barker on the scene, moving the story out of the studio to where it actually happened.

After a great deal of negotiation by Barker and Birnbaum, both permissions were obtained, for Saturday and Sunday, June 10 and 11. Only two weeks before the series was scheduled to begin.

Almost all our material had been shot on film, but for these central and crucial scenes, we decided to use two television cameras, connected to tape recorders, stationed in Oswald's window plus four cameras along the motorcade route. I asked Don Hewitt if he would produce and direct this crucial remote session and was delighted to have him answer he would be "honored" to do so.

On June 6, I told Salant I thought three hours would be enough, but after looking at the whole megillah two weeks later, we asked the network for *four* hours. And got them.

Vern Diamond, the director, ordered a large "window" hung in the studio behind Cronkite's anchor position. Into it he would put the questions we would pose and the answers we had arrived at.

Finally, all the complicated editorial and technical work was finished and we went on the air.

The first thing viewers saw was an open car moving slowly down a street, seen through a circle cut by crosshairs. The first thing they heard was Walter say, "This is what a rifleman would see from a sixth-floor window if he tracked an automobile down Elm Street in Dealey Plaza, Dallas, Texas."

The second thing they saw was a man on a tower firing a bolt-action rifle at a man-sized target. They heard Walter say, "This is a marksman firing three shots from a Mannlicher-Carcano rifle at a target below him and moving away.

"These two re-enactments represent the heart of the Warren Report," he went on. "In the view of the Warren Commission, they describe fully the assassination of President Kennedy."

After the opening titles, Walter continued with a brief description of the assassination and the appointment of the Warren Commission by President Johnson. Dan Rather then related, over film, the actions of Lee Harvey Oswald, as described in the Warren Report, from the time President Kennedy entered Dealey Plaza until Oswald was shot three days later in the basement of the Dallas police headquarters.

After some man-in-the-street comments reflecting public skepticism about the Warren Report's conclusions, Cronkite continued:

> Screening out the absurd and the irrational, we are left with a series of real and critical questions about the assassination, questions which have not been answered to the satisfaction of the people of the United States.

In this series of broadcasts, CBS News will try to cast light on those questions. They fall under four headings, which we will examine on successive evenings at this same time.

Tonight's question: Did Lee Harvey Oswald shoot President Kennedy?

Tomorrow night, we will ask: Was there more than one assassin firing in Dealey Plaza?

On Tuesday night, we will ask: Was there a conspiracy leading to the President's murder.

And on Wednesday night, we will ask: Why doesn't America believe the Warren Report?

As Walter posed the questions, they appeared graphically in the window behind him.

The first hour had fellow workers saying they saw Oswald on the sixth floor on the day of the murder, established that he owned a rifle found there, and went on with our re-enactment film and our tests of how fast such a rifle could be fired.

(Our own conclusion was that such a rifle could be fired fast enough to permit Oswald to get off three shots within 5.6 seconds and that, in fact, he might have had a second or two more time than that.)

Alvarez described his theories and Wyckoff explained his experiments timing the Bell & Howell cameras and the Zapruder film.

At the end of the hour, Walter said: "Did Lee Harvey Oswald shoot President Kennedy? CBS News concludes he did."

A point here. Dick Salant had decided early on that, departing from its traditional position of not editorializing, CBS News would in this case state its own conclusions.

Thus at the end of the second hour Cronkite said:

"Our own view, on the evidence, is that is is difficult to believe the single-bullet theory. But to believe the other theories is even more difficult...In the end, like the Commission, we are persuaded that a single bullet wounded both President Kennedy and Governor Connally."

And after the third hour: "Tonight, we've asked if there was a conspiracy involving perhaps Officer Tippit, Jack Ruby or others. The answers here cannot be as firm as our other answers, partly because of the difficulty, cited in the Warren Report, of proving something *did not* happen... but on the basis of the evidence now in hand, we still can find no convincing evidence of such a conspiracy."

(Contrary to general belief, the Warren Report did not state flat out that there had not been a conspiracy. Instead it said the Commission *had not been able to discover any evidence of one.* That is a ploy often used by the FBI and the CIA when they don't want to confirm or deny they have some specific piece of information; "they just can't find it.")

And at the end of the fourth and final hour:

> We have found that whenever you look at the Warren Report closely and without preconceptions, you come away convinced that it is the best account we are ever likely to have of what happened that day in Dallas.
>
> We have found that most objections to the Report—and certainly all objections that go to the heart of the Report—vanish when they are exposed to the light of honest inquiry. It is a strange kind of tribune to the Warren Report that every objection that can be raised against it is to be found in the Report itself.
>
> It is true that the answers to some questions leave us restless. The theory that a single bullet struck down both the President and the Governor, for example, has too much of the long arm of coincidence about it for us to be entirely comfortable.
>
> But would we be more comfortable believing that a shot was fired by a second assassin who materialized out of thin air for the purpose, fired a shot and then vanished again into thin air, leaving no trace of himself, his rifle, his bullet or any other sign of existence?
>
> Measured against the alternative, the Warren Commission Report is the easiest to believe and that is all the Report claims.
>
> But we have found also that there has been a loss of morale, a loss of confidence among the American people toward their own government and the men who serve it. And that is perhaps more wounding than the assassination itself.
>
> The damage that Lee Harvey Oswald did the United States of America, the country he first renounced and then appeared to re-embrace, did not end when the shots were fired from the Texas School Book Depository. The most grievous wounds persist and there is little reason to believe that they will soon be healed.

Good stuff by Steve.

This unique television enterprise had some interesting results.

First in the hearts of the television network bosses was, as always, the ratings. Much to their surprise, two of the series segments made the "Top Ten" that week and the Monday hour was Number Two, with a rating of 21.7. Number One "Gomer Pyle, U.S.M.C." had a rating of 21.9!

Reaction in the press was extensive and almost without exception laudatory. Especially from critics of the *Washington Post*, the *Christian Science Monitor*, the *Washington Star* and other highly respected papers.

Jack Gould, *The New York Times'* television critic, wrote:

> The Columbia Broadcasting System's four-part analysis of the Warren Report on the assassination of President Kennedy has been a thoroughly valuable social service. Taking up a controversy befogged by much confusing detail, the program has not only reminded the lay viewer of what actually was in the Warren Report, something that badly needed doing, but also, through its own initiative and resourcefulness, CBS independently established that the document's central conclusions remain far more impressive than the bulk of criticism of the Warren Commission's findings.
>
> Richard S. Salant, president of CBS News, is to be commended for recognizing that the controversy over the assassination called for the unusual step of investigating the soundness of the original investigation...
>
> From the tone and attitude of the program, Leslie Midgley, the executive producer, had another objective in mind. It was to invoke the resources of an impartial news organization, virtually the only instrument capable of doing the job, to restore a sense of much-needed balance to the controversy over the assassination, to make clear that the criticism of the Warren Report by such persons as Mark Lane should not be left to stand by itself...
>
> Walter Cronkite was at his best in reading the complicated narrative of the inquiry and invoking the right touch of inflection where CBS News elected to stay clear of flat declarations and

indicated that it rested upon the apparent reasonableness of circumstantial conclusions...

The CBS inquiry, extending over nine months and obviously involving the employment of a large staff, almost certainly is going to lead to a rise in investigative TV reporting. The trend should be beneficial because one of the blights of electronic journalism has been the overly tardy photographic reprises of material appearing weeks or months earlier in other media. Original reporting, confined not merely to a sensational crime but to all other areas of national interest, is what TV needs to recapture the sense of journalistic excitement that in recent years has been largely lost in hasty exercises in blandness.

In between these two projects about the Kennedy assassination, the first in 1964 and the second in 1967, I made several trips to Vietnam and produced reports which repeatedly cautioned that the US was getting deeper and deeper into danger there.

I kept reading about the "great power" of television to influence people. But these broadcast warnings about Vietnam, carefully gathered and authenticated, seemed to have no influence at all with either the administration in Washington or the American people. Where, I often wondered, was that "great power?"

But, after these four shows about the Warren Report were broadcast, I came to believe that they, at least, had indeed influenced how Americans perceived the assassination. The "buffs" blasted us, of course, claiming we were part of a huge conspiracy to conceal the truth, tools of a government trying to get the official version of the murder accepted.

But the buffs never regained their previous standing in public opinion, not even with young people, although the Vietnam war continued to escalate.

Maybe television is—sometimes—powerful. Maybe.

I got a great deal of satisfaction out of doing this job and the reaction to it. My favorite was this note to Salant:

> I was tremendously impressed by the job CBS News did on the Warren Report. I found it imaginative, painstakingly thorough

and altogether fascinating. Each program moved at a good pace and each built up anticipation for the next.

I've already heard many favorable comments from people who were as impressed as I was. I'm very proud of the program and of all those who had a hand in it. Congratulations.

It was signed William S. Paley.

Chapter 19

A Foot in the Door of the White House

THE YEAR 1967 brought me great personal satisfaction with the successful production of the Warren Report series. Which coincided with major changes in some matters both professional and personal.

My oldest daughter, Leslie, had dropped out of the University of Miami and was living at home in Crestwood and working at a Lord & Taylor branch not far away. Her sister, Andrea, was at Harcum, a girl's college in Pennsylvania. My son, Jeddy, named after his great grandfather, was at a boarding school for boys called The Nyack School. It was nowhere near Nyack but in the old Merrill mansion in Southampton, N.Y. He had had trouble learning to read and write in the early grades and needed both special instruction and a place to live, since there was no mother at home.

Miss Furness and I were very close. We spent all our time together socially and I spent many nights at her apartment. She is an early riser, and one morning when I was slugabed, she said, "If *I* had a contract with CBS, I would be down there at work!"

"You don't understand," I said from the pillow. "I am trying to work out the format of the third Warren show and that is work you do in your head."

She was not convinced. She was dying to get a job in television journalism but they wouldn't give her one. Because, she was told, she was still too closely identified with selling Westinghouse refrigerators on television.

One evening, she said she would like to be invited to the White House for lunch some day. I said I thought Bill Small, the head of the CBS Washington bureau, could arrange for such a social invitation.

Later that day, the phone rang in her apartment and someone said the White House was on the line. It was not an invitation to lunch. It was a man named John Macy who asked her to come down to talk about working for the government. She was hazy about what he had in mind, but one of her cardinal principles always has been to take any job she is offered.

She went to Washington and returned the next day. That night, we went to dinner at the Brussels, an elegant French restaurant on 54th Street. She was visibly up.

Mr. Macy, she said, was chairman of the Civil Service Commission and principal personnel recruiter for the President. What he had in mind was that she become President Johnson's special assistant for consumer affairs. There were only eight such assistants. The job would entail living in Washington and working with the President and his staff to further interests of consumers and get consumer protection legislation passed by Congress.

Betty had listened to a lot of my gloomy bitching about the Johnson war in Vietnam. But we both knew that, in addition to running a shooting war, Lyndon Johnson was trying hard to win benefits for ordinary people with what he called the "Great Society" program. It has been both more sensible and more successful than his programs in Indochina. She was to succeed a woman from Utah named Esther Petersen, who was a good friend of my brother Grant. Why he wanted to replace Esther and why Betty had been chosen had not been spelled out.

BF, as my kids called her, was obviously dying to go to Washington. The question was, if she did, should we get married as planned? The decision was that she would take the job and we would work out the marriage business somehow.

So on May 1, Betty's daughter Babbie, the Cronkites, plus yours truly and offspring assembled at the White House to watch her sworn in. Babbie held the Bible. It was a big moment.

A moment which grew into days and months of exciting work for her. She had a rather grand office in the corner of the Executive Office Building just across the alley from the White House. (It was called the State, War and Navy Building when I was in Washington in the Thirties. Because it then housed all those departments.)

There had been a lot of negative press reaction to her appointment, questioning whether this glamorous former actress from New York was a proper person to speak for the ordinary consumer. But as the months went on and she testified before congressional committees on behalf of consumer bills, the critics were disarmed and she was recognized as one of the most effective members of a troubled administration. At least *her* department was on the side of the angels.

She leased a studio apartment at the Watergate complex and we started to look for a house when she came up for weekends. I wanted one on Long Island Sound, where I could tie up my little sailboat. But we soon discovered prices for such locations were out of sight. We looked at a few dumb houses before an agent said she had a house which had just come on the market in Hartsdale, just north of Scarsdale. It turned out to be a smallish red colonial on a dead end street.

We walked through the house and then out onto the brick patio beside it.

"Take me through it again," Betty said to the agent. After the second look, she joined me on the terrace.

"I've got two words for you," she said. "Buy it."

Delighted to have *that* decision made, we returned to Scarsdale and signed the papers. Not knowing that our acre contained a brook and that the woods beyond it were part of a 500-acre county park, which could never be built upon.

We knew the problem with the house was that it had only three bedrooms, which meant the girls would have to share one. What we didn't know was that both Leslie and Andrea would be married and gone in only a few months. The house was just the right size.

Now that we had a house, a wedding was in order. Betty, very busy in Washington, enlisted Ellin Saltzman, a charming and smart fashion expert and long-time friend, to help plan the wedding. Ellin said to have it at the Hotel Regency on Madison Avenue.

Betty invited about a hundred people, her family and mine and friends, most of them from the broadcasting business. One name I wanted on the list caused her a problem. The name was Frank Costello. Betty said she just couldn't have such a notorious man attend her wedding while she working at the White House. We had some words about it, but, of course, the bride prevailed. Too bad, it was the kind of thing he would have loved.

Dave Parsons came up with a couple of tickets to London on Pan American, and I asked the Collingwoods if we could use their lovely flat in Belgravia. They said sure, they planned to be in Greece at that time.

The wedding was in the afternoon and all went well. We went alone to dinner at "21" and speculated whether we would make the papers the next morning. When we walked into the hotel after dinner, the early edition of the *Daily News* had arrived, and on page one was a big picture of the two of us and Babbie holding her son, Chris.

When we returned from London, Betty began a regular schedule of commuting from Washington to spend weekends in Hartsdale, and I started driving to New York every day. That routine continued until the day Lyndon Johnson left the White House in 1969. We found a long-distance marriage can work very well.

That highly visible national service indirectly propelled Betty into the television news career previously denied her.

In 1971, Governor Nelson Rockefeller asked her to organize a New York State Consumer Protection Board and become its executive director. She did that, and in 1973, Mayor John Lindsay invited her to take over as New York City's commissioner of consumer affairs.

Which led, in 1974, to an offer from WNBC-TV that she become the station's consumer reporter.

She has held the job ever since and happily appears several times a week on the local station and once a week on the NBC network's "Today" show.

Chapter 20

Evening News and Vietnam

A COUPLE OF WEEKS after the Warren Report series was broadcast, Dick Salant told me Ernie Leiser wanted to leave his job as executive producer of the "CBS Evening News With Walter Cronkite." Dick wanted me to take it.

The half-hour evening news was—and is—the most important function of a network news department. Cronkite had made his reputation as a great broadcaster at big doings such as conventions and elections, but it was his appearance as anchor man of the evening news five nights a week that anointed him the Number One correspondent of CBS News.

And the executive producer of that broadcast was the Number One editor at CBS News. I had never even thought about doing that job. I had put in a dozen busy, and professionally highly gratifying, years at CBS doing other kinds of broadcasts. But this assignment meant editing news every day for an audience of millions. I said yes. But I suggested to Salant that the job was extremely taxing and it would be a good idea if we agreed I would take it on for two years, then he could think about another producer. He said that seemed to make sense and we agreed I would start in August.

After Betty Furness and I got married.

Ernie and I simply switched jobs. He moved into my office and I moved into his.

During the four years and four months I produced the Cronkite news, Vietnam was on the air night after night. Public reaction against the war was rising visibly and I began to think maybe the "power" of television I could not discern in our "in-depth" shows might indeed be there in the nightly show, with its enormous audience.

In the late Sixties, "the living room war" provided a constant supply of stark images of American boys fighting and dying in a dangerous swamp halfway around the world. These images, repeated over and over, blew up a rising tide of opposition to the war, especially among the young, who saw on the tube what might be their own grim and dangerous future.

The most dramatic footage we put on the Cronkite news in the late Sixties came from correspondents and cameramen willing, indeed eager, to go out into the field, live and march with the grunts, and see for themselves what it was really like. There were many of them, like Morley Safer, and the veteran Peter Kalischer. (As the war went on through the years, many correspondents served there, including Dan Rather, Mike Wallace and Don Webster. In the early Seventies, Ed Bradley got some remarkable stuff in Cambodia and later about the "boat people," Southeast Asians trying to escape their ravaged land in perilous fashion.) But the one who seemed to get closest to ordinary soldiers was Jack Laurence. Perhaps because he was about the same age as many of them and had an empathy denied older men.

When I took over the "Evening News," Americans had been fighting in the jungles and mountains for two years. Although there were hundreds of thousands of them, things were getting very hairy. Even the big base at Danang on the coast—scene of the first landing of Marines in 1965—was occasionally hit by mortar fire, although it seemed secure.

But west of it were bases under constant attack, often in danger of being overrun. In September 1967, Laurence sent us a revealing background memo on the situation at Con Thien, a forward Marine outpost just south of the demilitarized zone.

Jack had just made a two-day visit to Con Thien. He reported that it had been under continuous artillery and rocket attack for *six months*. He noted that the Marines, basically trained to work with the Navy for amphibious assaults on beaches, had been forced to adapt to front-line fighting in trenches, foxholes and bunkers reminiscent of the First World War.

A lot of great reporting was being done in Vietnam, but Jack insisted this aspect of the war was not being properly covered. He and his crew were the first to stay overnight at Con Thien. Most reporters arrived in groups of 10 or 20 after a major battle, stayed an hour or two and then flew back to Danang.

Those visits were made by helicopter, the wonderful machine which whisked correspondents in and out of battle zones in the Vietnam for a decade. But Laurence had chosen to ride in a truck convoy on the single resupply road to and from Con Thien. The road was under constant attack by small arms fire and rockets.

And, he wrote, the fall monsoon would begin in a few weeks, and the Marines knew only too well that the supply road would be washed out by rain. They would be left only the air route for resupply.

Despite whatever cheery news was being passed out at headquarters in Saigon, the Marine officers at Con Thien knew they were in a very difficult position. Some said candidly they were not sure they could survive.

And French observers who saw the location of Con Thien, in a valley with enemy positions overlooking it from heights all around, saw striking similarities to Dien Bien Phu, scene of the final French defeat in their war in Vietnam.

The "official position" was described as "let them come." But Jack said a lot of privates and corporals and a "few" commanding officers were not all that enthusiastic.

One joke they told newcomers to the deep bunkers at Con Thien: "We used to call the enemy Charlie. But now he's known as MR. Charlie."

Con Thien held during that rainy season, but in a few months, there was grave concern over the situation at the Khe Sahn and it probably would be disastrous, opinions at "Pentagon East" in Saigon notwithstanding.

Danny Bloom, the Saigon bureau chief, warned us that most reporters thought an attack on Khe Sahn would be coordinated with attacks on Camp Carroll, the Rockpile and Con Thien.

As it turned out, these places were scenes of brutal and bloody fighting but all managed to hold, at great cost to the American defenders.

Over the years, Cronkite personally tended to be the side of those who believed the US should indeed be involved in Vietnam. But by 1968, he decided to go there himself. When the Tet offensive exploded.

Ernie went along as Cronkite's producer, in case the trip turned up material which could be made into a special report. It did. Walter and Ernie were in Hue, where bitter battles went on around them. They came home to put on a half-hour "Report From Vietnam by Walter Cronkite," during which he said the war was not being won and a peace should be negotiated. President Johnson was reportedly dismayed, seeing that show as signaling the end of public support for his Vietnam policy.

"If I've lost Cronkite, I've lost the people," he was quoted as saying.

The fact that the Viet Cong and North Vietnamese could mount uprisings all over the country, including Saigon itself, shocked an American public which was being told over and over again by its military and political leaders the war in Indochina was being won.

General Westmoreland maintains to this day that Tet was not a victory but actually a major defeat for the Viet Cong. He is entitled to his opinion but that is now how it was perceived at home.

The Tet attacks were unique, but Vietnam provided a day by day flow of news very attractive for television. Because most of it consisted of action—often very violent—which this visual medium eats up. In other words, plenty of "bang, bang." And, increasingly the stories were about the growing number of young Americans killed or wounded. It was indeed "the living room war" because for the first time in history Americans were able to sit home and watch their troops in battle action. We put an awful lot of it on the "Evening News."

The following year, Gordon Manning decided to make a tour of Vietnam and asked me to go along. In Saigon, the bureau informed us that MACV public relations had accredited us as "assimilated major generals," which meant we had high priority for such things as plane travel. The high rank was recognition of Gordon's position as news vice president. (For me a step up from assimilated corporal in World War II.)

We traveled, by plane and helicopter, the entire length of South Vietnam, from the delta in the south to the Demilitarized Zone, the border with North Vietnam. One of our stops was at the headquarters of a Marine general west of Danang. He lined up some GI's and insisted that we talk to them. "Ask them anything," he said. When we asked what they wanted, some boldly replied they just wanted to go home.

At midday, the general ushered us into his own helicopter saying we would fly up to his villa in the mountains for lunch. It would be cooler there. When we got into the chopper, it turned out to be carpeted, wall to wall. When we took off, the pilot went straight up several thousand feet. I was sitting next to him and asked how come. "The general doesn't like the idea of being a target for snipers," he said.

Although I always wanted to see it, I never managed a visit to the big naval base at Cam Ranh Bay. It had been built on a cost-plus contract by the Texas construction firm of Brown & Root, which put up the first big campaign money for young Lyndon Johnson. I always suspected it had been a multi-million dollar boondoggle with who knows what hanky-panky.

So on this trip I began to ask officers why that base had been built. Most said they didn't know, it really was not needed to service the aircraft carriers which launched bombers to strike at North Vietnam. At lunch, Gordon and I were seated with eight or 10 Marine officers who were, of course, involved with the Navy. When I asked my question, most of them said it was just part of normal strategy to have a very big base near where you were fighting a war. One of them said he believed it had been built to leave behind as a gift to the people of South Vietnam after the war ended. Some gift. Now it's a fine base for Soviet warships.

My own guess was that some admiral simply decided he would like to have a big installation in this deep-water bay and ordered it built. Anything went in Vietnam. Besides, it was a very nice contract for Brown & Root.

What impressed Gordon most in 1969 was the terrible sight of the Vietnam landscape viewed from a helicopter. Uncounted thousands of tons of poisonous defoliants had turned the green jungle into what looked like the dead surface of the moon. Bomb craters were everywhere.

What impressed me most was the sight of a small country overrun by vehicles of every size and description. In addition to machines of war, there were trucks and jeeps everywhere. The country looked like one huge parking lot at a General Motors factory.

As the years went by, the constant flow of Vietnam stories on the "Evening News," most of which inevitably reported young Americans killed in increasing numbers and no end of the war in sight, caused great unhappiness among the stations affiliated with the CBS television network.

The station owners and managers, being almost without exception rich and conservative members of their own communities, viewed us at CBS News as left-wingers whose liberal political views were probably being reflected in how we viewed and thus reported news of the war. They often complained about Vietnam coverage and we were aware that many owners wrote Salant and Stanton objecting to the coverage. But unless there had been an error of fact, we never got any fallout from those complaints. The protection afforded the editorial staff at CBS was highly admirable, in my opinion greater than that given the staffs of the biggest newspapers and news magazines by their bosses.

But acute discontent with CBS News was a fact of life, especially when the affiliates perceived us as "persecuting" Nixon while he kept saying he was winding down the war. (Actually, of course, he was expanding it.)

In 1970, we got a revealing look at just how the affiliate owners felt.

Each network shells out for a convention of the affiliates in the spring, during which they wine and dine the owners and their lovely wives. These lavish affairs are often held at the Century Plaza Hotel in Los Angeles.

The principal purpose of these gatherings is to showcase portions of the entertainment schedule for the coming season, giving network executives a chance to "hard sell" their affiliates on how great the upcoming season will be.

An additional thrill—especially for the wives—is the command appearance at cocktail parties and dinners of the network entertainment stars. Something to talk about back home!

For this convention, Salant, Manning and Bill Leonard decided to give the conventioneers something unusual. They told us to move the Cronkite News to Los Angeles during the week of the convention. They would then invite the owners and managers to watch us go on the air.

Television City is an excellent place to work. Our biggest problem would be to get the show ready by 3:30 P.M., Los Angeles time, since we were accustomed to go on at 6:30. It was only a matter of habit, since we would be doing it at 6:30 New York time anyway.

Cronkite, producer Sandy and Socolow and I moved the whole operation to LA. Once again, the stagehands set us up on the stage of one of the biggest studios, where entertainment shows go on before audiences. The idea was that after one of their lunches, the affiliate executives would take the audience seats and watch Walter perform live. Big monitors would display film and tape portions of the show.

Russ Bensley stayed in New York to assemble film pieces and take in satellite feeds from Europe and the Far East. He would roll these into the show on cue from our director, Ritchie Mutschler, who was with us in Los Angeles.

This gave me one problem. It was common practice to receive a feed very close to air time, when the only possible decision was to use it as is or not at all. (Given more time, a piece could be re-fed or re-edited if that seemed necessary.) But at least in New York I could *see* the pieces as they came in and knew in advance what we would be putting on the air. In LA, I would see them just like the audience—for the first time.

The big afternoon came. We got everything ready on the stage—just like putting on a *show*—and the audience seats were taken by our friends from the affiliates.

Cronkite duly led into a report by Gary Shepard from the western border of Vietnam, where he was seen interviewing young soldiers about to board helicopters for the invasion of Cambodia.

Gary asked several of the youngsters what they thought about this operation. Did they like the idea? Several of the GI's said they didn't want to go on the mission but must obey orders.

When the show was over, Leonard and other executives sat on the stage and invited questions from the audience. They got an earful:

"Shepard asked those boys leading questions, trying to get them to say they didn't believe in the war."

"This was typical of CBS News. Trying, as always to undermine the administration's war effort."

"A perfect example of exactly what this audience doesn't like about network news."

"Why are correspondents permitted to get away with this kind of stuff?"

And so on and so forth.

There was a second problem. This show for the affiliates was on Friday, and the Kent State campus killings had occurred just four days before. There had been follow-up stories about Kent State, and the sympathies of these owners and managers were not with the student demonstrators, even those shot down by the National Guard.

The bid for some affiliate approval had backfired.

But that night, a curious thing happened.

When I arrived at the Century Plaza to attend the final dinner of the convention, Eric Sevareid got out of a car just ahead. Dinah Shore, one of the stars of the evening, spotted Eric and began to gush over him, saying how much she admired his work. Other women crowded around to shake his hand and have a word.

After an hour or so at cocktails, the guests filed into a huge dining room before a stage that must have seated 40 people. The network had summoned its entertainment stars to sit there. And the *news stars* were up there too.

Each one was introduced with trumpet fanfares.

And the greatest applause—by far—was for Walter Cronkite.

The second greatest hand was for Sevareid.

Well, well, I thought. Those station executives don't seem to know what people in their own homes like.

I never afterward paid much attention to rumors of affiliate discontent with news. They should convert their wives first, I decided.

Chapter 21

Evening News Years

With Walter Cronkite

A FEW YEARS AGO at a seminar on Cape Cod sponsored by The Sloan Foundation, I screened some of our CBS News coverage of Jack Kennedy's assassination for an audience of distinguished academics and writers. I explained that I had been one of the two producers in charge during the "Four Dark Days" after the President was shot.

When the tape ended, one of the professors asked what was going through my mind while all that great drama was being put before the nation. He said he assumed I was trying to reassure the American people of the stability of the nation in this moment of great crisis.

"I wasn't doing anything like that," I replied. "I was just doing my job."

There was an immediate flurry of comment all around the audience.

These were very intellectual types, a former science adviser to the President was among them. It became clear that most of them did not believe an editor could simply "do his job" in such extreme circumstances without consciously trying to influence the way his audience should think. Bending their view to his, if you like. But it was indeed true. As far as I was concerned, it was up to viewers to decide what

231

they thought. My assignment was to give them the facts. Collingwood was there also, and he expressed his own agreement with my view; he understood.

Some of the comments concerned the question of how editorial decisions are made. Specifically decisions on what goes into a network evening news show. Decisions about what—from all the things going on in the world on a given day—should be included in a broadcast whose aim is to select and include the principal events of that day. And, conversely, what should be left out.

When I was asked to take over as executive producer of the "CBS Evening News," making those decisions was going to be the most important part of my job. The technical and administrative matters had to be kept in line, but the one big inescapable question every day was: What is the most important news?

During the years I did that job—1967-72—many people who write about television came to watch how the show was put together, especially after Vice President Spiro Agnew delivered his slashing attack on television news in 1969:

> A small group of men numbering perhaps no more than a dozen anchormen, commentators and executive producers settle upon the film and commentary that is to reach the public. They decide what 40 to 50 million Americans will learn of the day's events in the nation and in the world. . . .
>
> It's time we questioned such power in the hands of a small and unelected elite.

That brought reporters around to find out what we were doing. Their most frequent questions concerned where we got our information and how we chose what to put on the air.

Proper answers required incursions into all kinds of things such as the mechanics of television news gathering and presentation, professional practices and standards, personal philosophy and even simple honesty.

Some reporters asked about the physical process, as though understanding that would make everything clear.

I told them the first thing to realize was that for us a half hour really was less than 23 minutes when opening and closing copy and commercial announcements are subtracted. Those minutes amount to the small end of a funnel. Into the large end is poured, every day, a vast amount of information from all over the world.

The CBS news-gathering organization even then included a very large bureau in Washington, some 20 correspondents and the necessary support staff. Also big bureaus in places like Chicago and Los Angeles and smaller ones in Atlanta and San Francisco. Plus bureaus in London, Paris, Rome, Tokyo, Hong Kong, Bonn and Moscow. And, since Vietnam was the biggest continuing story, a large staff of reporters, cameramen and technicians was always working there.

We were connected to these places by telex machines and telephones. The bureaus reported overnight to the central news desk in New York what stories were being covered on any given day. A list—a long list—of available stories was compiled by morning. A basic menu of news for the early morning, midday and evening shows.

The "Evening News" was put together in a small newsroom where Cronkite and his editor, writers and technicians worked all day and broadcast from at night. Cronkite had a modest office in one corner and I worked in a little one nearby with a glass wall that looked out into our little newsroom. The staff called it the fishbowl.

I had been lucky to inherit from Ernie two super producers, Sandy Socolow, who had worked with Walter for years on big special events as well as the daily news show, and Russ Bensley, who had been the director of many special shows. He had become a producer, but his experience as a director was extremely valuable.

We worked so closely together that there were no staff meetings. It was actually one big meeting all day. Everybody, including Cronkite, was aware, almost instantly, of any big news break anywhere, or the arrival of newsfilm or videotape which might affect our show.

Socolow kept in constant touch with the bureaus, especially Washington. Russ was in charge of the associate producers and the film editors. He was the unchallenged master at getting film and tape edited properly.

One of the first things I did was institute a telephone conference call every day at noon, connecting all the domestic bureaus. Each bureau updated the status of breaking news. The call was valuable to us and a great service for the bureaus because it gave them a good idea of how stories in their areas were shaping up in comparison to others around the country. When not otherwise occupied, Walter got on the phone and everyone was clued in to what was going on that particular day.

Before I went out to lunch, I typed out a "pre-lineup," a list of the most promising stories of the day, in the order of their apparent importance. It was circulated to our staff, the news desk in the big general newsroom next door, and our bosses down the hall.

That list and its successor lineup was the only notice to our superiors of what we planned to do. The news director, Gordon Manning, and the news president, Dick Salant, let us decide what was the news of the day. That acceptance of our ability to make crucial decisions reflected Salant's confidence in Cronkite and me to do things right. He kept saying he was a lawyer, not a journalist, that we should do our jobs as we saw fit. Actually, he was a superb managing journalist in just the right role. After he left CBS News, intrusion into the daily news selection process by management types changed and damaged the show.

By 3 P.M., I refined the early list to a "lineup," the skeleton of the coming broadcast. It served exactly the same purpose as the dummy a newspaper managing editor uses to lay out his front page. (It has been estimated that the whole content of the evening news is equal to about three-quarters of the front page of *The New York Times*.)

By looking at the lineup, Cronkite and his editor, the steady and talented John Merriman, could see what stories I proposed we cover with film or tape or have reported on camera by correspondents in Washington or wherever. Then they could decide what other stories Walter should "tell" and where they should appear. For example, if a major story about an economic development was slated to come from Washington, they would position other economic news items adjacent to it.

In the early Sixties, it was common practice to "switch live" to places like Washington and Los Angeles and have pieces fed by telephone lines into the show while it was being put on the air. But after the development of videotape editing, we began to have pieces fed to New York in advance and rolled into the broadcast from tape machines. It was more reliable and gave us a chance to look at the pictorial content before it went on the air.

It was very hairy. Every day. Cronkite had Merriman and a staff of three writers to assist him. But he is a meticulous editor. He read and timed every item himself, decided at times to rewrite piece of copy in his own style. He often wrote a late-breaking story while we were on the air, during a commercial or while a taped story was on.

Socolow used to say that the miracle of the show was not that it was so good but that it managed to get on the air at all.

That was the physical process. When a newspaper or magazine writer watched it in action, he understood *what* we did but it didn't seem to enlighten him or her about *why* we selected a certain piece of news to appear on the show and ignored hundreds or even thousands of others.

I have described my discovery, years before, that for the readers of the *Washington Post* news was—for them at least—what John Denson thought it was. But that is too simplistic.

The editorial process is complicated.

A news story must, first, interest an editor—known, unfortunately, as a "producer" in the TV news world. The story would interest him because it fell within one of two categories.

One: Is it something a reader or viewer *should* know? Does it concern his safety, his health, his wealth, his future? Or that of his family, his city, his nation? If so, an editor has a professional responsibility to pass on that information.

Two: Is it something a viewer would *want* to know? Such as an item about an interesting or glamorous personality, an unusual crime, some scandal, a bit of humor. These things catch the attention of editors because they know such stuff attracts an audience. Call it, if you must, show business.

In actual practice, on any successful newspaper, news magazine or television program, the decision about what is "news" and what is not is made by very few persons, drawing on a body of knowledge and experience. Almost without exception, these people have been making news decisions for a long time and doing it well. Their skills are, in some ways, similar to those of highly professional internists or judges. It is, indeed, one of the maxims of the legal profession that "the law is what judges say it is." In the end, decisions about what is and what is not important news are likely to be made by drawing on experience and ability—indeed even on intuition—almost without the judge being aware of the process.

Why only a few persons? Because it is the only practical way. Each day, final, fast, decisions must be made. There is simply not enough time to submit them to group scrutiny.

I digress.

Gary Paul Gates, who was one of Cronkite's writers in the late Sixties, wrote a book in 1974 called *Air Time—The Inside Story of CBS News*, a factual and entertaining account of the way things were. With, of course, emphasis on maneuverings for gilt and glory.

One of the chapters was titled, "Discussing the Lineup With God."

Gary writes, "Midgley himself was not an especially creative producer. His strength was as an editor who knew how to draw out the talents of others."

He went on to observe that, in contrast to "Don Hewitt's flair for Hollywood hi-jinks" and "Leiser's stringent demands and curt manner," "Midgley was as decorous and restrained as a Boston banker...soft-spoken and serene in temperament."

Johnny Merriman was Cronkite's editor and Gary recounts that a "new man" asked about various people on the show and what they did. When asked what Midgley did, Merriman smiled.

"Mr. Midgley" he said, "discusses the lineup with God."

I exemplified the "Peter Principle in reverse," he said. "Born to be an executive producer."

I certainly accept these two old friends' and colleagues' observations about my demeanor in return for:

What a compliment!

He had me down cold. My overriding obsession was the *content* of the show. Was it indeed a proper distillation of the enormous flood of daily information into a useful—and above all accurate—account of the news of the world and the nation? Nothing, NOTHING, was more important.

John Denson would have understood.

Over the years, Walter and I used to talk from time to time about what we were doing and how well we were doing it. We both suspected that more action—sex and violence if you will—in the show it would attract bigger audiences. Salant always preached that the news department was interested only in facts, not ratings. But he knew very well it wasn't so. Every journalist wants the biggest audience he can attract, just like every politician. And, in television, big audiences translate into big bucks.

But our musings constantly came down to this assessment: If we were willing to believe what the ratings were saying, that more Americans depended on Cronkite to bring them the news of the world than any other source, then they, the people, had handed us a mandate to give them the most responsible news account within our power.

And surprisingly little discretion is actually available to the editor of a daily show. Because very important stories are obvious to everyone and cannot be left out. When they are all lined up, very few minutes are left for what we used to call "all else."

One of Spiro Agnew's dark suspicions was that producers of the network shows were in cahoots every day to agree on what the American public would see. That is why, he insisted, you always saw the same stories on different stations. It was not true, of course; I never even met Wallace Westfeld, who was my opposite for several years at NBC, until a decade later.

But Agnew was quite right in saying that the same news stories appeared on the competing shows. They did so because they were obviously the most important of the day and could not be ignored.

It was very difficult to find time for other things. As part of our format, Eric Sevareid wrote and read on camera a "think piece" three times a week. Since we were forbidden to editorialize, they were labeled "commentary," which didn't deceive anyone. And it always was hard to squeeze that two minutes and 15 seconds into the lineup.

Eric read his piece before a camera in the Washington bureau and was almost always recorded on tape and rolled into the show. A copy of his script was phoned up to my office and transcribed by a secretary. So we would know in advance what topic he planned to address.

In all those years, I can only remember once suggesting he change something. He had written a piece which involved the Secretary of State, Dean Rusk, and commented, "Rusk is drinking more and enjoying it less."

When I saw that, I picked up the phone.

"Eric," I said, "do you want to say that Rusk is drinking too much?"

"Absolutely not," he replied, and did the paragraph over.

A bit of a contrast to what is going on today.

Sometimes the editing became tricky, complicated by nuances of television. For example, in March 1968, in the darkest days of the Vietnam tragedy, President Johnson spoke before the National Farmers Union in Minneapolis. Dan Rather, covering the event, called it "his strongest fighting speech since the 1964 campaign, alternately pleading for and urging what he called a total national effort to win the war, win the peace and complete the job at home."

Rather's report was fed to Washington to be edited. It was our lead story in a lineup which also included Bobby Kennedy addressing a group in the midwest. The Senator had belatedly turned against the Vietnam adventure and was challenging a sitting President of his own party. And Johnson was under siege. He even had to arrive in Minneapolis unannounced, so that anti-war demonstrators would not have time to assemble and taunt him with "Hey, hey LBJ, how many kids did you kill today?"

As happened all too often, the editing was not completed in Washington until we went on the air at 6:30 P.M. for the first of our two nightly feeds. (Most stations around the country used this first feed but some of the largest cities, including New York and Washington, came on at 7 P.M. If the first version went well and no big news broke during that half-hour, we simply sat and watched a tape rerun of the first show. If changes had to be made, we either did the whole show over from the top or started on tape and came on live at the appropriate time.)

When the Johnson piece appeared, I saw immediately that our report did not show any audience reaction to what Dan had described as a ringing appeal for support. I had not been in Minneapolis. But I was absolutely sure the President *must* have elicited applause. Our version had him making a strong statement followed by a "cutaway" showing people sitting silently in the audience.

I picked up the direct line and asked our Washington producers about the editing. They checked the original tape feed from Minneapolis and, sure enough, discovered that an editor and an associate producer had cut Johnson's speech without including stormy applause from his audience. They fell to re-editing the story and I scheduled a repeat for 7 P.M.

Then—it had to happen—when our Kennedy spot came up a few minutes later it showed him being wildly cheered.

A critic of our reporting, especially one who was a supporter of Lyndon Johnson and/or the war, certainly would have every reason to suspect CBS News had misrepresented what had happened in Minneapolis. We had, in fact, done so in that 6:30 feed. They could contend we were trying to undermine the President, perhaps even to build up Bobby.

When goofs like this occur, they usually confirm Murphy's Law that if something can go wrong it will. In this case, the 6:30 feed was recorded in Los Angeles and *that* version instead of the corrected one found its way onto the local news on CBS-owned KNXT-TV at 11 P.M., Pacific time. Which prompted a letter by an irate viewer to the Federal Communications Commission complaining that CBS News reporting was "slanted" favorably toward Senator Kennedy and unfavorably toward President Johnson.

The problem came to the attention of Dick Salant, who asked how come we didn't know in advance what was going on the air. I explained that we did indeed get telexed copies of the words in reports from Washington but that didn't tell us exactly what the picture would show. One of the perils and pitfalls of electronic journalism.

When I took over the "CBS Evening News," it was just about to pass NBC's "Huntley-Brinkley Nightly News" in the rating race. At that time, ABC was not in the running.

Huntley and Brinkley, who had made their reputation by working very well together at conventions and on election night, had been ahead in the race for audiences since before both networks went from 15 minutes to a half-hour in 1963. But Cronkite was gaining steadily as he appeared with great success anchoring big events such as space shots. And the CBS backup correspondents such as Rather, Roger Mudd, Marvin Kalb and Harry Reasoner were plainly superior to their NBC counterparts.

I wish I could take credit for the CBS victory in 1967 but the truth is that Cronkite and Leiser and Hewitt had been moving the show up steadily. It just peaked as I arrived. Once it became Number One, the CBS show never lost that position. Our average lead over NBC was about 15 percent over the years. From time to time NBC would draw a little closer, and Cronkite, ever the driving competitor, would grumble that we should do better.

Since we really wrapped up the show by 6:30 each evening and only changed it in the following half hour if necessary, the staff habitually sat down in my office and watched what our competitors were doing. Walter either joined us to look at the three monitors in my office or looked at those in his own office. If he saw some story on NBC which he deemed superior to the CBS version, he was quick to conclude that we were falling down on the job.

"Let's do it better—and beat them!" he would cry. It was the old United Press warhorse speaking. The UP *must* come in first, ahead of the Associated Press.

Political conventions are great fun, and in 1968, I attended both the Republican Convention in Miami and the Democratic Convention in Chicago. Cronkite anchored not only the convention coverage but the evening news from his convention hall booth, so it was natural that I would be on the scene. In addition, I produced a one-hour prime time show the night before the Democrats convened.

That 1968 event was the scene of violence in the streets and parks of Chicago as Mayor Richard Daley's cops beat up on anti-war protesters. And there was great turbulence inside the convention hall itself.

I started the pre-convention show with the police battling demonstrators, during which the voice of Frank Sinatra was heard singing "My Kind of Town, Chicago Is..." Very effective.

Betty Furness had been a highly visible fixture of the Johnson Administration for a year. She had worked hard and successfully to get bills through Congress on truth in lending, meat inspection and other consumer matters.

So among the speakers assigned to address the convention one evening was the President's special assistant for consumer affairs. She had attended six political conventions doing sales pitches for Westinghouse appliances on television, but this was something else. Addressing the convention!

Alas, Mike Wallace, one of the "floor men" for CBS, was interviewing a delegate when she began to speak and continued to do so for most of her appearance. The delegates heard her in the hall, but not on CBS Television.

It was a strange convention. At one end of the great hall was an empty section of balcony seats set aside and obviously decorated for the use of the President. He never appeared but his presence hung like a ghost over the gathering. Hubert Horatio Humphrey was duly anointed the nominee of the Democratic Party and went out to do battle against another former Vice President, Richard Nixon. Humphrey had not been able to disassociate himself from the Vietnam policy of his chief before the campaign began. Nixon's victory was predictable and probably inevitable.

About that attack on us by Spiro Agnew.

One Thursday afternoon in November 1969, Bill Small alerted Salant and me that an Agnew speech set for that evening before a Republican Party meeting in Des Moines was going to be a blast against television news.

The speech was scheduled for 7 P.M., eastern time, which meant that if Salant decided to go live with Agnew, the Cronkite news would have to be carried by all stations at 6:30 P.M. That would put the Vice President on right after the networks' evening news, his target.

The strategists in the White House who wrote Angew's speech almost guaranteed they would get live air time by including in the advance text this sentence:

"Whether what I've said to you tonight will be seen and heard by all the nation is not my decision, it's their decision."

So all the networks had their cameras warmed up and waiting when he began to speak.

The Vice President made it very clear that "the instant analysis and querulous criticism" on television following a Nixon speech 10 days before had stung the administration into mounting this attack. Nixon had told the nation that he sought to rally Americans to stay the course in Vietnam, to support his policy of seeking what he called "peace with honor."

Public opinion polls taken after the President's speech show that a majority of Americans supported him. But Nixon and his advisors had been annoyed by what they took to be negative comments by Marvin Kalb, Bill Lawrence, Bill Downs and other television journalists after the President finished.

Agnew complained about the selection of stories on the evening news shows, saying, "Bad news drives out good news. One minute of

Eldridge Cleaver is worth 10 minutes of Roy Wilkins." He went on to blame television news for distorting the growing number of anti-war and anti-administration demonstrations, asking: "How many marchers and demonstrators would we have if the marchers did not know that cameras would be there to record their antics?"

He said some examination was in order to determine if television news, as a monopoly, should continue to enjoy First Amendment rights and privileges guaranteed to the press.

Perhaps more alarming to the broadcasting brass than the Agnew speech was an unusual request from Dean Burch, new chairman of the Federal Communications Commission, for transcripts of the discussions on air which had followed the Nixon speech. Especially since Agnew pointed out that the FCC had the power—and he said "indeed the duty"—to exert enormous influence on television in America.

All of which struck the owners of vastly lucrative broadcasting licenses as threats, pressure to get the networks to treat Nixon in a more friendly fashion. Very few licenses have been revoked by the FCC, but its power to do so always has made the broadcasting licensees uneasy.

And there *was* something to what Agnew said. We all knew it. We did have the power to "edit reality." We could use images on the screen to convey impressions that might not be stated in words. And we used that power. We could manipulate emotions and reactions.

Agnew was right in saying that decisions about the news were made by a few people who possessed unusual power to make them. He was wrong in implying that the men who made the decisions were part of the "Eastern establishment" and were under the influence of some liberal bias which distorted their judgment. Acting on motivations of that sort is for politicians, not journalists.

And, as a matter of fact, most of us came from places like North Carolina, Kansas, Utah and Chicago, far, far away from any "Eastern" influence.

One day, Charlie Kuralt came up with an idea for a continuing feature for the "Evening News." He proposed that he and a cameraman and a soundman just get in a van and travel around the country, looking for off-beat stories about ordinary people. We told him to go ahead and we would see how it worked out. And despite the difficulty of shoehorning anything but breaking news into our precious minutes, "On the Road With Charles Kuralt" became a regular fixture on the show. His first spot was about autumn leaves. The series was irresistibly good. Charlie's scripts and interviews were pieces of poetry. My wife says he is the only person on television who can make her cry. I've seen him do it.

The stuff was so good that after a year or two, Birnbaum began assembling collections of the best spots into a half-hour which not only got on in prime time but won critical raves.

My own favorite was a talk with an old black man in Winston-Salem, North Carolina, who made bricks. Kuralt always likes to talk to oldsters. This man and his brother were master brick makers and their bricks had for many years been put into the finest buildings in that tobacco town.

He told Charlie that when they started out as young men he said to his brother:

"We are going to make the finest bricks in North Carolina. That's the only way we are going to get them to call us Mister."

Much has been written about Walter Cronkite and how he functioned as the star of CBS News for all those years. Most of it by people who never worked with him and never had a chance to see him in action.

My association with him was congenial and highly productive. We worked together on a few rush specials on breaking news in the mid-Fifties, but the first really major production he anchored with my unit was "Where We Stand," after the Russian Sputnik orbited the earth in 1957. After that first space adventure, Walter went on to become intensely interested in the subject and was, by a wide margin, the most successful broadcaster covering the American space program. He's still a fan.

Our collaboration went on through the development of "Eyewitness," the Kennedy era, the Warren Report series and years on the "Evening News."

Walter had been designated managing editor after the evening news went to a half-hour. Salant said he thought that title appropriate because Cronkite was at the center of the action every night.

He took great personal interest in the content of the show, proposing we cover this or that, checking on who had been assigned to big stories, suggesting background interviews or follow-up.

He was in his office in the morning and more often than the rest of us had a sandwich at his desk for lunch. (That's where he was when Jack Kennedy was shot.)

Walter could be difficult, especially with writers who worked directly with him and correspondents whose work he found wanting. He was willing to work all hours of the day and night to do the job he thought should be done and he had little use for people who were not willing to do the same.

He is the most competitive person I ever met, always driving to win anything, from children's games to a yacht race to the television ratings contest. What he wanted, for himself and the show, was to be first and best. If NBC covered something that CBS did not have or did a better job on some story, he complained bitterly that our organization was falling apart and our people not working hard enough.

Cronkite thrived on deadline pressure. Sometimes he seemed to deliberately delay getting to his anchor spot to go over the news budget and read copy until it was so late, changing anything could become a crisis. Pressure seemed to act on him like a shot of adrenalin, revving him up to perform in a manner charged with energy. Which was very effective. He visibly enjoyed making changes live on air, adding a new story or cutting to make the thing come out exactly on the second. Which is, of course, the stuff of life for television.

We had differences from time to time about what should be in the lineup, but our news backgrounds were similar and almost always our judgments were the same.

We shared one common overriding goal: Make this the finest news show on television and nothing else. So problems of lesser import withered away.

I know only too well that Ed Murrow is always cited as the role model for television news aspirants. He did indeed do historic reporting on radio from London during the war. And Ed—along with his producer Fred Friendly—did some great things. Their radio program, "Hear It Now," became TV's weekly "See It Now," in 1951. They went on to grapple with many controversial subjects, the highlight being the unmasking of Senator Joe McCarthy in 1954. They also did "Harvest of Shame" about the plight of migrant workers, and reported on many foreign subjects including the Korean war, the Berlin Wall and Africa.

But those productions were carefully produced and packaged. Murrow never did well broadcasting live events such as conventions or election nights. They just didn't fit his style. Cronkite, on the other hand, loved to go on the air live, and he set the standard for how to do it. His successors still have not come up to his level of excellence. He, not Murrow, should be recognized as the legendary television broadcaster of *news*.

My description in these pages of how the "Evening News" is assembled and how and why news judgments are made might make the job of executive producer look like a routine function. It does of course operate with a routine, but it is enormously hard work to make crucial decisions about the content and length of news stories every day, constantly balancing the value of one story against another and, inevitably, dropping a lot of good stuff out of the show. All done with the inflexible deadlines looming and satellite transmissions failing and pieces arriving from far places not properly put together.

Responsibility is indeed taxing, and final responsibility lays a heavy burden on the nervous system. I knew this in advance and was quite serious about setting a two-year deadline on how long I thought it wise to do this job.

Well, *four* years later, I told Gordon Manning it seemed time to talk about replacing me. He was aghast.

"Everything is going beautifully," he said. For God's sake, don't change it now. We are Number One."

It was the spring of 1971, and Gordon and I were on a tour of the domestic news bureaus. I brought the matter up while we were flying to Atlanta and we continued to talk about it as we went on to Los Angeles and Chicago. He simply couldn't believe I was serious.

But I was. I don't know why. The show was indeed Number One and often something to be proud of. It was the top assignment for a news producer. Socolow and Bensley were a pleasure to work with and the staff was highly professional. It was satisfying to do a good job assembling headline stories but not exactly the most creative kind of journalism. I didn't have anything specific in mind to do. Produce my own shows under the "CBS Reports" umbrella, I supposed; Leiser was running my old production unit very successfully.

Gordon was so opposed to the idea of me leaving the show that for months he wouldn't even talk to Dick about it. I guess he thought I would change my mind. Later, I found out that he decided with Bill Leonard to use a change in executive producers as the lever for a major change in the hierarchy. He and Bill would get promotions to senior vice president and a whole new layer of vice presidents would be created.

So by November, Gordon had talked the matter over with Salant and they said okay. They also agreed I could take a trip to Europe and on to Egypt and Israel, where I had never been. Betty came with me to London and Paris and then flew back to work from Rome.

We had a fine time in London, dining with guys in the CBS bureau and my old friends Sy and Stiva Freidin and John Crosby and his new British wife. She was very good for him and he began a new family.

We stayed at the Plaza Athenée in Paris and dined at the Grand Vefour. In Rome, the hotel was the Hassler, at the top of the Spanish Steps, and lunch was with Winston Burdett, the finest American correspondent in Italy.

Winston had a garden apartment on the outskirts of Rome and he drove us there in his tiny Fiat from the CBS bureau, which was in the crowded and very fancy shopping district at the foot of the Steps. It seemed to me an odd location for a news bureau, but Winston explained Mr. Paley liked having his offices in fashionable areas. It was pleasant when he came to visit.

We were joined at lunch by Winston's wife and daughter. When I recalled he did a piece almost every year about the terrible traffic in Rome, it set him off on a long discourse about just how bad it was. Especially, he said, since everyone tried to get to work at the same time every day and many of them drove home to lunch.

When we walked down to the courtyard to drive back to the bureau, I discovered both Mrs. Burdett and her daughter were enroute back to jobs, both driving cars. Winston didn't seem to connect the idea of three cars traveling to lunch with the jammed traffic in the old and narrow streets of Rome.

In Cairo, our correspondent, Bob Allison, introduced me to some very suave guys at the foreign ministry. One of them remarked casually that Egypt would have another war with Israel.

"Why?" I asked. "To regain our national honor," he replied.

When I asked who would win, he said Israel. I was astonished but he was not joking. He really believed his country would—and should—go to war and that it would lose. Strange.

When I got to Tel Aviv, Danny Bloom, the bureau chief, was off on a breaking story somewhere in the Far East. The correspondent was Ed Rabel, who had been assigned to Israel from his native Atlanta. I have seldom seen two people as unhappy as Ed and his wife who, I suspect, had never been out of Georgia. They simply did not understand these Jews they were living among. All they wanted to do was get back home.

But I had the good fortune to find in Tel Aviv an old friend of Betty's, Julian Tomchin, a talented fabric designer. He had decided to put in a year trying to help the Israelis develop their textile industry. He was training young people how to originate new and exciting designs. It was Jules' way of paying some dues to Israel.

It was good fortune for the Rabels, too, because in addition to being witty and charming, Jules really knows how to live well. He took me and the surprised Rabels to excellent little restaurants and clubs they didn't know existed. They were delighted to discover something a little like home.

When I stopped in Rome enroute to New York, there was a cable from Bensley waiting for me at the bureau. It was the announcement of a series of promotions for CBS executives which mentioned as a sort of afterthought that Russ would succeed me on the evening news.

I was very surprised, since Socolow was personally closer to Cronkite than any of us and had literally been his right hand for years. We all had assumed that he would become executive producer. I couldn't figure out how Gordon had talked him into taking over as vice president and editor in charge of news gathering.

I discovered later Gordon had convinced Sandy it was a logical step up the ladder, that he was being groomed to eventually become director of news and perhaps even president of the division. What actually happened was that Sandy got sidetracked in administrative jobs in New York and Washington for several years before he finally did go back as executive producer. A rare selling job by Mr. Manning.

When I got back to New York, it was apparent that the way the announcement had been made by CBS caused many people to think I had been fired off the show.

The transition, after the first of the year, was painless. Russ knew exactly how the show operated there was nothing I could tell him about it.

So it was back to creating rather than just editing the news of the day.

Chapter 22

Documentaries
The Big Picture

BEING ONE OF the world's worst self-promoters, it never occurred to me to seek some agreement about a new assignment before I left the Cronkite show. Get something while you still have something, etc. I just assumed a worthwhile job would be forthcoming. After all, Salant had been quoted in *Variety* as saying, "Midgley can probably write his own ticket."

They gave me a dark office off the first floor corridor and suggested I draw up proposals for possible documentaries. Bud Benjamin, a fine producer and old friend, told me, with obvious reluctance, that he would be executive producer of whatever I did. So it was down a rung on the ladder. But since I always thought "executive producer" sounded terribly pretentious and "producer" should be changed to "editor," it didn't bother me. The news wouldn't dry up; there always was work to be done.

President Nixon was planning a trip to China that winter and another to Russia in the spring. It seemed an excellent time to put together another "Where We Stand" hour to provide some perspective on the state of the world and America's place in it. The idea was approved. Collingwood, now chief European correspondent, was available for it.

My first outline proposed a show which would examine where we stood in:

DIPLOMACY. We had been assured of an air date sometime between the China visit and the Russia visit, which meant the enterprise would have an account of diplomacy at its very highest level.

MUSCLE. The status of our conventional forces, especially in Germany. Indochina. The Poseidon submarine and the Minute Man missile system. Space.

THE ECONOMY. Inflation and unemployment, basic strengths and weaknesses.

NATIONAL STATE OF MIND. Black versus white. The decline of the cities. The old versus the young.

A tall order. But the first "Where We Stand" had been done 15 years before when we had a lot less experience and far fewer resources. Beside I always have maintained "we can do *anything*" on television, that its capacity to explore the most difficult subjects was limited only by our own ability and expertise.

It worked. Collingwood did his usual fine job on the script. We agreed in advance to avoid the obvious pundits, the Kissingers of the world, and instead talk to experts who really knew the score. The result was interviews with people like General James M. Gavin, a great soldier and Ambassador to France; Air Marshal Paddy Menaul, head of Britain's Royal Institute for Defense Studies; Professor Marshal Schulman, head of Columbia University's Russian Institute, and John Paul Vann, one of the ablest hands in Vietnam, chief advisor in beleaguered Binh Dinh province.

That summer, I once again got a chance to go to the Democratic Convention, this time in Miami. When the sessions began to run into the middle of the night—the McGovern people were so dumb, they didn't understand they were losing huge numbers of viewers by so doing—it began to be a strain on Leonard, Wussler and the other executives who were in the control room to make decisions about coverage. They needed *some* sleep. I was a kind of loose executive type so they asked me to sit in the decision slot each day until noon. Very little could be expected to happen that early.

I was there the next morning when we got a call from the remote unit at one of the convention hotels with hot information about the vice presidential race. Ed Fouhy, who was running that crew, said the winner was going to be Senator Thomas Eagleton. I notified New York that we would cut into whatever they had on the air with an "interrupt" bulletin. CBS got the story on well ahead of the other nets, which is the name of the game at conventions.

Conventions had been her first introduction to the worlds of television and big time journalism, and Betty loved them. She came with me and we had a ball wandering around the big zoo and seeing a lot of old friends. We were made most welcome in Walter's anchor booth and a good time was had by all.

The Democrats continued their folly of putting on a late, late show and things ran on until the wee hours. On the final night, I complained that I certainly would like a drink but only beer was available in the hall. Bobby Wussler promptly produced a bottle of scotch from his executive refrigerator and we sat out on the floor watching the hijinks with me feeling better.

I confess I was very impressed by the McGovern nomination. There was an aura of excitement in the great hall, a feeling that the party had been captured—or reclaimed if you will—by the rank and file.

Which gave Betty and me a warm feeling that democracy, with a small "d," was really prevailing. Only later did we realize it had all been a mistake, that the old system of big bosses was the best way for a party to operate.

The "reforms" which gave power to splinter groups and, inevitably, brought about the present chaotic system of primary campaigning, proved to be a burden rather than a blessing on the elective process.

Big Jim Farley could get a Franklin Delano Roosevelt nominated in 1932. One wonders if he could do so today.

The Leiser unit did a whole series of one hour shows about the campaign that summer in the 6-7 P.M. Sunday time period. "60 Minutes" was often scheduled in that time period but it was available in the summer when "60 Minutes" put on rerun shows. (That kind of time is simply not available now for news productions.)

Concerning pre-emptions of "60 Minutes." Don Hewitt was very savvy about where to go with his show. When Manning went charging over to Black Rock seeking an hour of prime time so CBS News could cover some big news development, he often got the answer: "You have your own hour, '60 Minutes.' Pre-empt yourself."

Sometimes Gordon tried to get "60 Minutes" to cover a breaking news story but Don consistently refused. "60 Minutes" had its own format, he said. It was not a news show.

"If you insist on pre-empting our time, let Les produce the show" was his standard answer.

Near the end of the political weekly series, Ernie resigned from CBS News and went to work for ABC. Ernie had been passed over when that batch of vice presidencies had been passed out and he was unhappy about it. Rightly so. As a veteran and talented producer and former news director, he had far more experience in the business than those who had been promoted. (Feisty Carolyn Leiser paid a visit to Dick Salant in his office to chew him out for not promoting her husband.)

Leiser left to follow Harry Reasoner. Harry had been, with Mike Wallace, a star of "60 Minutes." But Wallace was *the* star and egos loom large in television. And despite its excellence "60 Minutes" had not been given a regular time period and was still being bounced around the schedule at the whim of the boys from Black Rock. Who had *absolutely no idea* of what "60 Minutes" could and would become.

Reasoner was the regular substitute for Cronkite on the "Evening News" when Walter was on vacation or otherwise occupied but there was then little prospect of Harry being anything more than a pinch hitter for many years.

ABC was far behind in the evening news competition because many of its affiliate stations did not even carry the network show. ABC moguls figured, rightly, that a star of Reasoner's brilliance would attract more station clearances. In addition to their evening news, ABC agreed to give Harry a half-hour in prime time each week for "The Reasoner Report." Ernie was hired to produce that show.

So I moved into my old office and went back to putting on special shows about big breaking news, plus occasional documentaries.

As an executive producer.

Chapter 23

The Elusive Peace

BACK DEALING WITH NEWS big enough to warrant prime time specials, I found the Vietnam War still right on the front burner. During Christmas week of 1972 we did an hour, "The Elusive Peace," a hard look at what was going on after Henry Kissinger pronounced "peace is at hand" during the Paris peace talks.

Peace failed to arrive. The North Vietnamese left the talks and President Nixon ordered the "Christmas bombing," which has gone into history as an unexplained brutal attack on Hanoi by B-52 bombers. The White House apparently was convinced that such force would finally bring the North Vietnamese to negotiate seriously on terms favorable to the regime of South Vietnam President Thieu.

Collingwood was the principal reporter and wrote his usual excellent script.

Even in hindsight, this show was strong stuff.

(ON CAMERA)

DR. HENRY KISSINGER: We believe that peace is at hand. We believe an agreement is within sight...

PRESIDENT THIEU: When is a just peace, a guaranteed peace. There is no one single obstacle in Vietnam...as long as is the non-just peace, a surrender peace, a peace which give South Vietnam to the Communists, there will be not only one Thieu but seven million and half Thieus who are against that.

LE DUC THO: [speaking in French]

KISSINGER: How do I get out of here?

[I don't know where we got that last line, I guess you might suspect it had been taken out of context.]

Then:

COLLINGWOOD: Good evening. Just two months after the administration announced that peace in Vietnam was at hand, there are now more bombers over North Vietnam every day than ever before in the history of the war. Premature proclamations of impending peace have been made often enough before, but never with such confidence. American reprisals had been undertaken before, but never with such fury.

Bob Schieffer, the Pentagon correspondent: "The difference in this campaign is that scores of 52s are being used for the first time in concentrated attacks around North Vietnam's heavily defended population centers...

"Ironically, the raids were not urged by either military or civilian officials at the Pentagon. In fact, authoritative sources say, Pentagon officials raised serious questions about resumption of the bombing... they also estimated that for every 100 bombers sent over Hanoi and Haiphong, three would be shot down.

"But, in the end," Schieffer said, "these officials bowed to the President's wishes."

Bob Pierpoint from the White House: "All the signs here indicate that President Nixon is frustrated by his failure to bring the war to an end, angered by the refusal of the North Vietnamese to meet what he considers fair terms for a settlement but, above all, determined to force the Communists back to the bargaining table.

"He is aware that much of the world considers the destruction now raining down on North Vietnam to be a savage and tragic mistake. But he is convinced that only when Hanoi has suffered sufficiently will it be willing to negotiate seriously."

Marvin Kalb reviewed the situation at the Paris peace talks, saying Kissinger had believed he could persuade President Thieu to go along with his plans but the Vietnamese leader had balked, fearing his sovereignty was being bargained away. Bernie Kalb reported that Thieu had welcomed the bombing because his power—perhaps his very existence—depended on the continuation of the war.

Former Undersecretary of State George Ball told Bill Plante that bombing had never been successful in destroying morale, that it actually drew people together, gave them a sense of a common danger, a common enemy.

While putting this show together, we tried hard to get official spokesmen from the Pentagon and the White House to explain and/or defend the bombing. We got nowhere. The big wheels had left Washington for the Christmas holiday, but Senator John Tower said he would agree to an interview if it could be done in Texas. It could.

Tower said that he thought the bombing "could have the effect" of bringing the North Vietnamese back to the bargaining table. He said he did not believe the bombing would "stiffen resistance." And when Plante reminded him that 13 B-52s had been lost in the current attacks the Senator said, "Well, this is a risk you always take . . . when you consider that 97 percent of our B-52s get through, I would say that's an acceptable percentage."

Two wives of prisoners of war who had been shot down in previous bombings were interviewed. One said she supported the President in whatever he did.

Mrs. Jeremiah Denton, whose husband had been a prisoner for seven years, said, "I've always tried not to react politically but this time I don't know. It seems to me that this was one of two things, either Dr. Kissinger is not the expert we thought he was—because if—he should certainly have anticipated the hangups, or we were deceived."

[Jeremiah Denton came home to a hero's welcome and was later elected to the United States Senate.]

Collingwood wound up by stating we simply did not know what effect the bombing would have and that peace had eluded the negotiators because both sides were still seeking advantages for themselves.

He said, "The main war, at least, in Vietnam is fitfully approaching its terminal phase, although the hour, the date and the manner of its ending cannot now be foretold."

Charles had been in Vietnam too many times to be more optimistic than that. None of us had any idea then that the date would be as far away as another three years.

I have put down here perhaps too much about this one show but I do so because there was for me a surprising aftermath.

Five days after the show, I got the following memo from Salant: "As I told you on the phone, I thought that 'The Elusive Peace' was first rate. Many thanks.

"For the record (and the mail is already beginning to indicate that we will need the data in answering letters and criticism), can you and Soc, as well as Bill Small, to cover Washington end, give me memos recounting our efforts to find spokesmen from the administration, or on the administration side, on the issue of the resumption of bombing."

Rightly or wrongly, I read into that at the time—and still do—the unspoken message that someone in our higher echelons was getting flak from the White House.

I answered Dick the next day:

Concerning our efforts to get administration spokesmen for "The Elusive Peace":

The week before the broadcast I had conversations with Richardson (Small was away for a few days) and Schieffer about the desirability of having administration and pentagon views about the bombing. Both felt that there should be no problem as we got closer to air.

On Tuesday morning, I got to Small first thing and explained that this was our top priority. We had very strong comments from Clark Clifford and had a date with George Ball and should really have administration comments on what was going on. Small agreed and took the matter up with the White House.

At the same time, I alerted Marvin Kalb to the problem and he talked to Ken Clawson in Herb Klein's office. Small told me later that day that John Scali was working on the matter. Scali agreed someone should appear and thought it could be arranged.

But by Wednesday morning, the word came back—through Small—that Scali had struck out everywhere. (Small had suggested on Tuesday that we go after Admiral Moorer. I enthusiastically urged him on. By Tuesday night, the word was that any Moorer appearance had to be "cleared with the White House."

By Wednesday morning, the only person Scali was able to get was Senator John Tower and he was in Wichita Falls, Texas. We were now only one day away from air, but a call to Senator Tower confirmed that he would indeed appear, that he would go over to the local station if it would be convenient for us. He allowed as how he had "been in touch with the White House" on this matter. Obviously he had talked to Scali.

Marvin told me later that he had seen Scali Tuesday night and that he was surprised that we weren't jumping on the Tower offer with great interest and enthusiasm. But, given that only option, we did indeed get Bill Plante to Texas and cut and fed the piece on Thursday from Dallas.

[Even as I write this, I shudder to think that we even tried to do such things on *the day of air*.]

In the wake of this, some correspondence between Socolow and the New York and Washington producers of the "CBS Morning News" revealed that administration figures had been consistently refusing to appear on the show or comment about anything concerned with the resumption of the bombing.

And just 10 days after our broadcast, Socolow wrote this memo: "On Wednesday, January 10, Bill Small spoke to [White House press secretary Ron] Ziegler and asked him, again, for someone, anyone, from the Administration to explain and/or justify the bombings and Ziegler told Small that he would call when they were ready to go this route. All indications are they are not going to be ready for some time."

And three days later, I sent the following to Gordon Manning:

First, in my view—which is shared by Dan Rather—the real motivation for the bombing is unknown to anyone except the closest circle of Presidential advisers and they are not talking at all. Dan even thinks that only one man, the President himself, knows. We could go around the country and report on the reaction to it—mostly revulsion I would expect—and do the same thing abroad. We could talk to military experts outside the Pentagon about the virtues of bombing. But the real WHY cannot now be discerned.

Second, I think that this bombing campaign has now become, particularly in view of the suspension announced today, another episode in the saga of the Indochina War, just as Tonkin Gulf is one. If it ever is revealed that this terror bombing really worked, that it was the biggest factor in getting the talks going again, that will be a big story. And if it ever is revealed that the losses in planes and pilots were the motivating factor in the renewal of talks, that is the other side of the coin. A story. But that may await the revelations of historians.

There were a lot of terrible things done during the war in Indochina. This "Christmas bombing" must stand as one of the worst.

We did a good job with it. In days.

Exactly 30 days later, we produced a show "The Signing in Paris." The United States had given up on the Indochina war and agreed to leave it to the South Vietnamese.

As a result of that signing, we put on "Operation Homecoming: The Prisoners Return" 16 days later—live in the middle of the night to cover events in a time zone halfway around the world.

America's preoccupation with Vietnam had ended, replaced by concerns over the oil embargo and the problems of energy.

We did no special shows whatsoever about Vietnam in 1974.

But the next year...

Chapter 24

We Lose Frank Stanton

THE YEAR 1973 was very big for news, what with Watergate and Vietnam boiling on the front burner, Agnew resigning in disgrace, and long lines at the gasoline stations caused by a cutoff of oil supplies from the Arabian fields. The re-designated Midgley unit put on 23 shows, one almost every two weeks. One of my basic contentions about television news is "The name of the game is time on the air."

That was a year we really got it.

In the spring, something happened across town that would profoundly affect the news division. It was announced that Frank Stanton would retire as president of CBS Inc. when he reached 65. It was company policy that all employees retire at that age, but when Mr. Paley had become 65 in 1966, he proposed to the board of directors that they ask him to stay on as chairman. They dutifully did so. Stanton knew then he probably never would succeed to the Number One spot.

We in news felt especially bereft because Frank always had taken a close interest in what we did and encouraged and protected us.

It was a custom at CBS to have large parties, often in one of the studios, when long-time executives retired. The studios are huge and great places for parties.

When nothing of this kind was scheduled for Stanton, I told Salant

258

we owed him a great debt and should give him a proper farewell. Dick
said he already had told Frank we wanted to do just that but Stanton had
declined.

"You ask him," Dick said.

So I did.

Sensing that Frank would not agree to a big party, I asked him if
some old timers in the news department could give him lunch. He said
sure.

I drew up a list of about 40 people like Cronkite and Doug Edwards,
Allen Jackson and Eric Sevareid and told them to kick in the necessary.
Everyone was delighted. I booked the Hunt Room at "21" and we had a
fine lunch. Made more festive because that very day a batch of
Nixonian scoundrels who had given Frank a hard time about our
reporting of Watergate were indicted. He arrived in high good humor.
The only speech was by Sevareid, the most eloquent in this bunch.

So if the great corporation couldn't manage a public thank you and
Godspeed, at least the news division could organize its own.

(One of the things Frank Stanton habitually did which endeared him
to workers in the news vineyard was to write notes about the shows we
put on. I got scores of them over the years and even continued to receive
handwritten messages after he left and became head of the American
Red Cross. "Good job last night. Best regards," they would typically
read.)

Stanton was succeeded as president of CBS Inc. by Chick Ireland, an
executive with ITT. Ireland died suddenly not long after taking the job
and was succeeded by a young financial expert named Arthur Taylor,
who came from the International Paper Company and had been an
executive with First Boston Corp. My first experience with his regime
was gratifying and somewhat amusing.

At that time, the news divisions of the three television networks all
earned far less than they spent. They were all big losers—financially,
that is.

When the time came for the various divisions of CBS to present their
annual budget estimates to Mr. Taylor, he discovered the news division
was forecasting it would *lose* about 20 million. He couldn't believe it.

"I have been with companies that lost 20 million," he said, "but I
don't go along with *budgeting* a loss of that size."

Taylor appointed a committee headed by Sheldon Wool, a guy he had brought into the company, to go over to the production center and conduct an inquiry into how these news types could possibly draw up plans to lose a pot of money.

I was told to meet Mr. Wool in Bob Chandler's office one afternoon to explain how the Special Reports unit operated. I arrived to find several people sitting around amid the dregs of a sandwich lunch. Wool and his assistants had just interviewed Casey Davison, who ran the camera crews, editing rooms and technical support staff.

By chance, I had produced one of our rush specials the night before, and Mr. Wool immediately announced he thought it had been great. How much had it cost? he asked.

"Oh I guess about $5,000," I said.

"What," he cried, "they keep telling me it costs up to $100,000 or more to produce a documentary. I thought the show last night was better than almost any hour I have seen. What's going on?"

So we explained that if you had to do something in a few hours or days, there was just *no way* you could spend a lot of money. The only real costs were some staff overtime, payments to the technical crews and rental of a studio and its support facilities. (CBS Inc. charged the news department the same rentals it asked from producers of soap operas. So the technical department's books could show profits. At the expense of the news department.)

Documentaries ran up big costs, we told Mr. Wool, when film crews, producers, writers and their assistants spent weeks or even months traveling to distant locations. They habitually filmed about 10 times more material than appeared in the version which went on the air. (Called shooting 10 to 1 in the trade.)

Such lavish shooting meant a lot of time had to be taken to edit and re-edit a show. The expenses of all this production were written off against a show budget, for accounting reasons. Since a show could not be scheduled until it was ready, the costs simply kept going up and up until the night it actually appeared on the air. When it was written off the books.

Mr. Wool kept mumbling that all our documentaries should be done like the one he had seen the night before. I was amused and, of course, pleased, while knowing all too well it was impossible.

I never saw any report from the Wool Committee but finally someone—most likely William S. Paley—explained the facts of life about news budgeting to Mr. Taylor. In due course, the news budget was approved—with a planned $20 million loss.

I suppose what Arthur did not know then was that news was regarded by Mr. Paley and Dr. Stanton as a very valuable "loss leader." When they went to Washington to talk to the FCC or to congressional committees or other power centers, it was very useful for them to be able to point out the great public service they were performing by keeping the American people informed by a news service that cost the company 20 MILLION DOLLARS A YEAR. It also was good public relations.

This state of affairs was all right with us, although it led to a lot of scornful grumbling from television network honchos like Jack Schneider and Mike Dann.

Look, they said, we make great gobs of money with entertainment shows in prime time and soap operas for housewives during the day, only to see a lot of it turned over to a wasteful news division. Dann even used to maintain that if he had control over news, he would show us how to attract bigger audiences and thus make money. He never got the assignment.

But since these chaps controlled the precious time on the air, Salant and Manning had to go to them each time they wanted to pre-empt time for special broadcasting.

What Dann had in mind, of course, was more "show business" in the news broadcasts. And television news has, willy nilly, adopted many of the techniques of entertainment broadcasting, especially the glitz and glitter effects pioneered by the producers and directors of television sports.

And the anchor persons on television news have become great stars, often outshining and certainly outlasting their counterparts in entertainment. Paid now not in the hundred of thousands but in the millions a year. Which is the acid test of celebrity.

And, curiously, what gave television news the biggest shove toward show business was that old debbil money.

Twenty-five years ago, the news department of CBS operated with an annual budget of around $50 million.

But over the years, news began to earn more and more, and in 1977 came a great turnaround. There were no deficits and news actually became, first, profitable, then very profitable. A 30-second spot in the

Cronkite evening news which had been sold for $25 thousand began commanding $60 thousand. And when "60 Minutes" finally moved into its 7 P.M. Sunday night slot, it became almost immediately the most profitable show on television.

News became what the industry calls a "profit center." And, inevitably, when budget time came around, the question to news executives was not "What can you get by with this year?" but "How much *more* money are you going to make this year than you made last year?"

A new generation of news executives seemed willing to accept as their first priority the production of profits. Which require big audiences. And if big audiences require show business techniques, so be it.

And it is.

Chapter 25

Watergate
Nixon Down the Drain

WHETHER TELEVISION NEWS was fair to him or not, Richard Milhous Nixon had been re-elected President in 1972 by a whopping majority, but his administration began to come apart the following year. The Watergate affair scandalized Congress and it became evident that if the President did not resign, he would probably be impeached by the House of Representatives.

While busy during the winter putting on shows about the peace talks in Paris, the withdrawal of Americans from Vietnam and the subsequent return of American prisoners, I also put together a documentary, "The Long War—Congress Versus the President."

We had two natural stars. Nixon and his buddies thoroughly detested Dan Rather, the White House correspondent. The President himself had boosted Dan's status as a celebrity by asking, at one of his carefully orchestrated campaign press conferences: "Are you running for something?"

"No, Mr. President," Dan came back, "are you?"

And Roger Mudd was well established as the best broadcast correspondent on Capitol Hill, knowledgeable, precise, unflappable. He liked to make a little fun of the distinguished lawmakers. They didn't seem to resent it; they admired Roger.

"Congress Versus the President" was a good example of documentary treatment of a breaking news story. The subject matter and the issues involved were very much on the front burner. And we put it together fast.

It began with reports on two current flaps between the President and the Congress: One, the attempt by Nixon to "impound" funds appropriated by the legislators and thus thwart their will, and, two, the President's contention that he had the right of "executive privilege" which could be extended to his personal aides to prevent them from being questioned by congressional committees.

These segments were followed by an historical review of the seesaw relationship between the two branches of government which sometimes saw a strong President dominating a weak Congress and sometimes the reverse.

Then came profiles of and interviews with Senator Sam J. Erwin of North Carolina speaking for Congress and John D. Ehrlichman, Nixon's domestic affairs adviser, defending his boss.

In his *New York Times* review, John J. O'Connor wrote that the subject matter almost dictated that the show have a lot of "talking heads," which he and other critics of television always have decried. (These fellows seem never to notice that "60 Minutes" is almost nothing *except* talking heads.)

O'Connor followed that observation by writing, "for the occasion, Mr. Rather and Mr. Mudd were given a new and elegant setting by Leslie Midgley, the executive producer."

"On a large and spare set," he wrote, "the two correspondents sat between giant mockups of the seals of the Presidency and Congress. The seals were designed to revolve and filmed portions of the program would begin on their reverse sides. The result was just a touch too elegant and both correspondents seemed suitably self-conscious at times."

Mr. O'Connor obviously caught something going on but did not discern what it was. What he saw but did not grasp was a powerful mutual antipathy—or something stronger if you like—between Rather and Mudd.

It was kind of him to credit me with the "elegant" set, but it had actually been copied from one developed by Leiser for Harry Reasoner's ABC show. As the big seals turned around, new pictures were supposed to be revealed in the circles before they filled the whole screen. This was before the days of a lot of electronic trickery and the seals, which were about three feet in diameter, were physically turned by electric motors.

When we got set up in Studio 41, the biggest in the production center, the stars were on their stools, the four cameras warmed up and ready, the control room and tape machines manned and up to speed— and the director, Joel Banow, couldn't get pictures to appear as the seals turned around.

One of the problems with television technicians is that they love to play with their gadgets. It is a game of electric trains for grownups. Banow became totally absorbed in the problem of the turning disks and simply didn't pay any attention to what was going on out on the studio floor.

Paddy Chayevsky portrayed this phenomenon brilliantly in his great movie *Network*. When the crazy anchor man announces that he is going to kill himself on television, the director and his assistants are chatting up a girl in the control room, totally oblivious to what is going out over the air. It does, believe me, really happen.

As Joel continued to fiddle and a 15 minute delay became an hour, Mudd and Rather were getting very restless and unhappy. Their mutual dislike, perhaps rooted in competitive aspirations, began to surface more and more clearly.

I simply had to overrule a director in his own control room, insist that the delays be ended, and tell everyone that the taping would start in five minutes whether or not the turning seals worked. I warned Banow that he was leaving his show on the studio floor, but he didn't understand what I was talking about.

We finally got the thing taped and it worked well. Even the turning seals, as Mr. O'Connor noted.

As soon as we got "Congress Versus the President" on the air in March, I was told to get going on an hour about Watergate to be broadcast two months later when the Senate Select Committee would begin its hearings into the Watergate scandal.

Socolow, now the boss of the news gathering organization, told me he had long ago instructed the Washington bureau to organize a master file of material about Watergate which he was sure would be of great value.

In Washington, I found that Bill Small, the bureau chief, had turned the assignment over to his assistant and confidant, Sylvia Westerman. She had, I was dismayed to discover, simply told one of the associate producers of "Face the Nation" to do it. But the woman had "been so busy," nothing had been assembled.

Dan Schorr, CBS News' principal reporter on Watergate, told me he had extensive files but they proved to be almost all clippings from the *Washington Post*, whose Woodward and Bernstein team had broken the story and covered it far better than any other reporters.

I had known Schorr before he went to work for CBS, and in my opinion, he was not by a long shot the best reporter on our staff, although *he* seemed to think so. Dan had been given the assignment because he didn't have a regular Washington beat and it was not seen early on as a White House story. Clouded crystal ball.

So we had to do our own research.

By this time, I was confident about my ability to size up a story, get a staff going on film and script and have the thing on the air fast. But this was a VERY BIG story, full of pitfalls—such as administration wrath if we got anything wrong—and we had just seven weeks to get it together.

I suspect the experience of 15 years in television news and making a thousand lineups for the "Evening News" had entered my subconscious when it came time to organize this one. In any event, things worked out well. The show was a big winner.

It opened with Dan Rather against a black background. He said:

Unfolding before this country is what many people now regard as the worst political scandal in our nation's history—the Watergate Affair. That scandal will be the subject of a special Senate hearing, set to begin Thursday.

In the next hour, we'll take a look at that committee and what it hopes to accomplish, and at these other aspects of the Watergate story.

THE CASE OF THE WATERGATE itself—a burglary that opened a Pandora's box.

THE CASE OF THE COVERUP—attempts to keep the lid on the box.

THE CASE OF THE MONEY—lots of it available in cash for suspicious enterprises.

THE CASE OF DANIEL ELLSBERG—whose trial has been connected to the Watergate burglars.

THE CASE OF CAMPAIGN '72—and how it may have been sabotaged.

And THE CASE OF THE PRESIDENT—what are his chances now of governing successfully.

That tease staked out clearly how the show was constructed and needs little further elaboration.

Rather set up the basic premise of the show and led into Roger Mudd, standing in the Senate Caucus Room, where the hearings would be held. He explained the powers of the Senate Select Committee and then went into the niftiest series of short profiles I ever read or heard.

About the chairman, Sam Ervin: "Magnificently mobile eyebrows. Is believed, by the Senate at least, to be its greatest Constitutional lawyer."

About Howard Baker: "Known back home as Harrad...no longer regarded as the administration's water boy."

Herman Talmadge: "Said to be very smart. Does his homework. Self-contained, independent. Smokes big cigars and chews tobacco."

Joseph Montoya: "A professional politician since the age of 21. Said to be a lightweight."

And more.

Schorr reported on the alleged coverup and Fred Graham, CBS news legal specialist, did an excellent job on the Daniel Ellsberg robbery case, produced on the West Coast by David Browning.

The show was very well received by newspaper critics, especially for the manner in which it was presented. And by TIME magazine yet!

"The Senate and the Watergate Affair was distinguished by brilliant organization. Its juxtaposition of denials by leading Nixon Administration officials with the facts as subsequently confirmed pointed up the spectacular sordidness of Watergate far more graphically than can be done by the printed media."

From the guru of the print media!

And it won an Emmy award.

Rather called me a few months later to say he had found out Spiro Agnew had been caught in corruption so flagrant he would either be forced out or, more likely, resign.

"I can't believe it," I said. "Agnew too?"

"Absolutely," he said. "The case is stronger than the one against Nixon."

The Agnew story broke one afternoon and was covered by news bulletins in regular entertainment programming. I was told to put together a special hour at 10 P.M. *That very night.*

Cronkite was the anchor man. We put together a summary of the Agnew case—cash kickbacks from his days as Governor of Maryland, some of which had actually been delivered in his vice presidential office—plus a history of the vice presidency, an analysis by Graham of how Agnew's court plea would affect his future as a private citizen and lawyer. We had an interview with Paul Freund of Harvard, the nation's leading expert on constitutional law and a wrapup and analysis panel with correspondents Rather, Bruce Morton, Bob Schakne and Eric Sevareid.

Salant raved about the show.

And, finally, as the Nixon regime was falling apart and he prepared to depart the White House for California, we put on "The Embattled President."

It was the end.

Chapter 26

The Trouble With Rock

COME SUMMER OF 1974, I was handed a very hot potato that involved not only different areas of CBS News but separate divisions of the CBS Inc. conglomerate.

A grand jury had been convened 12 months before in Newark, N.J., to look into charges of corruption and payola in the phonograph record industry. CBS Records was the industry's leader in pop music sales and the most profitable division of CBS Inc. Leaks from the grand jury indicated CBS Records was being investigated.

Clive Davis had been president of the record division for six years. He was well known for being able to spot rock and roll talent and have them cut records which turned into smash hits. and thus made a bundle of money.

But in 1973, David was fired by CBS, which alleged he had "misappropriated" some $80,000 of the company's money. It turned out that most of the dough had been used to pay for a lavish bar mitzvah for Davis' son at the Plaza Hotel. Scores of rock stars and other music industry figures had attended, and Davis maintained it was just an expense account item. The company didn't buy that and used the "misappropriation" as an excuse to get rid of him. But there was more to it than a big party.

David Wynshaw, one of Davis' assistants, had been called before the grand jury and questioned about the distribution of some $300,000 in various ways to stimulate sales of CBS records. There were rumors that drugs had been provided for rock stars and record distributors. Wynshaw was fired.

There really wasn't anything all that new about the story. References to drugs were made openly by the biggest rock stars and some of them, like Janis Joplin, had died of overdoses. Code words for drugs were inserted into song lyrics. It was common knowledge that some "artist and repertoire" men, as people dealing with musicians are called in the industry, paid off radio station disk jockeys to get certain songs played on the air.

Such shenanigans upset Arthur Taylor and not just on moral grounds. CBS Records was part of an organization that owned enormously valuable broadcasting properties, licensed by the federal government. Any suggestion of scandal was to be avoided lest the licenses be put at risk. The television quiz show scandals of the Sixties had not been forgotten and broadcasters were very sensitive about their public image.

And there was another angle. Watergate was still a hot topic and revelations about it on television news had not endeared the broadcasters to conservative Republicans and their friends.

Pat Buchanan, a right-wing syndicated columnist, wrote a piece complaining that network TV news departments were always ready to expose and condemn corruption in other people's affairs, but seemed to have a blind eye when something funny was going on in their own back yards.

Which prompted Dick Salant to tell an interviewer that CBS News would conduct an investigation into the allegations of corruption in the record industry and would put the results of the inquiry on the air. No matter who was involved.

When the story about the grand jury first broke, I wrote a memo proposing we produce a documentary about it. The proposal was turned down because, Salant said, a decision had been made to develop a multi-part series on the matter for the Cronkite news.

Stanhope Gould, a talented producer, was put in charge of the series. Stan's hippy style of dress and hair didn't exactly fit the image of a Harvard man, which he is. And he had enjoyed pot and other exotic things with thrilled younger members of the staff.

Gould got Linda Mason, a fine associate producer, assigned to work with him, and Bob Schackne was appointed on-air talent.

Almost a year later, Stan finally showed Cronkite, Paul Greenberg, now the executive producer, Socolow and others involved rough cuts of five parts which he proposed be shown on successive nights for a week.

There were interviews with "a former employee" who said on camera he had handed out drugs while working for CBS. Another interview was with "a sales representative for a black record company," filmed in shadow because he was afraid to be identified. He said he had paid off disk jockeys for radio play, claiming it was done all the time. Davis and Wynshaw had refused to be interviewed, as had officials of CBS Records. Gould had material linking Wynshaw with one Pat Falcone, said to be a Mafia figure in New York. Falcone had many dealings with Wynshaw, some of them right in Black Rock.

The Cronkites simply couldn't see it as worth time on their show. The Newark grand jury investigation had fizzled out and the story had been dormant for a long time. To them, it just wasn't part of daily news. I don't think for a minute that Walter or any of the others were concerned about the involvement of CBS Inc. On the contrary, if they thought it was legitimate news, they would have been delighted to have it.

But there was still the promise by Salant that CBS News would investigate the story and make it public. Bill Leonard asked me to look at the material to see if it could and should be made into a documentary. Stan and Linda brought their reels to our screening room, and, now the "soft news" vice president, I looked at the stuff. After which I took Stan to lunch.

Stan was upset and angry. Not at me especially, although he obviously suspected I was ready to emasculate his big story. He felt he had been let down by old comrades on the Cronkite show and by Leonard and Salant because they were afraid his revelations would displease the big brass.

I asked Stan flatly what he wanted now. He said it was to have his material about corruption in the record business go on the air.

Would he be satisfied if I managed to use it in the context of a larger framework, which would include a look at the whole phenomena of the rock music explosion? He said yes—*if* the corruption angle was not squeezed to meaningless proportions and that section of it dealing with CBS was not watered down or dropped.

I said I thought we could work it out, although I didn't think much of the allegations by nameless and faceless men and thought Schackne's script had too many "according to sources" lines.

I told Leonard we could produce an hour about the record business which would be informative and very entertaining, because we would naturally work into it performances by the most popular rock stars. And we could use the Gould material. He said to give it a shot.

I suggested that David Culhane, one of our best young correspondents, be given the assignment. Schackne was delighted to be relieved of this hazardous duty. Culhane, not all that happy to be involved in what might turn out to be a nasty intra-company brawl, started to work.

The first thing I did was have a long talk with Bob Jones, my close friend from Salt Lake days. Bob had recently retired as art director of RCA Records to play with his beloved Glad Hand Press in Stamford.

Jones had started designing covers for Columbia Records after being discharged from the Army and had gone on to supervise the production of covers at RCA Victor. He knew the business inside out and I asked him to tell me just how it worked.

Bob explained that pop records, especially those made by the new generation of rock and roll stars, could be turned into gold mines by promotion and exploitation. This was so, he said, because it only cost about $50,000 to rent a studio and cut a master disk with a singer and some musicians. And if an album or a "single" sold only about 50,000 copies, it could essentially break even.

BUT. If its sales could, by hook or crook, be pushed up into the millions, the profits were enormous. And it happened all the time. Because the cost of the master disk was the whole investment, innumerable copies could be squeezed from it and they cost very little.

This presented the A&R men with irresistible temptation, Bob went on. They would do *anything* to get a release up into the big sales leagues. Anything.

Sure there was a lot of payola to disk jockeys, he said. There always had been. It was part of the business. The head offices looked the other way while the field men paid off with whatever was necessary. Dough, girls, drugs, you name it.

Since Bob knew the whole score and was totally trustworthy, I had a pile of valuable free research.

The second thing I did was call Goddard Lieberson, who had succeeded Clive Davis as president of CBS Records. Goddard was a fine guy, the most intelligent and cultured man in the music industry. He had been president of Columbia Records for many years before Davis took over during the rock era. Goddard's principal interest had been serious and classical music and he had been instrumental in building up Columbia's catalogue of fine recordings. He had been called back after the Davis/Wynshaw scandal.

Ever the gent, Goddard received me pleasantly, listened to my problem and politely declined to have anything to do with a show about problems in his business.

"What good would it do me?" he asked. "After the show, everyone would say, 'Gee, I saw you in that show about scandals in the record business.' No thanks."

He said no one at CBS Records would appear on the show but that Bob Altschuler, the public relations vice president, would provide us with the standard "press information." Bob, obviously unhappy, said the records people couldn't figure out why the news division was after them.

I heard later about an incident that might have affected Lieberson's attitude, although I would not have participated either had I been in his shoes.

When Gould had been putting his material together, he took a film crew and Bob Schackne over to Sixth Avenue and positioned him so that the famous CBS "Black Rock" building was the background for Bob standing across the street.

Bob read for the camera opening and bridge lines that went something like: "The spreading scandal in the pop music business has involved officials of CBS Records, whose offices are here in midtown Manhattan... among the matters being investigated are allegations of payola to have records played on radio stations and claims that some CBS Records employees not only used drugs but dealt them out to rock stars..." etc. etc.

Irwin Segelstein, a very smart and funny man, was then an executive at CBS Records. One day, he looked out the window and saw Schackne and a film crew across the street. He took the elevator down to the ground floor and walked over behind the camera to listen to what Schackne was saying.

He came back upstairs, went to the CBS Records offices and said: "You guys wouldn't believe what is going on down there."

Irwin was right; they wouldn't believe it.

When my own enterprise was nearing completion, Salant phoned to say that Arthur Taylor wanted to see the two of us in his office in Black Rock. Arthur asked us to describe for him what the show would consist of. I told him the kind of material I had inherited from Gould and how we had fleshed it out into a report on the whole record industry.

He was obviously unhappy to have one part of the company he presided over saying nasty things about another part. But when I mentioned Wynshaw, he sighed and said he had ordered his own investigation and had concluded that Mr. Wynshaw was "perhaps the worst person" he had ever met. He did not give us any instruction whatsoever about how to proceed.

We did interviews with people who knew the score about the record scene and finally stitched a rough version of the show together using Gould's interviews with pop music critics like Albert Goldman and Richard Goldstein. They were very good.

The Culhane script started out by noting that the record industry had *tripled* its income in three years—to TWO BILLION DOLLARS A YEAR. More than 75 percent of it came from rock hits.

The dimensions of the industry were almost incredible. Its income exceeded *all* the receipts from professional sports combined. Baseball, football, racing—everything. Culhane explained that radio play had become the key to creating a big hit and A&R men would do anything to get a record played over and over again.

Critic Goldman's opinion:

"Rock is the most important cultural event in American history. It cracked a shell and out came a generation of freaks."

The last half of our rough cut included Gould's corruption charges, which I found far less interesting than the out-in-front aspects of this weird business.

Since no one from CBS would appear, Culhane read statements from CBS Records management denying any wrongdoing. Only Joe Smith, the president of Warner Records, was interviewed from high executive levels. Smith said it was against his and other companies' policy to have anything to do with payola or drugs, but that he could not deny they might have been used by individuals anxious to promote record sales.

Morris Diamond, a West Coast record promoter, told how a disk jockey handed his insurance payment book to a record promoter, who promised to send in the payments on time. "Payola on the installment plan," Culhane called it.

Culhane had rock superstar Mick Jagger saying, "People in all industries graft and rock's another industry to a lot of people and so they graft. It seems it's part of business, part of the American way of life."

We decided to put Culhane in a recording studio rather than on a television set to do his opening and closing narration. While he was doing that filming, I got a call from him.

"You better come over here," Culhane said. "We have a lot of trouble with Stan. He's threatening to take his name off the credits and 'go public' with complaints about the show."

I got in a cab and went over to the studio. Stan was objecting—somewhat late, I told him—to the way the show had been organized. I finally got him calmed down and he agreed not to make any trouble. At least not then. David was very nervous, fearing that if Gould told reporters the show was a whitewash, he, Culhane, would be in big trouble with the press and public. And he knew, of course, that the whole project was resented by some people high up in the company.

"The Trouble With Rock" finally went on the air at 6 P.M., Sunday, August 11, 1974. Late, but fulfilling Salant's pledge to investigate the scandal and broadcast the results no matter who was involved.

We got some complaints in the press that the show had been "buried" in the middle of summer and had not been sufficiently publicized in advance. Because, ran the speculation, it involved CBS Inc. I was surprised that it didn't get huzzahs for just that reason. But I had learned long before not to worry about what was written about television news. Most of the "critics" were astonishingly misinformed and often just plain lazy. At this point in the history of television, there were no Jack Goulds or John Crosbys around.

Morris Diamond, the aforementioned record promoter, sued CBS, claiming he had been maligned and that his business had suffered grievously.

As is usual in such cases, CBS did not have its own legal department defend the case, but retained instead Cravath, Swaine & Moore, an expensive Wall Street firm. Cravath lawyers interviewed all of us at great length, often at expensive restaurants which they could bill as expenses. The case was finally tried in Los Angeles and thrown out of court.

I produced about 1,500 shows for CBS News, and this was the only one that resulted in a law suit.

"The Trouble With Rock" was lively, entertaining and informative about a huge, popular cultural institution. Birnbaum and I had a lot of fun working on it and were pleased with the result. I still am when I look at the tape today.

There was a postscript.

At the next meeting of the CBS Inc. board of directors, one member of the board—I presume Goddard Lieberson—said he would like to raise a question about why one division of CBS would go about investigating and broadcasting information detrimental to a sister division.

Another director spoke up.

"Listen," he said, "the man promised we would conduct the investigation and put the results on the air. It was done and the building is still standing. Let's go on to other business."

They did. That director was William S. Paley.

Chapter 27

We Lose Jack Benny

With a Great Goodbye

THE SPECIAL REPORTS UNIT ended 1974 with what can only be called a bang. On Sunday, December 29, we had *two* one-hour shows on the air. One from 7:30 to 8:30, another from 9:30 to 10:30. Maybe a record.

The second one was the traditional "Television Album," a review of the year's greatest pictures, written and anchored by the talented John Hart. Good show.

But the 7:30 hour was one of my all-time favorites among the hundreds I produced for CBS News. It was done in three days.

Christmas was on Wednesday that year, and the next day came news that the great comedian Jack Benny had died in Los Angeles. There were the usual tributes on the daily news show. Then something else hove into sight.

Betty and I were having dinner in our apartment in New York on Thursday night when Fred Silverman, programming director of the CBS Television Network, called. He asked if we could put together a special show as a tribute to Benny. I—as always—said of course, we could do anything. Silverman had never before called me directly about programming.

Betty and I began to talk about how we might get in touch with Benny's family and associates. She said John Green, the composer and her first husband, was a close personal friend of Jack and Mary Benny and would know who to call. John did indeed know and gave me the names and phone numbers of Benny's agent, lawyer and others.

The next morning, I was in my office alone. My secretary, along with most of the staff, had taken Christmas week off. The phone rang and it was Bill Small, who said that if we were going to do anything special about Jack Benny, William S. Paley would like to be part of it.

The minute Bill said those words I knew beyond the shadow of a doubt there was no "if" involved. CBS News was indeed going to "do something special" about Jack Benny. Bill gave me a phone number in Nassau and said to call Mr. Paley.

Now I also knew who was going to do the "something."

I called the number and found myself talking to The Chairman. He said he was writing a tribute to his old friend. I told him we would get a correspondent and a crew to Nassau to record it on video tape. He said okay and asked that they be sure to bring "idiot cards" with his words spelled out in big block letters which he could read off-camera. He said he didn't want to try to memorize the tribute.

He called me back in the afternoon and read what he had written. He then asked, anxiously, if I thought it was all right.

I said yes.

I took the statement down on my typewriter as he dictated and read it back to him. Then I took it down to the art department to get the cards lettered.

This was not some whim. Jack Benny meant a lot to him, personally and professionally. After the war, William S. Paley had returned to New York to take back the reins of his Columbia Broadcasting System. His biggest challenge was to overtake the National Broadcasting Company, which was far ahead in the race for audiences in the entertainment part of radio broadcasting. The part that was beginning to make big money. CBS was very strong in news because of its excellent work covering the war, but NBC had the most popular entertainers under contract.

In 1948, Paley began a serious campaign to sign up NBC's biggest stars for CBS. One of the first pieces of major talent he bagged was

Jack Benny, whose Sunday evening radio program was a national institution. It was reported in later years that one reason for Paley's success in this talent raid was that he figured out how entertainers with big incomes could defer payment of federal income taxes, which were beginning to reach very high levels.

After Benny moved over to Paley's network, they became close personal as well as business friends. Which was why The Chairman wanted to pay a tribute to Jack Benny.

Silverman and his boss, Jack Schneider, decided Friday that the Benny tribute would appear on Sunday evening. Which meant we would at least have one very timely element: The funeral was scheduled for Sunday afternoon, and because of the three-hour time difference between the coasts, we would have it on very soon after the actual ceremony. (The eulogy was to have been delivered by George Burns, but Bob Hope took over when Burns became too emotional to continue.)

Other potential elements that went onto my yellow pad were interviews with Benny's close friend Danny Kaye, and actors who had been in his comedy troupe on the air. Such as Eddie Anderson, who played his valet, Rochester; Mel Blanc, who had a great repertoire of comic voices; Frank Nelson; Dennis Day, the singer who was a regular foil for Benny's wit, and Don Wilson, the announcer.

And, of course, the Paley tribute.

All of the above were practical and possible and did indeed turn out well. But what we needed most was the toughest to get, films of Benny's comic routines after he went on from radio to television. Bernie Birnbaum went into action and proved again his skill at getting things done. He quickly found a few brief film excerpts in the CBS film library and other film archives around New York. But the great bulk of the stuff was in vaults in Los Angeles. And this was Christmas week with almost every entertainment office closed.

After hours on the phone, Bernie determined that Wayne & Schuster had produced a Benny omnibus show a few years before which, as he put it, "has done our work for us." It was a compilation of the greatest punch-line sequences of the Benny years. But the 35mm film was in the Hollywood vaults of Universal pictures, which owned it. Bernie somehow got a print out of the vault and into the hands of our LA bureau, promising over and over we would not use it without permission from a certain Universal vice president who was off somewhere for the holidays. The print was shipped to New York overnight.

I had originally decided to send Kuralt to get the Paley tribute and, hopefully, also an interview. But Bernie pointed out that Charlie was the ideal man to write the script and anchor the broadcast. As I say, Kuralt is a poet and the script was lovely.

So David Culhane went to Nassau. Let Mr. Paley read his prepared script, I told David, then try to get him to answer a few questions. Zeke Siegel, the Atlanta bureau chief, went with the tape crew to meet Culhane on the island. The tape was recorded on Saturday, and Zeke flew to Miami and fed it to us in New York.

When we looked at it, Charlie said we should throw away the prepared statement and use Paley's answers to some questions Culhane had posed. He was certainly right, the big boss stumbled trying to read from the cards and had to go through several takes. But he really came alive answering Culhane's questions.

I told Charlie that if Mr. Paley wanted to write and read a statement on his own network he was entitled. But in the end, I used a combination of some of the formal statement and some of the interview. It was fine.

So was the stuff from Universal, which we had transferred from film to tape. It contained sequences that would work beautifully with the Mel Blanc and Dennis Day interviews and others which showed Benny delivering his most famous laugh lines.

Bernie was on the phone most of Saturday arguing with people at Universal Studios. He explained, loudly, to the vice president's assistant how the use of this material on our show would be a great thing for the studio, that its exposure on a network show would increase its value, that the studio owed it to the American people to let them see Jack Benny at his best on this sad occasion. And so on and so forth.

My memory was that we used the stuff without the required permission, but Birnbaum says he did finally get an okay. Maybe. Anyway, nobody squawked.

Kuralt, as he often did during our many collaborations, came up with the perfect opening for the show. He told the director to have the prop department find an old, cathedral-shaped radio and put it on a table beside his stool.

We should open, he said, with the sound of a scratchy violin playing the Benny theme, "Love in Bloom," followed by the familiar, "Hello again. This is Jack Benny..."

The set was dead black with a huge blow-up of Rene Bouche's famous caricature of Benny leaning pensively on his left hand.

Kuralt began by evoking memories of all those Sundays we gathered around the radio set to laugh at the master of comedy.

Followed by some great routines, such as Jack trying to pick up a salesgirl—Mary Livingstone—in a women's clothing store. A song-and-dance with George Burns and Bing Crosby.

And:

Stickup man holding gun:
"Your money or your life."
Silence from Benny. Laughter from audience...wanes.
More silence, more laughter.
Stickup man:
"Well?"
Benny:
"I'm thinking, I'm thinking."
Prolonged laughter.

Then came Dick Threlkeld's coverage of the funeral attended by Bob Hope, George Burns, Jimmy Stewart, Cesar Romero, Rosalind Russell, Milton Berle and Governor Ronald Reagan. Followed by the Danny Kaye and Bill Paley interviews.

At the end came a pair of violin performances, Jack Benny playing Bach with Issac Stern at a benefit performance to save Carnegie Hall and what Kuralt described as "that unforgettable duet with Giselle MacKenzie" of "Tea for Two."

A great show. Maybe my favorite among the hundreds I put together.

The phones began ringing in the control room as we went off the air. One of the callers was Betty, who said Fred Silverman had called. He wanted to tell me what a great show it had been. When she told him I was at the studio, he seemed astonished. We had done the show live? I guess that's one difference between news and entertainment programming.

Salant's memo the next day contained the lines: "The Benny special last night was magnificent—absolutely stunning. Freddie Silverman called me to say he couldn't understand how we had done so marvellously well so rapidly—it was the best thing of its kind he had ever seen."

From Frank Stanton (in retirement): "Beautiful job on Benny. Congratulations."

Wire from Bob Wood, president of the television network: "Tribute to Jack Benny was at the same time a true tribute to CBS News. Simply superb."

From Jack Schneider: "Please accept my rave and add it to all the others you have undoubtedly received. This was a very tasteful and skillful effort which is all the more remarkable since it was done on such short notice."

Zeke Siegel discovered on Saturday that the CBS affiliate in Miami had scheduled a local sports event for 7:30 P.M. Sunday and didn't plan to run the show. Since the only way Mr. Paley could see it in Nassau was a relay from Miami, we got the CBS brass to change the station's plans and, at least, put the show on after their sports event.

The next morning, I found a note on my desk:

At 10:01 P.M. Sunday night, Mr. Paley called from Nassau to say the Jack Benny show was 'just great.'"

Chapter 28

A War That Is Finished

THE WHOLE SAGA of the Americans in Indochina—58,000 men dead, countless thousands wounded, vast treasure expended, civilian morale torn apart—seemed, at last, to be coming to an end.

In March 1975, we did a show about Cambodia, which was falling to the Communists after the flight of the US-supported dictator Lon Nol. Fearful slaughter and destruction were being inflicted on what had previously been a peaceful and tranquil kingdom.

Vietnam appeared to be on the same course, and on April 8, we put on an hour, "Indochina 1975: The End of the Road?"

I got the go-ahead for this show on March 24 and had just 12 days to get it together.

One of the first things I did was to ask Bob Simon, who had done brilliant reporting in Vietnam, to leave his post in London and fly immediately to Saigon to work on the show. I told him to take along Jim Clevenger, who had done a great job with John Laurence in the boonies. Clevenger would be our producer in Saigon, and Bernie and Hal Haley would work in New York.

These are classy people and the result was my own idea of just what an up-to-the-minute television documentary should be.

It had a fine script and performance by Collingwood in New York and dramatic, sometimes daring, coverage from our correspondents in Vietnam. It turned out to be a perceptive forecast of what happened exactly three weeks later. And the task of putting it together gave us a leg up on what we had to do then.

"End of the Road?" started with Charles explaining, with a map, that Thieu had decided to abandon positions held by his troops in the central highlands. The ARVN soldiers pulled out of a small but strategically important place called Ban Me Thout in great disorder and a sense of panic seemed to sweep through the whole army. Soldiers began to throw away their arms and join a huge river of refugees fleeing down the coastal roads toward Saigon to escape what they believed to be imminent capture by the North Vietnamese army.

Actually, both the retreating ARVN troops and even the refugees were moving faster than their pursuers, but rumors turned the retreat into a rout as officers left their commands, leaving no one in charge.

When the fleeing people got to Hue, they thought they might be safe, only to be told to go on south.

Bruce Dunning was in a plane on the airfield at Da Nang when frightened men, women and children tried to clamber up the rear steps even while the pilot was gunning the craft down the runway. There was wild confusion as people fell or were pushed off the steps. After the plane lifted off, Dunning reported grimly that 90 percent of the passengers were not women and children but deserting South Vietnamese airmen.

The great rout continued through Da Nang, Na Trang and on to the naval base at Cam Ranh Bay. The base was supposed to be strongly defended but it turned out no troops were there at all. The whole place was wide open.

Simon gave us a dramatic piece from Vung Tau, where a ship from Cam Ranh had arrived packed with starving and dying refugees. The South Vietnamese navy had abandoned even this death ship. Vung Tau was a beach resort favored by the rich of Saigon.

Collingwood reprised the collapse of Cambodia, and Dick Threlkeld, a young CBS News star, gave us an update from Phnom Penh, Cambodia, then being turned into a ghost town by its captors.

In answer to the question of why this was all happening, Collingwood explained that the United States had "created in Vietnam an army in the image of its own." With the same uniforms, artillery and planes, "The *fourth largest* air force in the world."

The Vietnamese pilots were okay, he went on, but there never were enough mechanics to keep the planes flying, although Americans went back there to work on them under contracts as civilians.

Air Marshal Nguyen Cao Ky, who had been ousted from the government by Thieu, said on camera, "I am afraid we picked up a lot of bad habits from you Americans. When things got hot in the field, you always called for artillery and air support. So did we. But that is not the right way to fight a war here."

Bob Simon also gave us a piece from the ARVN base at Tay Nihn, just north of Saigon. There had been 800 planes on the base two years before, he said. Now only 250 remained. What the Vietnamese really expected, Bob reported, was to have their allies the Americans suddenly reappear and save them from disaster.

From Washington we had Henry Kissinger deploring the lack of that US aid, saying "The question is, will we destroy an ally?" And President Ford: "It's a tragedy. We are frustrated by the Congress not responding to our requests for military aid to Vietnam." Defense Secretary James Schlesinger: "It's a question of national honor."

Final scenes from Vietnam were the attempted airlift of Vietnamese war orphans out of the path of the advancing enemy. One of the planes crashed on takeoff and several hundred children were killed.

Collingwood's summation was that the collapse of the South Vietnamese government would lead to questions from America's other allies about our credibility and will to carry out an enterprise once begun. But most of our allies never were enthusiastic about America's Indochina adventure. A tragedy for all, he concluded.

The Midgley unit had done some preliminary work on a documentary about the US commitment to Israel, but I suggested to Bill Leonard we put it aside and get ready for a very big, probably multi-hour, broadcast to be put on when Saigon fell. Which, I told Bill, might well come in only a few weeks.

Russ Bensley, who was now commanding the election and live events unit, and I sat down and worked out plans for a TV spectacular. It was an off year for politics, so Russ and his troops were available. We agreed that he would put together a history of CBS News coverage of

Vietnam. Memorable coverage would be reprised and correspondents who had been involved with historic events would write and record new narrations. Russ was the best supervising editor in the business and had, over 11 years, himself edited much of the finest reporting by CBS men.

(In 1988, he completed a series of 11 one-hour shows about Vietnam, Walter Cronkite narrating, which appeared on cable channels and on cassettes, which sold briskly.)

Russ had himself been wounded in Vietnam. Twice. He was hit by shrapnel while visiting one of the beleagured camps and then again while in a tent hospital awaiting evacuation. You might say he had a personal interest in the story.

Russ put on a full-court press, working day and night. He wound up with about an hour and a half of marvelous stuff, which included not only scenes from the reporting of younger men like Jack Laurence and Bob Simon but also pieces done by Peter Kalischer, Morley Safer, Mike Wallace, Dan Rather—and Walter Cronkite.

I put my own people to work on the breaking story, keeping track of every foot of film and tape which arrived from Vietnam. As noted, the "End of the Road?" show had already given us a running start.

Finally, at 3 A.M. on April 29, President Ford gave the order to abandon the American Embassy in Saigon. It was now perfectly evident that the city was about to fall. The plan was to airlift as many Americans as possible to Thailand or Guam as long as planes were able to use Ton San Nhut Airport, then have helicopters fly the rest to Navy ships off the coast.

We were on. The decision was that we could have two and one-half hours *that very night*, from 8:30 to 11 P.M.

Excellent. Almost all of Bensley's material could be used and we still would have an hour for the latest stuff. We knew, from monitoring satellite feeds for the "Evening News," that great pictures would be available.

Later, one reviewer for a small newspaper noted—perceptively— "Walter Cronkite must have a new chair. He was sitting straight up." He certainly was, but not because of any chair. Walter suffered from serious back pains from time to time and on this historic day he was in bed at home, hurting a lot. But nothing was going to stop him from doing *this* broadcast. He arrived accompanied by a doctor who had strapped up his back so firmly he could hardly move. The doctor stayed right there while his patient went on the air.

The show opened with Walter saying 81 helicopters were—as he spoke—transporting some 900 Americans and several thousand Vietnamese from Ton San Nhut and the roof the Embassy to the waiting ships.

Bob Schieffer reported from the White House that tension had been high there "until a half hour ago" when word came that a final band of 11 Marines had left the Embassy roof safely.

Bill Plante came on live from a television studio in Hong Kong. He had managed to establish open telex communication with the CBS office in the Caravelle Hotel and got from the Vietnamese "night man" still working there a description of total shambles in the streets of Saigon. No police or ARVN troops were to be seen, he said.

Bruce Dunning reported from Guam, where Vietnamese who had worked for the Americans had been taken for their own safety. Terry Drinkwater described the scene at Camp Pendleton, California, where a steady stream of refugees was arriving.

Henry Kissinger came on saying, "We do not believe this is a time for recrimination...what we need to do is heal the wounds and put Vietnam behind us." (Sure.)

Collingwood reviewed the history of the American involvement, beginning with President Eisenhower.

Walter explained we had organized the show as a history of CBS News reporting from Vietnam with some of the correspondents who had served there recalling their experiences and replaying historic scenes.

The first was from Safer, who incorporated some of Kalischer's material into his own piece. Then came one from Walter himself, on a bombing run over Hanoi in 1965. Kuralt appeared with a dramatic scene from his "Christmas in Vietnam."

Then came the historic film of American GI's setting fire with a Zippo lighters to a village, reported by Safer.

Bruce Morton recalled the big buildup in 1966. Five thousand Americans died that year.

Cronkite led into a Rather piece from 1967 about the politics of

Vietnam. Ike Pappas told of war atrocities. Stories done by Mike Wallace, Don Webster, Jack Lawrence, Bob Schakne, Eric Sevareid and Collingwood were reprised.

From the files of 1968 came reports from Bernie Kalb on Viet Cong atrocities during the Tet uprising, Cronkite at Hue during Tet, and Collingwood in Hanoi.

The review of 1970 included pieces by Bert Quint and Gary Shepard, and the work of correspondent George Syvertson and producer Gerald Miller. Both were shot to death in Cambodia. Thirty-three other CBS staffers were wounded in Vietnam.

Cronkite continued with scenes at the Paris Peace Talks in 1972 and his own reporting of the release of American prisoners of war in Hanoi.

Bruce Dunning described the wild refugee flight out of Da Nang. Ed Bradley told about the final death throes of Cambodia. Scenes of the aerial escape from the embassy roof were reported by Wallace and Bill Plante.

At 10:35 P.M.—with 25 minutes to go in the show—Walter said:

"Whatever the cause in South Vietnam, it is now a lost one.

"The bulletin has just come in from Saigon: The war is over.

"South Vietnam's new president, Duon Van Minh, has announced an unconditional surrender to the Viet Cong."

The war ended. Live on our broadcast!

Timing is everything.

After the report of the surrender, we went to a group of "wise men" commenting on what it all meant.

Father Hesburgh said it "proves that we are not infallible."

Pat Moynihan: "Are we going to hate ourselves too much? Will we over-respond?"

John K.Fairbank: "I hope we have learned that Vietnam is an entirely different culture from our own. You can't operate if you don't know the culture of the people."

Barry Goldwater: "This divided us like nothing except the War Between the States—the Civil War. Most Americans are ashamed. Our honor is tarnished."

Then Cronkite set up another group to address the question: Where do we go from here?

W. Averell Harriman: "Policy can't succeed without popular support. Vietnam created disastrous divisions in the country."

Dean Rusk: "What we need now is a great national debate on our role in international affairs."

Senator John Tower: "This is going to result in a loss of confidence in the United States around the world."

George Ball: "We should not commit to a policy without careful examination of what is involved. We should not commit our forces where a government is fragile. And we should not assume that every civil war around the world is dominated by communist policy."

There were some final scenes of the last days of Saigon. And President Ford saying "Vietnam is a war that is finished." He spoke on a New Jersey Campus to an assembly of students—the first President to dare appear on a campus since 1967.

Walter's closing:

As we were putting this broadcast together today—and tonight—I wondered what possibly could be said to conclude it. After two and a half hours of the grim highlights, what more could possibly be said. Two and a half hours, of course, only touched the highlights. There is no way to capture in one evening's broadcast the suffering and grief of a 30 years of a sub-continent at war.

There is no way to capture the suffering and grief of our nation from the most divisive conflict since the Civil War. We embarked on this Vietnam journey with good intentions, I think. But once upon the path we found ourselves having been misguided. Many of us—myself included—in our private, personal opinions of the rightness of the course came half-circle around.

Perhaps that is our big lesson from Vietnam, the necessity for candor. We, the American people, the world's admired democracy, cannot ever again allow ourselves to be misinformed, manipulated and misled into disastrous foreign adventures. The government must share with the people the making of policy. The big decisions.

In Vietnam, we have finally reached the end of the tunnel and there is no light there. What is there perhaps was best said by President Ford: "A war that is finished."

And ahead, again to quote the President, "The time has come to look forward to an agenda for the future, to unify, to bind up the nation's wounds and to restore its health and its optimistic self-confidence."

This is Walter Cronkite. Good night.

Several times during the show Cronkite warned viewers that it included many scenes of explicit violence and were not for children or the queasy. Scenes of corpses piled high. Broken bodies piled in graves. Legless children trying to walk again. Death and destruction.

The legacy of war for the Vietnamese.

"A War That Is Finished" got some critical raves. Cecil Smith of the *Los Angeles Times* began:

"CBS threw out all of its prime time programs Tuesday night to devote the evening to a riveting two-hour backward look at what Walter Cronkite called 'the first televised war.'

"It was journalistic achievement of the highest order, speedily assembled and thoughtfully and soberly presented, delving into the bloody mess of that 30 years of war in Vietnam, now thankfully finished."

He concluded:

"The face of war is something you cannot compress into words. CBS brought the whole meaningless, empty, hideous spectacle back to life, back to the living room, a final look at this gruesome chapter of human misery.

"It's a look we *should* take again and I'm grateful to CBS News and producers Russ Bensley and Leslie Midgley for so skillfully presenting it and to the network for giving them the time to do so."

Right.

The Montreal Star's Joan Irwin began:

"CBS News made broadcasting history in the US last night with a two-and-a-half hour retrospective of the war in Vietnam which must rank as the most powerful and moving prime time program yet attempted by an American network...

"It might be wise if last night's program were to be carefully preserved and shown annually to US government leaders, the Joint Chiefs of Staff and others in key position, just to remind them of what happened between 1964 and 1975."

John J. O'Connor wrote a piece for the *Sunday New York Times* 10 days later that was less enthusiastic. He allowed, after noting that NBC had some transmission and other troubles with its special: "On CBS, all was precision and smooth professionalism...it added up an extremely polished slab of television."

O'Connor went on to complain that we had "strayed too close to being a commercial for CBS News" and had failed to "properly explore the sources and many dimensions of the biggest blunder in American history."

He ended:

"Electronic journalism may be forever doomed to superficiality. On one slick, often very effective level, the CBS retrospective worked impresssively. But at the end of two and one half hours, even Walter Cronkite had to concede that the program offered little more than highlights, the grim highlights, of the Vietnam tragedy. The occasion demanded more."

He may have been right, but I, at least, do not know how to put on a more honest and revealing account of the Vietnam decade.

New York Times opinions are important to television news organizations because New York is where the networks have their headquarters; the big bosses read the *Times*. And those bosses decide whether or not to give precious time on the air to news. On this occasion they did. But O'Connor's criticisms might have led them to be more stingy in the future.

The men and women of CBS News loved the show, of course. Even some members of the CBS board of directors and affiliate owners who had been critical of our war coverage told Salant they were proud of it.

Television shows traditionally end with a list of credits, the names of the producers and directors, cameramen, editors, and television technicians and assistants of all kinds. Many of these credits are mandated by union contracts, but in any event they are greatly prized by those of us who do not appear on the screen. It is indeed the only "credit" we get.

But this show had a different ending.

During my last visit to Saigon I asked the bureau manager, David Miller, if by any chance the office had kept a file of the names of people who had covered the war for CBS News. To my surprise he said that such a list had indeed been kept, and included not only Americans but the names of Vietnamese and Japanese technicians who had worked for us. And, also, the name of every CBS person who had passed through Vietnam. I don't know why, but I asked him to send me a copy.

When we were editing this show, I had an inspiration. Instead of winding it up with a list of production credits, I asked the art department make up a crawl of *238* names of those who had contributed to CBS' effort to report the enormous tragedy. The names were superimposed over scenes of its beautiful skies and landscapes, scenes of its terrible agony. It was a marvelous way of saying a great big thanks in public to so many people who had worked so hard.

Chapter 29

Assassins
The Murderous 12 Years

I THOUGHT we had gone the last mile with the story of the Kennedy assassination, but continuing public interest led us back to it.

President Nixon was re-elected in 1972. Dan Rather, who began covering the White House during the administration of Lyndon Johnson, had some sharp exchanges with Nixon, and many Nixon fans believed he was personally hostile to the President.

Dan was an excellent White House correspondent, but after Nixon caved in, he was taken off the beat. Many people at CBS News believed Stanton and Paley had been uneasy about Dan's abrasive relations with Nixon, but they would not change his assignment as long as it would appear they were caving in to White House pressure.

Rather moved to New York as chief correspondent of the "CBS Reports" documentary series. This, he was assured, was certainly not a demotion but an honor; he was stepping into the broadcast shoes of Edward R. Murrow.

The "CBS Reports" unit did some fine shows, but most of the producers took a year or so to get a one hour show ready. We called them the basket weavers.

One day early in 1975, Dan called me and suggested we have lunch; he had an idea he wanted to talk over. What he had in mind was a multi-hour review of the shocking series of assassinations over the last dozen years, the murders of John F. Kennedy, his brother Robert and Martin Luther King, Jr., and the near-fatal shooting of Governor George Wallace.

I pointed out that CBS News had done everything I could think of to investigate Jack Kennedy's killing and I didn't have any idea what we might do about the others, although that had never deterred me from any subject.

Dan said he had become interested in this project because when he lectured on college campuses, the questions most frequently asked by students were about the assassinations. It was indeed often suggested that *all three* murders might have been linked in one enormous conspiracy.

When I asked how we could get time on the air for such broadcasts, Dan said he would make it his business to have several of the hours budgeted for "CBS Reports" diverted to this subject.

As a matter of fact, I did know about two important pieces of evidence available in 1975 that were not in 1967.

Time, Inc. had given Abraham Zapruder's film of Jack Kennedy's assassination back to his family and they might permit us to study it. TIME never would.

And the autopsy X-rays and photographs in the National Archives could now be examined by qualified authorities; the five-year embargo imposed by Bobby Kennedy had expired.

So we started down the road again. Beginning with the Jack Kennedy story, the assassination of a President and thus the most intriguing of all.

I quickly verified that if CBS News commissioned a qualified pathologist, he could indeed study the X-rays and photographs. I asked who was the *most* qualified and signed up Dr. James Weston, chief pathologist of the state of New Mexico.

Birnbaum got in touch with the Zapruders and they agreed—for a fee of $6,000, I believe—that we could have photo analysts study the film. The *original* Zapruder film, not a copy. It was a breakthrough. When Bernie asked who were the most qualified photo analysts, the answer, almost without exception, was the Itek Corporation, a Boston outfit which did very sophisticated work for people like big oil companies. And for the Defense Department and the CIA.

Bernie and I went to Boston and talked to John Wolfe, an Itek vice president. He said the firm would be extremely interested in the project, primarily because they would get to work with the *original* Zapruder film. It was the kind of thing their technicians loved.

So we had good reason to believe it would be profitable to go ahead with at least the John Kennedy part of the project. Other research indicated that much could be done to explore the other crimes, especially the Martin Luther King story. (It always seemed to me even less likely that James Earl Ray had killed Dr. King all alone than that Lee Harvey Oswald had done the same thing in Jack's case.)

I proposed four one-hour shows with the overall title of "The American Assassins." The first two hours would be "Lee Harvey Oswald and John F. Kennedy." The first hour would consider the evidence that Oswald was the killer. The second would be devoted to the question of conspiracy.

The third hour would be "James Earl Ray and Martin Luther King." The cases of both Bobby Kennedy and George Wallace would be considered in the fourth hour.

A project of this size required more help than I had. Two additional producers were available and I was delighted to get them.

The first was none other than Ernie Leiser. After working at ABC as producer of Harry Reasoner's weekly show, then the "ABC Evening News," he had returned to CBS. Bill Small, who had moved from Washington to succeed Gordon Manning as news director, had hired Ernie to organize a very big programming schedule being planned for the nation's 200th birthday in 1976.

The second was Lee Townsend. Lee had been the newsroom assignment editor until Manning abruptly made him the producer of the "CBS Morning News" when Sally Quinn, a *Washington Post* reporter, joined Hughes Rudd on the show. Lee was an experienced newsman—a *Herald Tribune* alumnus—but he had no experience as a producer. The Rudd/Quinn team, which was supposed to "knock Barbara Walters off the air" was a disaster and Lee was available to work on the Bobby Kennedy segment. Hal Haley would produce the George Wallace half-hour. Birnbaum, Bartels and Midgley would, again, take up the tangled matter of John F. Kennedy.

I decided to give the conspiracy theorists their say in front of the cameras. Not the real crazies but responsible people who believed that there had been—at least—one other gunman and thus a conspiracy. Like our old friend Dr. Cyril Wecht, the Pittsburgh coroner, who had never changed his mind and was eager to get back on the air.

Another was Josiah Thompson, a professor at Haverford College, who had produced a well-written, somewhat persuasive book advancing theories about how Kennedy had been killed which did not jibe with the Warren Commission's conclusions.

Charles Groden had become a celebrity on college campuses showing a film he had put together which he said "proved" Oswald hadn't been involved at all or had been firing along with other gunmen. He brought the film in and showed it to us. It was well-done and made me suspect most of his young audiences bought his theories of multiple gunmen in a conspiracy.

With Dr. Weston examining the Archives material, the Zapruder film tests at Itek, the Wecht and Thompson interviews, plus some new firing tests to re-check the "single bullet theory," we had good material for another look at the Kennedy assassination. Especially because now, for the first time, we could work with the most important pieces of physical evidence.

Ernie began to get the King/Ray story together and Lee took off for the West Coast, where he and associate producer Brooke Janis would spend a couple of months looking into the Bobby Kennedy/Sirhan Sirhan matter.

Late in the fall, we got air dates. They were not good. The 1967 series ran on four consecutive nights, at the same time each night. And the audiences had continued to build each night. I pointed this out to Bill Leonard and I am sure he did the same to the programmers at Black Rock, but to no avail. We would have to make do with two consecutive hours in late November; the other two hours would go into the first week of January 1976. Some series!

I asked for Arthur Bloom as director. Artie was the best young director at CBS News. Don Hewitt had him directing "60 Minutes." Artie's first job had been office boy for "Eyewitness." (As a matter of fact, all the top directors in the news division had begun as my office boys: Harry Mutschler, director of the "Evening News," Dick Knox, director of "Weekend News" and Kenny Sable, director of "Sunday Morning With Charles Kuralt.")

The opening of the first show laid out what we were planning for the series. The Rather script began by noting that in the last dozen years, the country had been through "a national nightmare," a series of experiences that had shaken confidence in the foundations of the government. He listed the disastrous war in Asia, Watergate, the assassinations of the Kennedy brothers and Dr. King, and the shooting of Governor Wallace.

We had commissioned a poll for this series and the results revealed, Dan said, that "An astonishing 46 percent of the persons polled believed that there is some connection between the three assassinations and the attempt on Wallace. Only 38 percent believed the crimes were unconnected incidents. The others had no opinion."

The opening show continued with Dan reviewing the John Kennedy assassination and our inquiry into it. Governor Connally said again he did not accept the single bullet theory. Professor Thompson said he was convinced only two shots came from the book depository and that the shot that hit the governor came from an entirely different building. Charles Groden insisted his film showing the President's head movements "proved" he had been hit by a bullet fired from in front.

John Wolfe told Rather their analysis had convinced technicians at Itek that the head movements were consistent only with shots fired from behind. Dr. Weston said his examination of the autopsy materials indicated the same. Asked whether he was willing to stake his professional reputation on the statement that President Kennedy was not struck from the front, Dr. Weston replied, "Absolutely. Yes."

Thompson insisted there was no way the famous single bullet number 399 could have inflicted serious wounds on both Kennedy and Connally and emerged almost whole. Dr. Alfred G. Olivier, who conducted firing tests for both the FBI and CBS, said it could have.

Dr. Wecht explained his theory that there had to be at least two gunmen because the trajectory of the bullets ruled out just one. Dr. Weston said there was no way the trajectory could be determined accurately.

Near the end of the show, Dan said, "Was there only one gunman? There is positive evidence of one gunman. Twelve years after the crime, the evidence points to one gunman. As far as we can determine now, the answer is yes."

Then Dan continued, "There are frayed ends to the Oswald story, bits and pieces that are bound to keep suspicion alive."

The show ended with one such tangled thread. An interview with Robert Ray McKeown, who had run weapons illegally to Fidel Castro. McKeown told Rather, on camera, that Oswald had come to visit him a few weeks before the President's murder, accompanied by "a Latin . . . I think his name was Hernandez." Oswald, McKeown said, wanted to buy "four .300 Savage automatic rifles with a telescope sight on them." He said he would pay $1,000 for each one.

McKeown said he told Oswald he had been in enough trouble and had no guns for sale. He was absolutely sure that his visitor was Lee Harvey Oswald, and a friend who had been there that day said he, too, was positive about the identification.

The story had, Rather concluded, "Mind-boggling implications. Why four guns, for example, unless there were plans for more than one assassin? It is mere coincidence that Cuba figures in McKeown's story?"

McKeown, Dan said, had never been interviewed by the Warren Report staff.

The second hour was devoted to the question of conspiracy and more information about Lee Harvey Oswald's background and history. I myself never believed that he had no connection with the CIA. It seemed incredible that a man could learn to speak Russsian in the Marine Corps, leave the corps and go to live in the Soviet Union, and then return with a Russian wife without *some* contact with the country's foreign intelligence organization.

Dan and I went to see William Colby, the director of the CIA, in his office at Langley, Virginia. We asked if the CIA had ever employed Oswald or had assisted him going to Rusia or returning from it. He gave us the dusty answer, "We have not been able to find anything in our files concerning Oswald." Dan, who is one of the most courteous men you ever will meet, told Colby flat out that his statement was very hard to believe. We got nowhere except to get Colby's agreement to appear on the show. When he was interviewed on film, Rather asked if the CIA had recruited Oswald and sent him to the Soviet Union. The answer was:

"No, we had no contact with Mr. Oswald."

Rather: "No contact before he went to the Soviet Union?"

Colby: "No contact with him before he went to the Soviet Union and no contact with him after he returned from the Soviet Union. No contact with him while he was in the Soviet Union."

I never believed those statements.

For this show, we had managed to get a lot more information about Mr. Oswald. A Marine officer who had worked with Oswald in Japan said he had a "secret" classification. His job was to plot aircraft flights, including those by U-2 spy planes. When he defected, codes were changed.

After he got to Moscow, Oswald went to the American Consulate and said he wanted to turn in his passport. When he came back two years later with a Russian wife, the consulate made arrangmeents for travel to the USA and lent them money for the passage.

Just five months before the Kennedy killing, Oswald applied for a new passport in New Orleans, indicating he wanted to visit Cuba and, again, Russia. And, in one of the many questionable incidents in Oswald's life, he got a passport in one day. (The State Department said later someone had made a clerical error, his name should have been "flagged" in case he came back for a new passport.)

Two months before the assassination, Oswald traveled by bus to Mexico City, where he visited the Cuban and Russian Embassies. A former CIA agent who was in Mexico at the time told Dan that Oswald was rebuffed at both places. They wanted nothing to do with him.

But the CIA continued to insist he was not their man.

We knew Oswald had been interviewed by the FBI after he returned from Russia, and there was speculation that he might have been working for that agency rather than the CIA. A New Orleans bar owner told correspondent Bruce Hall that he had been an informer for the FBI, and had seen Oswald with FBI agent Warren deBrueys. The agent denied he knew Oswald or that he had ever met him.

But a former FBI security code clerk in New Orleans said he knew Oswald was an informant for the Bureau. Pressed by Dan, he said, "I'm positive."

We also had known for years that Marina Oswald had been visited on November 1, 1963, by FBI agent James P. Hosty. The FBI failed to tell the Warren Commission that after Hosty's visit, Oswald went to the FBI office in Dallas and left a note threatening to blow up that office and Dallas police headquarters if the FBI did not stop bothering his wife. The note apparently failed to alert the FBI to any special precautions in connection with the forthcoming presidential visit, and the FBI did not tell the Secret Service anything about the note.

Hosty later claimed that within hours after Oswald had been shot by Jack Ruby, he (Hosty) was called to his boss' office and ordered to destroy both the note and a memorandum he had written about it. Because they didn't make J. Edgar Hoover look good.

Dallas Police Chief Jesse Curry told reporters soon after the murder that his department was not aware of Oswald's presence in Dallas but that the FBI knew he was there. And, Curry said, Gordon Shanklin, the FBI special agent in charge, called and asked him to retract the statement. He said he would not.

The show ended with two of President Johnson's associates, Joseph Califano and Leo Janos, recalling that Johnson several times expressed the belief that the Kennedy assassination had somehow been associated with the CIA's attempts to kill Fidel Castro. Ironically, Robert Kennedy had an active role in that operation.

As part of his summation, Rather advocated congressional investigation of the activities of the CIA and the FBI in this matter, especially what they failed to tell the Warren Commission. He also said:

"We have cast some new light on the event and on the activities of the alleged assassin—and still the case cannot be closed. To discover a conspiracy, and other gunmen, in the murder of John F. Kennedy would have been a journalistic coup almost beyond imagining. We tried to do that in 1967 and could not. We couldn't do it this time either."

Right again.

The other two shows in the "American Assassins" series were broadcast the following January. They were meticulously researched and very well produced but, again, we could not come up with compelling evidence of the conspiracies in the Robert Kennedy, Martin Luther King, Jr., and George Wallace cases. None has surfaced since.

When the Peabody Awards were presented the following spring, the two hours about the John Kennedy assassination won one. And when the dean of the University of Georgia School of Journalism handed me a plaque and a scroll he said, "Maybe you'll be back next year to pick up something for the last two parts of the series."

It didn't happen.

Chapter 30

Serious Stuff
Busing and Energy

THE MIDGLEY UNIT produced 27 shows in 1976, including those two dangling parts of the "American Assassins" series and 12 specials during the presidential contest between Carter and Ford. Plus a profile of Bill Colby, the CIA director, a fast re-creation of the daring rescue of hostages from the airport at Entebbe, Uganda, by Israeli commandos, and Patty Hearst's own story about her kidnapping. Mostly News.

Our major documentary effort concerned the busing of school children to achieve racial integration, a subject which aroused powerful emotions in the parents of white children who were taken far from their own neighborhoods and black parents who believed that children must start in school together if they ever were to live together in harmony.

(I myself—no expert—believed then that if children five or six years old studied together, they *might* be able to live peacefully together when they were older. Five years later, I screened part of an NBC documentary about race relations that disabused me of the notion that education could bring about desegregation when children were grown.

(It was a sequence showing how black students were getting along at Harvard University. What they were doing was eating with blacks, studying together, socializing with other blacks. Not with white students. It struck me forcefully that if young people intelligent enough to attend our finest university couldn't find ways to get together, there probably *was* no way. I still fear that is the case.)

We decided to devote the hour to examining how school busing was operated in two cities, Boston, which was deeply troubled, and Charlotte, N.C., where some accomodation, however uneasy, had been reached between the advocates and opponents of busing.

Collingwood spent weeks in both places doing field reporting and interviews and wrote an excellent script.

Both cities were engaged in school busing because they had been ordered to do so by the courts. United States District Judge James McMillan, who had handed down the original busing decision—the classic case which was appealed to the Supreme Court and upheld— told Charles he didn't think a court was the best place to regulate school business, but it had turned out to be the only place.

"The courts catch all the garbage other people don't want to take care of," he said.

Collingwood's conclusion was that despite much resistance from white parents and hasty organization of some segregated white private schools, "the situation in Charlotte has calmed, the education process had resumed... in an extraordinary community decision they came to the conclusion that, whatever its imperfections, busing was preferable to constant turmoil. So they decided to make busing work."

Not so in Boston. There he found one-third of the city's white school children had withdrawn from the public schools. Parents, students and educators were bitter, especially in South Boston, an Irish-American enclave.

But although polls had shown that a majority of Americans were opposed to busing, they were even more concerned abut the *quality* of American education. It was not good enough, Charles concluded, for either blacks or whites.

As noted, our unit produced 27 shows in 1976, but the next year was a different story. There were only four shows, although one was an extravaganza which took over an entire evening of prime time on the network.

The first major project was "The Retirement Revolution," a look by Collingwood at the rewards and trials faced by people at the end of their working lives.

What made this one different—for us—was that it was "filmed" not on 16mm celluloid film but on three-quarter-inch magnetic video tape and edited on the small Sony decks which were being used increasingly by the daily news organization.

The use of the tape, which doesn't require any processing, has become routine now, but it was revolutionary then and quite primitive by today's standards.

One of the oldest members of CBS News, I found myself urging people half my age to try new techniques. Most people, understandably, want to work with familiar tools. Many film editors feared that tape might endanger their jobs if they were ordered to change the working habits of a lifetime and found they couldn't adjust. Some never did make the transition and were phased out by attrition.

There were union problems. The tape recorders were light in weight and required fewer men to function efficiently. The unions always had insisted that four men be assigned to a documentary crew. Sometimes five men for an elaborate shoot. But this tape equipment required only a basic crew of cameraman and soundman, with a lighting man added only if necessary. Usually not, because the tape cameras required less light than the film cameras.

The Special Projects unit had for years been in a gray area in this matter. Although some of our productions were full-scale documentaries, others were clearly news shows. As a result, we often got away with production short cuts which caused much grumbling at union meetings.

Casey Davidson, vice president in charge of the technicians, agreed with me that tape was the tool of the future and was eager to see us make a full documentary with it. The orthodox documentarians at CBS were not receptive to such ideas; most of them still contended— strongly supported by their film editors—that tape could not be edited as well as film. We knew they were wrong. The unions agreed we could proceed with tape cameras on the retirement show "as an experiment."

When she began researching the subject, Jane Bartels found, to her and our surprise, that most people don't move to places like Florida and Arizona when they retire. The great majority stay put, most right in their familiar communities. The 1970 census had revealed that while

Florida was indeed the state with the most people over 65, it was followed by Nebraska and Iowa, right in the heartland.

Jane and Bernie found some feisty oldsters in Iowa and did a lot of taping in Des Moines. It was an interesting, often entertaining, show. Certainly of value to millions of Americans thinking about their own futures.

Collingwood got a personal touch in the script, saying that working on the show had started him thinking about his own retirement "in not too many years." He said he had resolved to put his financial affairs in order, try to figure out what to do with his time, get in better physical shape, nurture and cherish good friendships, and "start cutting down on a lot of things I don't need."

Which may have prompted this in John J. O'Connor's review in *The New York Times:*

"CBS News current concern with retirement may not be entirely coincidental. Several veteran producers are hovering around the 60 mark. Eric Sevareid, 64 years old, will retire officially next fall, Richard S. Salant, 63, president of the news division, and Walter Cronkite, 60, have reached that point where speculation about their professional departures has become part of the gossip mills."

We learned a lot about tape editing putting this one together. Bob Rheingold, our best editor, had been a bit uneasy about moving over to tape, but he adjusted rapidly and became very good at it.

The biggest problem was that each time you made an insertion or a deletion on a piece of tape the whole reel became another generation. And after it went down several generations, the image was badly degraded.

The solution was to make a copy of every reel—in this case there were more than 50 of them—and use the copy as a "work print" to make a rough edited version of the show. We put the original tapes in a rack until all editing decisions had been made. At that point, we could "cut the original," just as negative matching is done on film.

Another executive change had occured at CBS Inc. Arthur Taylor, who despite our differences about "The Trouble With Rock," seemed to me to be a fine executive, had been abruptly fired as president of the company by William S. Paley. Not being privy to the deliberations of the board of directors, I didn't know why, but the scoop was that Mr. Paley visited the Washington corporate office one day and discovered that Taylor had ordered a lavish suite of offices built and decorated handsomely for his own use in the capital. Paley was quite put out.

So the new president of CBS Inc. was John Backe, boss of the flourishing CBS Publications Group.

One night in the spring, Dick Salant called me at home. He said Backe was very interested in the energy problem and had enquired whether CBS News could fill one whole evening, from 8 to 11 P.M. with a show about the subject. I told Dick, as ever, that we could "do anything."

Dick didn't exactly say so, but I got the impression John Backe wanted to do something important, perhaps even spectacular, to mark his new presidency. It was certainly a timely subject. President Carter had created a whole new Cabinet entity, the Department of Energy. The lines at gas stations had disappeared, but the price had roughly doubled at the pump and energy was the biggest domestic issue.

I told Dick the next morning I could organize a three-hour show and it could be put together in a couple of months if I could borrow some additional production help. We agreed that Bill Small, the director of news, would be in charge of this one, because it would be on such a tight schedule.

My first step in getting this big project underway was to organize production teams, to which I could farm out specific projects. Producers work with film or tape crews as reporters in the field and with editors to get material into shape to go on the air. They are the workhorses of television news.

I had Ernie Leiser as senior producer and asked Russ Bensley to help out. Hal Haley and Birnbaum were my two regular producers and I recruited seven more. They were David Buksbaum, an expert in the technical area, Bill Crawford and Charlie Thompson from the Washington bureau, Mark Kramer from "The Morning News," Judy Hole and Ken Witty from the "CBS Reports" staff, and George Murray, one of Bensley's assistants.

Cronkite would be anchor man for the three hours. Nelson Benton and George Herman had done most of the reporting on energy from Washington, so we signed them up. In addition, I got seven other correspondents assigned to the project. They were David Culhane, Mort Dean, Eric Engberg, Phil Jones, René Poussaint, Bob Schieffer and Dick Wagner.

We started out seeking answers to the basic questions. How much oil was the U.S. burning? How much of it came from foreign sources?

How secure were those sources? What could and should be done to increase domestic production? Was natural gas a practical substitute for oil? Could coal, which was in plentiful supply, replace oil? How about energy from the sun?

Were our buildings being designed to make the most efficient use of energy? How about automobile design? What could a program of conservation accomplish? Was the federal government developing proper programs to cope with the energy problem?

And, what did the public think about all this?

I decided to use statements from ordinary people expressing their opinions about the energy problem as chapter headings for the subjects listed above. I asked all the bureaus around the country to send crews out to shopping centers and record brief interviews with men and women. Man-in-the-street segments were nothing new, but when these reels came back to us, it was evident they would work very well.

Instead of having Walter anchor the three hours in a studio, I decided to charter a jet plane and fly him all over the country during the two days before we were to go on air. He would meet on location various correspondents who had done reporting in the field and together they would open and close each report on video tape.

Unfortunately, one of Walter's children had a medical problem and could not leave New York. But we still stayed out of a studio and had him anchor from the huge central control room of the Consolidated Edison Company in Manhattan. Good, but not the same as covering the nation.

As part of our man-in-the-street taping, I asked the bureaus to have people address one question directly to President Carter. We took tape of the best questions to the White House and the President himself answered them on camera. Very effective.

"ENERGY...The Facts...The Fears...The Future" went on air August 31. Press comment around the country was favorable, but most TV writers said they didn't think the public would watch three hours of this subject. They were reasonably right. When the figures were in we began with a 10.2 share of audience for the night. ABC had a 24.7 and NBC an 11.22.

But something funny happened. For the last hour and a half that night, our show edged out NBC's entertainment schedule and moved into second place.

Chapter 31

The Long Form
Three Hours About Education

ALL TELEVISION PROGRAMMING and scheduling goes through faddish cycles and news programming isn't isolated from current fashions. Backe liked the three hour energy show—it was of course his own idea—and Salant and Small thought it was very successful. So they suggested we continue to work in the then currently fashionable "long form." Meaning more than one hour.

Collingwood and I had talked on and off ever since the school busing show about the state of basic American education. One of his conclusions in "busing" had been that the *quality* of education was more important than the location of the real estate where teaching was being done. And we were convinced that American youngsters were not being properly educated.

He wrote a basic outline explaining *why* a lengthy television examination of education should be undertaken and what it should cover, and I wrote one proposing *how* it should be put together. With these, we got a go-ahead for a multi-hour series on the subject. And, happily, it was agreed that if the series turned out to be worth three hours, it would not be put on in a single night but in one-hour segments on sequential nights.

307

After casing a variety of locations, I decided to focus on the schools, students, teachers, parents and educational establishment of the city of Denver. I was dubious about Colorado at first, fearing it might be too white and unrepresentative of the whole country. But research surprised me. There were a large number of blacks and chicanos in the Denver school system. After the war, many big federal bureaus and installations were established in Denver. And, as required by law, those bureaus had hired black people. Which meant black kids in the public schools. The chicanos had always been there.

I told my associates that although some other locations would be necessary, we should make every effort to concentrate the story on the situation in Denver, especially in the junior high schools, which seemed to be where many students got into trouble. The series would be more understandable if it could be kept in a location which would become increasingly familiar to viewers.

I assigned producers Haley and Bartels and Emily Lodge, an associate producer, to concentrate on classrooms. Who the teachers were, what were their qualifications and how they taught. Who the students were and what was the state of classroom discipline. Was violence common in the schools and were drugs present?

Birmbaum would work on students and parents at home, racial and segregation problems and the relations between parents and teachers and administrators.

Leiser and Margaret Ershler, an associate producer, would look at the effect of television on education, the quality of books and other teaching materials, and the attitude of employers and college administration officers toward graduates of the public schools.

We had, naturally, decided again to "film" this one with video tape and had hired Ron Eveslage, based in San Francisco, as the principal cameraman. Ron is an excellent cameraman, good enough to shoot feature films, which he has done. He was one of the new breed of freelancers who were beginning to buy their own video equipment and rent it to clients like CBS on a daily basis when they were given assignments.

This system had been developed by Walter Dumbrow, who started with "Eyewitness" and had gone on to become a star with "60 Minutes." It made a lot of sense for guys like Ron and Walter. They charged hefty rental fees which they used to pay back bank loans taken out to buy the equipment. Being in business for themselves, they enjoyed a lot of tax advantages not available to those on a company payroll. The television networks went along because they didn't have to tie up capital in expensive technical equipment.

Bernie always tended to overshoot film, and now that he had tape, which needed no processing, he went wild, shooting roll after roll until he had accumulated a huge amount of footage. When the editors in New York seemed to be drowning in the flood, I went out to Denver to stem the tide. I sat down in the Brown Palace Hotel with Collingwood, Eveslage and the producers and told them to stop shooting everything that moved, to plan in advance what would be most useful. After all we only had three hours! They cut down on the volume and I got a good look at how tape was used in the field.

This whole project had grown out of the memo written by Collingwood, and he did almost all the reporting. But, inevitably, anything this large had to involve Walter Cronkite, the network's Number One correspondent. It is the star system, which has grown even more pervasive since the late Seventies. The theory is that stars will themselves attract larger audiences. It may well be true, but it is to be deplored.

Walter didn't push himself into situations like this. Indeed, he was reluctant about moving onto another correspondent's turf, especially that of his old comrade Collingwood. But management was adamant; his presence on the show was vital. Walter was helpful and cooperative, and Collingwood understood the system. The only thing he asked was that he not be required to write copy for Cronkite. We brought in Charlie West, one of the "Evening News" writers, to work on Cronkite's portion of the narration. Leiser, who loves to write and does it in fine style, did some of it himself.

We commissioned a CBS News/*New York Times* poll as part of the project. Results were that 41 percent of those polled said the education their children was receiving was not as good as the one they themselves had obtained in the public schools. Seventy-six percent wanted a "return to basics" in education and 82 percent favored minimum competency testing—that is no automatic awarding of diplomas until tests had proved a level of learning to justify one.

The series went on air almost as originally outlined. The first two hours were devoted to problems in the schools, principally high schools, and the third hour examined some proposed solutions. (William Given of the Associated Press wrote that we had done it wrong. He believed we should have had one hour about problems and two about solutions.)

During the second hour, we looked at the effect of television. Our conclusion—not very surprising I admit—was that young people spent too much time watching television instead of studying.

The three hours were well done, and the report certainly was a valuable public service. Some administrators and teachers in Denver thought we had been too rough on them. But we got a lot of letters from other teachers saying our reporting on lax discipline and behavior, use of drugs and failure of students to make even minimal efforts to learn was not strong enough. Things were worse than we portrayed, they wrote.

We got a lot of favorable attention in the press. The *Wall Street Journal* review had this headline: "A Serious Look at the Educational Slag Heap."

An article by William A. Henry 3rd in the *Boston Globe* contained a major misstatement about the participation of Collingwood in the series. He wrote: "Walter Cronkite and Charles Collingwood read the narration (as is usual with reporters on all network documentaries, they had little to do with research or filming or even interviewing the people on the screen)." Dead wrong. Charles initiated much of the research, wrote all his own script and did all the interviewing in Denver, our principal location. Too bad some reporters can't bother to check their "facts."

Chapter 32

The Old Order Changeth

We Lose Salant

AS THE SEVENTIES wound down, some changes inevitably began in the ruling structure of CBS News. A new federal law prohibited companies from arbitrarily retiring people at 65, although it was permitted in the case of a person who was in a major policy-making position and had a pension above $35,000 a year. Others could stay until 70, if they so opted. Under the rules, I wouldn't have to retire in 1980 and neither would Walter and other correspondents when they reached 65. Ironically, Sevareid had attained that age before the law was passed and he had been retired, much to his displesure.

But Dick Salant was in the category of those who could be replaced at 65, and it was announced he would be, in March of 1979. There was, of course, a lot of gossip about who would be the new president of news. Then six months before Salant's birthday, the company announced that Bill Leonard would get the job. Bill, who had been very successful as the CBS corporate lobbyist in Washington, was told to move to New York and prepare to take over. It was a very difficult time for both Dick and Bill and a rather silly way for a corporation to behave. Bill had been for years a vice president of news, after serving

311

as a correspondent and producer. He knew the company inside out and didn't need any breaking in. And Salant didn't need anyone looking over his shoulder.

At the same time, other executive changes were made. Bud Benjamin, who had been executive producer of the "Evening News," was named vice president and director of news. Bill Small, disappointed by not getting the top job, was sent back to Washington to succeed Leonard. Sandy Socolow—finally—was named executive producer of the Cronkite news. Ed Fouhy took over the Washington bureau from Sandy.

March 1 was the date set for Dick's formal retirement, and I began to ask around what was going to be done about it. He had been our president for 15 years and a better one never existed. Bob Chandler said there would be a party in the biggest studio in the production center to which everyone in the news division would be invited. Plus a lunch hosted by Mr. Paley which senior people would attend. Sounded good.

Bernie and I decided to put together a video report on "The Salant Years," showing Dick in action and the highlights of his career.

Kuralt wrote and recorded a lovely script.

"This", he said, "is about a man we admire. 'Love' is not too strong a word. But most of this is about what he did, not how we feel about him.

"What he did was take over a little band of journalists—ourselves—and make us into a great news organization starting 18 years ago in some dusty rooms above Grand Central Station..."

The tape was shown on monitors during the party in the studio on the afternoon of March 1. Everybody, especially Dick, loved it

This was supposed to have been the day of the Paley lunch, but we discovered it had been abruptly cancelled. Because The Chairman was furious to be told only the previous day that Dick was going to NBC to become vice chairman of the board of directors. Although Salant had been forced to retire—very much against his will—Paley still thought some kind of disloyalty was involved in his joining the old enemy.

At NBC, Dick would join Fred Silverman, who was the chairman. Fred had left CBS after many successful years as program boss and had gone to ABC. There he had engineered a string of programming victories which made ABC Number One in the entertainment ratings race. NBC, which had sunk to third place under a series of dim and dismal chief executives, had hired Silverman, hoping he would work his programming magic to get them out of the cellar. Fred, who knew Dick well at CBS, thought he might be just the man to straighten out NBC News, which also was in the doldrums.

Dick was unhappy with Paley's displeasure, but he looked forward to moving over to Rockefeller Center in a big executive job, complete with a limousine and chauffeur to drive him to and from New Caanan, Connecticut, every day. He had become very attached to that perk as CBS News president. Limousines are, apparently, addictive. I wouldn't know.

A few months later, Small surprised a lot of people at CBS by resigning his Washington job to join NBC as president of the news division. Actually, his move should have been expected. Having been passed over in favor of Leonard, he very likely figured that the president's job never would come his way. Salant had been dissatisfied with Les Crystal's performance as head of NBC News and he held Small in high esteem. And Silverman also knew Small well.

Chapter 33

Duke and Dick
A Pair of Tributes

DURING 1979, Kuralt and I worked together again on a couple of sweet/ sad specials in prime time. The first was "The Duke," a tribute to John Wayne, who died in June after a long bout with cancer. The second appeared on New Year's Eve. It was a tribute to my friend, the great composer Richard Rodgers, who died after a long illness.

Kuralt did his usual excellent script for the Duke show, although it was not to everyone's taste. After noting that NBC and ABC had scheduled tributes to Wayne at 11:30 P.M., while CBS did one at 8 P.M., Tom Shales of the *Washington Post* wrote:

" 'The Duke' began badly, with Kuralt in his usual fully unfurled avuncular fervor. 'Good evening,' he said, 'you know how life is.'

"But the program improved steadily . . . and for all his flights of bombast, which have grown almost tolerable over the years, Kuralt ended the program with a welcome touch of pastel eloquence, saying of John Wayne, 'life can't be lived without at least a dream of daring and high spirit. That's what he gave us.' "

Shales' review made one amusing point: "Viewers who watched all three networks saw three different versions of one *True Grit* scene, the wild face-off between Rooster Cogburn, as played by Wayne, and a trio of bad guys on the other side of a field. Wayne takes the reins of his horse in his teeth after shouting 'Fill your hands, you son of a bitch' and begins his charge.

314

"Only CBS News, still the last word in class among network news operations, had the simple sane decency to leave the line and its harmless expletive intact. On ABC, traditionally the network of the most slipshod and insensitive censorship, the expletive was removed with a jerky cut. On NBC, the expletive was replaced with an insipid bleep."

Shales is entitled to his opinion of Kuralt's writing, but it should be noted that the line he scorned, "You know how life is" was followed by... "It is full of doubt and hesitation and compromise. We make a virtue of courage but the emotion we all know best is fear. That is what made John Wayne so different. He never doubted and he never hesitated and he never compromised and he was never afraid. Not so far as we could see."

And Kuralt wound up: "In a John Wayne movie, it was always John Wayne who decided how the story came out in the end. He would ride away over the ridges or go whistling off into the dark like that, not only alive but undefeated.

"Life isn't like that. But it should be. It should be honest and courageous and bold, probably, and full of shining symbols, nerves of iron and hearts of oak and when evil contests with virtue the goodness should always win and confidence and certainty should crown the close of every day.

"Life is also dreams you know, like in the John Wayne movies. Nobody can live without at least a dream of daring and high spirit. That's what he gave us."

Too bad an actor couldn't hear words like that spoken about him. And Mr. Shales should write like that...

Between Kuralt's opening and closing segments, Mort Dean narrated a profile of Wayne which observed that he had strong opinions about patriotism, was always to be found among political conservtives, and was much loved by the likes of Ronald Reagan and Barry Goldwater. And was by far the most successful actor of his time, appearing in nearly 200 movies to enormous acclaim.

The show about Dick Rodgers was a labor of love, and I was delighted to see it on the air even while mourning the occasion. He died on December 30, and the show went on the following night.

Dick and Dorothy Rodgers had been Betty's good friends for more than 40 years. Betty's closest friend, despite an age gap of 15 years, had long been Judy Crichton, one of Dorothy's nieces.

Judy, a talented producer and writer who had moved from producing game shows to "CBS Reports," called me with the news that Dick was sinking and the doctors feared he would not last more than a few days. I said I wanted to put together a tribute to him on the network and asked if she would help. She was delighted to be involved.

I went to Leonard and he agreed to try to get time on the air. He succeeded, bless him, telling me we could have a half-hour on Monday, December 31, if that turned out to be appropriate. Dick died on Sunday.

Judy was, of course, completely plugged into the Rodgers & Hammerstein office. They knew the content and whereabouts of every film and television special that ever had been done about Dick. As a result, we had at our disposal a lot of marvelous stuff complete with the rights to use it as we chose. Harold Gold, a talented tape editor, worked day and night through the weekend getting the material ready, with Judy's invaluable assistance.

By now, Charlie and I seemed to have television obits down to a science. I hired a piano player certified to know every Rodgers and Hart and Rodgers and Hammerstein song, and the director ordered a piano brought onto the set. Over it, we hung a big blowup of a lovely photograph of Dick at work at his piano.

On the day of air, Charlie showed up in the morning and I explained what we were planning.

"You didn't tell me we were going to have a piano player," he said.

Then he went into an empty office and shut the door. He emerged two hours later holding the usual poetic and practical script. He would stand, he said, in the bend of the grand piano beneath the photograph.

The show opened with the pianist playing, "Oh, What a Beautiful Morning," and Charlie explaining that the great composer had died last night. Then came a film montage of ordinary men and women, in the street or working at construction jobs or whatever, singing stanzas from some of the great Rodgers songs. Amateurishly and off-key but wonderfully. The sequence came from a special that had been done years before by David Susskind. The street singers bumbled through "I Enjoy Being a Girl," "Some Enchanted Evening" and "Oklahoma!"

Then came a segment of the last interview with Rodgers, done by James Day for the Public Broadcasting System before Dick's larynx was removed in an operation for cancer. Day asked him if it were true he wrote the music for "Bali Ha'i" in a few miniutes at some dinner party. Dick said no, it was at a luncheon at Josh Logan's apartment.

Oscar came in, he said, and handed him the lyrics. Dick said he went into a bedroom for a few minutes, then came out and played the song on a piano. But, he insisted, it had been incubating in his mind for weeks. It was just waiting to be born.

Dick had two great collaborators, but he wrote both the music and lyrics to one of the lovely songs in *No Strings!*, "The Sweetest Sounds."

Beautiful Diahann Carroll sang that song on this show, as she had done in the Broadway production. Yul Brynner appeared in the "Shall We Dance?" sequence from the movie of *The King and I* and, in a brief interview, recalled how Dick would have a chair placed in the wings during a revival of the show and watch with great satisfaction while it went on. Sold out.

There was a segment from the television series "Victory At Sea," for which Dick had written the score. Followed by a smashing medley of Rodgers and Hart/Hammerstein songs by Peggy Lee, Lena Horne and Vic Damone. "My Funny Valentine," "Happy Talk," "The Gentleman Is a Dope," "The Lady Is a Tramp."

Brief on-camera tributes were paid by Josh Logan, Alfred Drake and Celeste Holm followed by the memorable opening scene of Julie Andrews singing "The Sound of Music" from one of the most popular movies ever made.

Charlie closed by noting, "Richard Rodgers wrote the scores for 42 Broadway shows, and when he died last night, one of them was a big hit on Broadway."

It was a revival of *Oklahoma!* and we had sent a crew to the theater to tape a scene from it. So, in a sense, Dick was both dead and alive.

It all ended with the pianist reprising "Oh, What a Beautiful Morning" while the camera closed in on Dick's picture. Lovely.

Chapter 34

After the Ball Is Over

FACING UP TO the traditional retirement age of 65, I began to wonder what *to* do next. I had a couple of talks with Leonard. He could not have been more helpful or sympathetic. I tentatively suggested I might work six months a year for a while. He said he could live with that; I could continue to work full time, half time or retire completely, just as I pleased.

I might have opted for the latter, but Betty was working hard as hell for NBC, loved every minute and hour of it, and wouldn't even think about retiring. So we couldn't go traveling or move south or other things couples in their sixties are supposed to do. She had become very popular with consumer pieces on the local NBC-TV station and was on the *Today* show once a week. We were both in excellent health and so busy working, our social life was almost non-existent.

One day in October, I had lunch with Bill Small. I told him I had heard that Nigel Ryan, the vice president in charge of "soft" broadcasts for NBC News had resigned and was going back to London.

"Hell, I can give you more as a producer than that job pays," he said.

"Bill, I know that," I answered. "I know some producers get more than executives and on-air talent gets a lot more than producers. But I have a feeling the job might be interesting."

He said he would think it over, but he certainly wanted me at NBC in some capacity.

When I got back to the office, I found Dan Rather sitting on the couch smoking a cigar from my humidor. He said he wanted to talk to me about his future. HIS future! Dan tended to ask a lot of people for career advice, me among them. He said he had been receiving some "unbelievable" money offers. I gathered they were coming principally from ABC, although Dan had been very close to Small. He asked whether I thought he should try to get out of his CBS contract. I said I wasn't qualified to make a judgment for him, but CBS was the biggest fish in the network pond and he had a great future with it.

The phone rang and it was Bill Small.

"I'm on if you are," he said. "Two years firm."

"I'll get back to you," I answered.

Then I told Rather about the NBC proposal. He was fascinated. I don't know whether he had talked to Dan, but I did know Small was already negotiating with other CBS correspondents, including the Kalb brothers and Roger Mudd.

"Well," I told Rather, "now I've got to go see Leonard."

Who was furious.

"I agreed with everything you proposed, right?" Leonard said.

He was indeed right. All I could say was that this was something that interested me after years of producing shows. The coincidence of my turning 65 and the conclusion of a five-year contract with CBS seemed to make for an orderly leave-taking.

I asked if he wanted me to work until the contract was up at the end of January or leave now. Work until it is up, was his answer. He was very annoyed. Justly so.

A few weeks later, I got a note from Bill saying that if I wanted to go sooner, it would be okay with him. My answer was that it would be neater if everything went according to the book. I would stay until January.

Jack Carmody wrote a very complimentary piece in the *Washington Post*, saying I was "the man who practically invented 'instant specials,' was executive producer of the 'CBS Evening News With Walter

Cronkite' for seven years (WRONG) as it climbed to the top (RIGHT)... and is regarded as perhaps the most experienced off-camera man in the business, with more than 1,600 broadcasts to his credit..." and so on and so forth. I got a lot of good wishes from my friends and fellow workers, although Carmody had written that my move "shocked the organization." Hardly.

But there was work to be done in the old shop.

In November, the Iranian crisis, which had been building up since the flight of the Shah nearly a year before, came to a head. "Students" had seized the American Embassy and taken 60 State Department people hostages.

We did three specials, one on November 12, one on November 20, and a third the next night. All, I am sorry to say, in the 11:30 to midnight time period. The days of big special programming in prime time appeared to be over.

The "big news" in the first show, anchored by Cronkite, was that President Carter had retaliated by announcing that the United States would not buy any more Iranian oil. Some retaliation! That and urging Americans to cut down on consumption seemed the only things this frustrated President could do.

The second half-hour, anchored by Rather, considered the possibility of armed intervention. Not much chance, was the conclusion.

The next night, "Day of Crisis," Cronkite anchoring, concerned the continuing problem of the Teheran hostages, now down to 49, plus the destruction of the American Embassy in Islamabad, the capital of Pakistan, by a mob. An American marine had been killed. And the great mosque in Mecca had been taken over by terrorists.

The only positive thing Cronkite could report was that two aircraft carriers and their escorts had been ordered to the Persian Gulf area.

One afternoon when all this was going on, I ran into Casey Davidson in the hallway. He said he had just left Leonard's weekly executive meeting.

"Bill gave you a great tribute," Casey said. "He said here you were about to leave the company, but instead of coasting, you were busting your ass to get shows on the air. In the great tradition of CBS News."

I went off to find Bill and thank him for the kind words. "All of it highly deserved," he said. Damn nice of him.

Our little production unit, which had worked together for more than 20 years, did one last prime time documentary on January 5, 1980. It was "The Energy Crunch...The Best Way Out." That way, we concluded, was to conserve it. Rather anchored the show, with contributions from Collingwood, David Culhane, Morton Dean and John Sheahan.

My 65th birthday was on January 18, and two nights before, CBS News took over Alfredo's restaurant on Central Park South to throw a farewell party for one of their people who was going off to join the opposition.

The place was mobbed and scores of old comrades from the TV news battles were there. Sevareid, with whom I had started, came up from Washington. And, maybe best of all, Frank Stanton.

Many extravagantly kind words were said by Bill Leonard and Walter Cronkite, which rendered me even more inarticulate than usual.

But between gulps I managed to say that leaving CBS was both an occasion for deep regrets and deep satisfaction. One of the regrets was that the eloquence of Sevareid and Kuralt had not rubbed off onto me. The greatest satisfaction had been working with those assembled. I recalled that several years ago, I had occasion to write a note to Mr. Paley in which I observed that an excellent definition of a good company would be that it was a group of companions. CBS people were just that, I told him. My companions. The finest.

There is a postscript to the Iran story.

When the Emmys were handed out in 1980 "Showdown in Iran," a prime-time hour we had produced in January, 1979, was a winner. I stepped up to receive the award but had nothing to say. It should not have gone to me, of course, but to the great CBS News organization. By then, I was a vice president at NBC.

CODA
The Last Word Flies
Through the Air

I WAS LUCKY ENOUGH to work first in print and then in television news when they were performing stylishly as The Fourth Estate, our greatest institution outside government itself. When they were telling us what was going on in the world.

Maybe newspapers had seen better days than before my time, but there were lots of big city papers around in the Thirties and they were a very important and visible part of the nation's life.

Individual giants like Hearst and Pulitzer, and the passel of Pattersons, McCormicks and the rest who walked in their tracks may have been more interested in big circulations to grab political power and influence for themselves than in any sort of public service.

But, willy-nilly, they did inform people. Certainly the crochets of individual newspaper owners were preferable to today's money-grubbing by corporate giants. And much more fun.

When I got started, there were still great papers owned by the families of their founders or those who had built them. A Bonfils was on the masthead of *The Denver Post; The Courier-Journal* was in the hands of the Bingham family; Colonel Robert McCormick ruled over his *Chicago Tribune*, and Colonel Frank Knox the *Chicago Daily News*. In New York, McCormick's cousin, Captain Joseph Medill Patterson, had built the *Daily News* into the nation's number one paper in sales. The *Times* was in Ochs family hands and the *Herald Tribune* was run by Reids. Harry Chandler hewed to his unique idea of public service, but his *Los Angeles Times* flourished.

I loved working on newspapers and served a lot of them. But, when radio began delivering news all day, especially late news of war and sports and financial markets, the afternoon newspapers went on the skids. Television inevitably followed and did them in.

But let's not shed too many tears for newspapers. The Gannett, Chandler, Knight-Ridder and other chains are rich; publishing newspapers can be very, very profitable if one is in the right market. Especially in a monopoly position.

And fine papers are still with us. *The New York Times, Boston Globe, Philadelphia Inquirer, Washington Post* and *Los Angeles Times* justly deserve great respect. And, I am happy to observe, the little *Paris Herald* is available now all around the world by satellite transmission. It is jointly owned by the *Times, Post* and none other than William S. Paley.

But, the big fact of life in journalism today is television.

That baby stirred in its cradle as the decade of the Fifties began, then shot up like Jack's beanstalk. Because it brought into American living rooms entertainment, great events as they actually occurred, sports— and daily news.

But news was not the greatest elixir of change in the heady draught of television.

It is entirely possible that advertising, the commercials, had more affect on American society than anything else about television. Because they showed a way of life suspected but not really seen before by millions of the less privileged. Inevitably, many of those millions wanted the cars and houses and furniture and shiny kitchens they saw other Americans enjoying right there on the screen.

The whole ball of wax of television and its effect on society cries out for a Gunnar Myrdal to explain what it *really* is and what its future is going to be.

I wish I could.

Television has, in the last 40 years, opened wide magic windows through which the entire citizenry, down to the youngest, the most impoverished and the least educated, can watch—and hopefully in some degree understand—what is going on.

Almost nothing can be more important to this nation's future than what is told and shown to them.

Television news was not left behind. It grew into a great force, right alongside the entertainment and commercial content. Because its audiences swiftly came to be counted in the millions, dwarfing the impact of any vehicle which offered printed words.

Twenty years ago, we were told by the number crunchers that more Americans got their daily doses of world and national news from "The CBS Evening News With Walter Cronkite" than from any other source.

That's heady stuff. Certainly it was for Walter and me, and I am sure for the owners of CBS. How could it not be? And at the same time, in addition to the daily news report, those owners paid for the production of, and made available time on the air for, dozens of serious documentaries, the Murrow/Friendly "See It Now" series, Bud Benjamin's classy "The Twentieth Century" and scores of prime time hours about breaking news.

That cost money. The news department was subsidized by dough the entertainment department raked in. About 20 million a year, in "sounder" dollars. Because Messrs. Paley and Stanton said to do it.

CBS was not alone. General David Sarnoff at NBC, Leonard Goldensen at ABC and Robert Kinter at both ABC and NBC marched their troops down the same high road. All deserve huzzahs.

But, as the new breed of television news managers like to say, "That is *yesterday*. Let's get on with *today*."

I reply, "Okay, let's by all means . . . but the way things are going, maybe you better look at yesterday."

I was the producer of the half-hour "CBS Evening News" longer than anyone else, at least to date. So I have a deeply ingrained habit of watching it every night. Or maybe I should say *had* a habit. Because a couple of months ago, something appeared that made me wonder what in hell was going on.

Mention was made early on that the program would include something very good, "so stay with us." Such language is called a "promo," a contraction of promotion.

The spot came at the end. It was about a dog which had been trained by his master to climb trees. It showed the dog in action, time after time. A tree-climbing dog.

This is not the kind of stuff that appears in a lineup made in consultation with God. I can say without fear of contradiction He prefers big news stories reported with skill and put together with care and distinction.

Lest I judge the talented dog too harshly, let me admit that we men of "yesterday" were not averse to wrapping up a broadcast with something lighthearted or funny—*when the flow of news gave us time for it.*

But our idea of the right stuff in such a situation tended toward Charlie Kuralt's delightful series, "On The Road." Sometimes, when there was a lot of news, we found it tough to find time for Eric Sevareid's classy essays. Because breaking news came first.

When we started the half-hour news show at CBS in the fall of 1963, NBC's Huntley and Brinkley led in the ratings. It took four years of hard work by Walter—and Don Hewitt, Ernest Leiser and the whole CBS News organization of talented correspondents and producers, editors and technicians—to make CBS Number One in the ratings. But they did it. By putting on a quality broadcast night after night, year after year.

There is no other way.

If you think there is, let me point to the example of "60 Minutes."

Don Hewitt and his band of merry men tell me, with straight faces, that they have *absolutely no idea* of why their program is so popular. They know it *is* popular, but swear they don't know *why*.

They know of course.

It is popular because it is so damn good. Week after week.

"60 Minutes" is by far the most successful show on television. Not in television news. Television.

It has been at or near the top of the ratings for years. It is the most *profitable* show on television, probably accounting for around $50 million a year. Which might well be the difference between a profitable and a losing year for the whole network. And it is not owned by any Hollywood producer but by CBS itself. Glory, glory hallelujah!

There is no other way.

During the unfortunate reigns of Van Gordon Sauter and Ed Joyce at CBS News in the early Eighties, deliberate decisions were made to copy the patterns of local news shows. They decided more flash, more emphasis on a system of star performers on the screen, would be the right stuff for the network news. To get bigger ratings.

Their hearts were not in putting on a quality news report every night. What they sought was to maneuver themselves up the corporate ladder to bigger jobs, offices and limousines. They believed a diet of news the public "wanted" rather than one it "should have" would raise ratings and thus profits and thus their positions on the ladder. Neither Joyce nor Sauter lasted long, but the tree-climbing dog gives off a lingering whiff of them. Mysteriously, both men were handed huge sums to go away.

It is true that by the time Sauter/Joyce took over, the local stations' position vis-à-vis the network had changed drastically. Devoting more time to news, the locals began looking past their own cities and states and filling up the time with world and national news. Which tended to make the network report, coming later, look like old stuff.

We used to have the power to withhold reports by network correspondents in Washington and other big news centers from early local news. They could use such material only in their 11 P.M. shows. But constantly growing pressure from the affiliates inexorably forced the CBS syndication operation to make almost every single bit of news in hand available for local use.

Then, you might ask, what can and should the network news do?

It should try to make sure that the great news-gathering organization does first class reporting. Every day. And that the editors who control the final use of its work accept their responsibility to the correspondents, field producers—and the public—and do right by it.

I would say to the news executives of the networks: Since nothing can be done about what the local stations broadcast, ignore them. Just do what you are hired to do. Give the millions of Americans who turn to the "CBS Evening News" every night a responsible review of world and national news, as complete as your assigned 22 minutes permits.

There is no...

I always did think that the network evening news was an anomaly. That, sooner or later, the affiliate stations would tell the networks to roll over into an electronic version of the Associated Press. The stations would buy the output of a worldwide news-gathering service, but *they* would decide, in their own offices, what would go on the air. If they didn't like what Eric Sevareid said, they wouldn't use his stuff. Just like a big newspaper. It hasn't happened yet. But someday, kid.

When the 15 minute network evening shows were expanded to a half hour, news executives hoped they could someday get their hands on a full hour. That never happened either.

Because local stations affiliated with the networks had discovered that news could be very profitable even if they had to go out and get some of it themselves. And they kept all the advertising money. Why should they give any of *their* time back to the network?

Television stations are very powerful in their communities and get respectful hearings from the Federal Communications Commission, which in theory is supposed to regulate them. And if the FCC doesn't bow to a station owner, the congressman from his district will rap their knuckles. He wants the station's approval—and support. And the commission doesn't want to get its budget cut or be harassed by congressmen.

As local news shows became increasingly profitable, the stations yearned for more time in the evening and scornfully rejected any suggestion that the network news be doubled to an hour. They were tough enough to want some kind of written guarantee. So in 1975, the FCC dutifully passed the access rule, which reserved the hour between 7:00 and 8:00 P.M. for local use. No longer could that be "network time." (The stations could, if they chose, trade some of that time for their own news show at 6:30.)

That hour, it was piously stated, was set aside to be used for public service programming in the community served by each station. Some local public service-type programming was tried but it cost quite a lot of money. So the time slid into the trash barrel, with game shows and other syndicated stuff which can be purchased very cheaply and, sorry to say, draw large audiences.

They never had *much* of a chance, but from 1975 on, the networks had *no* chance whatsoever of obtaining time on the air for a one-hour news show in the evening. (Walter and I used to talk wistfully about having an hour between 10:00 and 11:00 P.M. but we knew perfectly well it never could be.)

During the past year, the "CBS Evening News With Dan Rather" was moved in New York from 7:00 P.M. to 6:30. (Most affiliates always did carry it at the earlier time.) But this station, WCBS-TV, is not a local affiliate. It is the flagship of the network. Which chose to make more money with cheap programming than to keep the network's premier program on later. As I write, Dan is on at 6:30 and a pseudo news ("reality") show and a game show occupy the 7:00 to 8:00 period.

The networks are now the property of very large corporations whose mothers did not raise them to lose money. General Electric owns NBC, the Tisch conglomerate of various real estate, tobacco and other interests holds CBS, and ABC has been swallowed by Capital Cities, the only one which amassed its big-time money from broadcasting.

On the day in 1989 the DuPont Awards were handed out at Columbia University, there was an afternoon symposium with the presidents of the three network news divisions. ABC News was reported to be already profitable and the other presidents said that by the decade of the 1990s they, too, would be operating in the black. They didn't say it right out loud, but that's what their new owners have decreed.

The commercial television networks are steadily losing chunks of their audiences to the rapidly growing reach and technology of cable and VCR. So everything, including news, has to be a "profit center."

The Public Broadcasting Service puts on quality shows occasionally, but only recently has any serious attempt been made to create first-class entertainment. It has for years been dependent on British television for that. It develops and buys lots of documentaries and some of them are excellent. But independent producers say that if they approach a PBS station, or the parent organization, about getting a show on, the first question they are asked is where the money will come from. They must go to the public system with funds already in hand.

As a result, hard, controversial subjects get short shrift.

PBS never did fulfill the hopes of its original prospectus, "Public Television, A Program for Action," published in 1967 by the Carnegie Corporation of New York. (And written by Steve White.)

That was a proposal for a non-profit public corporation which would develop broadcasts not for commercial use and not for classroom use, but quality stuff to be seen "by the tens of thousands and sometimes by the tens of millions."

It envisioned lots of production by local stations in regional program centers and interconnection of the stations. Maybe even a national dramatic repertory company.

James Reston wrote at the time that if the goals of this proposal were fulfilled, it might have as much influence on the nation's welfare as the bill to set up the great land-grant colleges.

PBS was set up by public stations as a collective to distribute programs. Federal money is allocated to the stations and to state public television organizations through the Corporation for Public Broadcasting. Commercials have tiptoed in on tiny "brought to you by" feet.

Mostly institutional commercials now, but wait around for the hard sell. It's coming.

I have a suspicion that the richest—and I don't mean just in money—future lies in cable. Certainly the richest future for news, which the networks seem to be sluffing off.

I was sitting on the floor in front of a television monitor the morning of January 26, 1986, trying to learn how to make a VCR work, with the dubious help of a manual obviously translated from the Japanese. Probably *by* a Japanese.

Not interested in the soapy morning fare, I punched up CNN. And saw the *Challenger* blast off into the sky for a few seconds before those terrible explosions filled the screen. As plumes of white smoke began to trace patterns downward, I turned to the network stations, one by one. None was showing the launch. It was morning, a time for small audiences and minimum loss for a brief network special without commercials. But they were not on.

(If you watch television I have to put this to you.

(*Challenger* exploded in full view of cameras set up at Cape Canaveral. The comparatively few who saw it live, and the multi-millions who saw it replayed on tape over and over again later in the day and evening, felt the full force of a dramatic picture in color and motion and sound. It triggered a staggering emotional reaction.

(My question is:

(Would that reaction have been anywhere near the same if the accident had happened out of sight, beyond the range of cameras?)

So things aren't what they used to be in the news business. So what?, you may well ask. Why take the time to heed an old rewrite man muttering about it?

Because methinks news programs offered to the public through the three large commercial networks are not getting better in *editorial* quality, despite dazzling *technical* advances. Those are increasingly employed, skillfully, to enhance show business content.

That invaluable ingredient, time on the air, may add up today to about the same number—or even more—of hours and minutes it did during what I am reluctantly willing to call the olden days. But that precious time is more and more filled by magazine formats wistfully panting after the fabled successs of "60 Minutes." Long gone are serious examinations of breaking "big news" developments in prime time. Too expensive, they say. Not to produce. Expensive in lost revenue.

In May of 1989, a series of almost unbelievable events took place in Beijing, during and after Mikhail Gorbachev's state visit to China. Perceiving this as a big world news event, CBS and CNN decided to set up satellite equipment to transmit their coverage. CBS sent a group of top correspondents, headed by Dan Rather and Charles Kuralt, to anchor the network's daily and Sunday broadcasts from the scene. NBC and ABC decided to go through China's own broadcasting facilities.

But the state visit sparked something much greater and unforseen. A vast outpouring of students filled Tiananmen Square and demonstrated day and night, demanding less corruption in the government and "democratic" reforms. Ordinary Chinese joined in, and even police and soldiers were openly sympathic—on camera.

When the demonstrators refused to disperse, the government (after Gorbachev's departure) finally brought in troops from outlying provinces who would obey orders. Hundreds of demonstrators—perhaps more—were shot.

What a story for television!

Memorable events—dramatic and highly visual—happening right in front of live cameras!

Many special "interruptions," bulletins, were broadcast and the evening news shows and ABC's "Nightline" were filled with the story every day. CBS had the edge with its own satellite setup—until government agents arrived to pull the plug, right on air!

The network spokesmen expressed pride in what they had done to cover the story. Should they?

Highlights on CBS were: Kuralt's "Sunday Morning," on May 14 before the big events. A special edition of Rather's prime time series "48 Hours," done from China (a great show). Special inserts into "West 57th" and "60 Minutes" and a full hour reprise of Mike Wallace's coverage of China over the years on "60 Minutes."

NBC did a one-hour special at 7:00 P.M. on Sunday, June 4, and a special half-hour at 11:30 the next night. Tom Brokaw went to China after the event and got a strange interview with Yuan Mu, a Chinese official, who smilingly declared that not one civilian had been shot.

ABC had "Nightline" on every night, did many special brief broadcasts and an hour at 7:00 A.M. on June 4. (Both the ABC and the NBC hour were opposite "60 Minutes," which guaranteed them small audiences.)

I don't regard this as doing justice to an event of this magnitude, especially when those on the scene had all the wonderful modern tools of broadcasting at their command.

What was going on in the executive suites?

It was summer, in the repeat season, losses caused by covering the story in important time would have been minimal.

They should have been on at 10:00 P.M. every single night. *That* would have been in the *public interest*.

The latest attempts to get "reality" shows on the networks came in August 1989. Introduced were a shabby pair, "Yesterday, Today and Tomorrow" on NBC and "Primetime Live" on ABC.

Both arrived with the kind of overblown promotion and advertising that ushers in expensive entertainment projects. They were embarrassingly bad.

In addition to the Nielsen ratings, which purport to measure how many people are watching a particular show on commercial television, there is something called a "Q" rating. This purports to be able to determine what percentage of the audience "likes" a particular person on the air.

At the time these two shows were introduced, the glamorous Diane Sawyer was "liked" by 18 percent of the audience and her straight man, Sam Donaldson, by 19 percent. The same report had Barbara Walters liked by 21 percent and Connie Chung by 22 percent.

Walter Cronkite, who handed over the "CBS Evening News" to Dan Rather in *1980*, was liked by 36 percent.

Won't someone please tell me why he is so seldom on the air?

The daily newspapers have been squeezed down to a handful in the big cities by the crushing power of television to deliver enormous audiences for advertisers. Too often their response has been to print shorter, what they call "brighter," stories about what they call things of "reader interest." Presented in jigsaw makeup style with, whenever possible, color here and there. (Advertisers like it.) The art director sits beside the news editor's chair.

Why all this moaning?

Because most important to our present and future welfare is not what the wizards of Wall Street are doing to the nation's treasure by shoving vast sums of our money back and forth among themselves. Nor what obviously corrupt windbags in Congress are doing to the country while making oily deals in our name.

The greatest service that can be done for the American people is to give them honest, complete information about what the hell is going on. By greatest I mean THE greatest.

All is not lost. Despite the blight of multiple corporate ownership, some television stations, some newspapers and some magazines still strive manfully to do that job. May they grow and multiply!

As Harold Ross used to say, God bless. I submit that, beyond doubt, they are engaged in the most honorable of professions.

Maybe even the *true* work of The Lord.

Index

335

LESLIE MIDGLEY has had a long and distinguished career in print and broadcast journalism. Most recently he was a speaker at the Yale University seminar in modern journalism. He is married to NBC News correspondent Betty Furness, and lives in Hartsdale, New York.